'A surprise appointment as High Representative – effectively the EU's Foreign Minister – and initially dismissed as too inexperienced, Catherine Ashton became recognised as a brilliantly effective diplomat and negotiator, winning international acclaim for two personal triumphs: her brokering of an agreement between Serbia and Kosovo in 2013 and her leading role in the Iran nuclear deal of the same year. This riveting, deeply personal and wonderfully accessible book takes the reader inside the room during the successes, setbacks and personalities of this turbulent period of history.'
  Sir Kim Darroch, former British Ambassador to the USA, National Security Advisor, and UK Permanent Representative to the EU

'A riveting, absorbing account of modern diplomacy by one of the greatest international diplomats of recent times. *And Then What?* is hugely informative, full of tremendous insights, and a truly great read!'
  General David Petraeus (US Army, Ret.), former Commander of the Surge in Iraq, US Central Command, and NATO/US Forces in Afghanistan, and former Director of the CIA

'Cathy Ashton's gripping memoirs are not only a perfect combination of very precise facts and touching personal emotions, but for all foreign policy observers they convey important lessons of the past to serve for the crises of today.'
  Pierre Vimont, former French ambassador to the EU and the USA

'As I read *And Then What?* I couldn't help but think of the bar scene in *Star Wars*. A prerequisite for future diplomacy among such characters, including our progeny, is the success of diplomacy such as Cathy Ashton reports here, in lieu of war and a dead-end future. If generations of Earthlings-to-be do indeed engage in cosmic negotiations with other lifeforms, it will be because of the success of Cathy and her diplomatic compatriots in bringing us to realise we are Earth-life, together.'
  Rusty Schweickart, Apollo 9 astronaut

'Cathy Ashton was not a diplomat, but she became the EU's top diplomat overnight in 2010 and was immediately plunged into a host of global crises. Her account of some highlights of her time in and away from Brussels makes fascinating and illuminating reading. From Haiti to Libya, reconciling Serbia and Kosovo, the Iran nuclear deal and the start of the Ukraine drama, she was immersed in the hard grind of global crisis management. Modest but highly professional, she made a major impact – and this book is truly remarkable history.'

Lord (George) Robertson, Former Secretary General, NATO

'This is not an ordinary diplomatic memoir. Cathy Ashton worked tirelessly to mitigate the devastating consequences of real and political earthquakes while the EU's de facto Foreign Minister. She combines acute analysis with moving portraits of the many people she engaged with, from dictators to shopkeepers; from overworked civil servants to distressed toddlers searching in vain through rubble for their parents; from the revolutionary youth of Tahir Square to jaundiced negotiators who wanted a deal but didn't know how to strike it. During her time in office, Ashton eschewed the limelight. While avoiding self-promotion and deflecting the arrows of appalling misogyny from the quivers of the media as well as of some of the EU's male establishment, she was at the heart of at least two of the most important international agreements of the early twenty-first century, the Iran nuclear deal and the first major step towards rapprochement between Kosovo and Serbia. Perhaps most surprising is her story-telling ability – each episode in this book has the element of a thriller combined with that of the most perceptive travel writer. And together it throws an entirely new light on the monumental political processes that shook the globe in the wake of the 2008 financial crisis. A must for students of politics and a treat for lovers of general non-fiction.'

Misha Glenny, Rector of the Institute for Human Sciences, Vienna, and author of *McMafia*

AND THEN WHAT?

INSIDE STORIES OF 21ST-CENTURY DIPLOMACY

CATHERINE ASHTON

Elliott&Thompson

First published 2023 by
Elliott and Thompson Limited
2 John Street
London WC1N 2ES
www.eandtbooks.com

ISBN: 978-1-78396-634-9

Images have been sourced from the author's personal collection and from the EU Services, and the publisher would like to thank all sources for their reproduction in this book.

9 8 7 6 5 4 3 2 1

A catalogue record for this book is available from the British Library.

Typesetting: Marie Doherty
Printed by CPI Group (UK) Ltd, Croydon, CR0 4YY

To Robert and Rebecca, who finally know
what I was doing all those years

CONTENTS

Foreword ix

Introduction xiii

1   The Journey to Brussels 1

2   Somalia and 21st-Century Pirates 19

3   Natural Disasters: Haiti and Japan 33

4   The Arab Spring I: Egypt and the Fall of Morsi 55

5   The Arab Spring II: The Collapse of Libya 87

6   The Western Balkans: Serbia and Kosovo Dialogue 109

7   The Iran Nuclear Negotiations 147

8   Revolution in Ukraine 179

Afterword 217

Acknowledgements 221

Index 225

FOREWORD

When I was a little girl, I had a blue plastic pencil case on which I wrote my name and address. After the usual street number and name, village and county, I wrote England, UK, Europe, The World, The Universe. I wasn't an aspiring internationalist, just a small child in a sleepy village near Wigan in the north-west of England writing down what was obvious then and now. For good or ill, we are all connected to each other.

Decades later I would be given the chance, first through trade negotiations and later through diplomacy, to connect with more than a hundred countries across every continent, and to represent the views and values of twenty-eight nations. It was a tall order. The period involved, from 2009 to 2014, was one of the most turbulent in living memory. What had seemed certain for decades was swept away in days. Hope for better things rose and fell regularly – sometimes several times in a matter of hours. I struggled, along with everyone else, to respond effectively while working with the smartest, most dedicated diplomats and politicians it has been my privilege to know. I encountered dictators and murderers aplenty, but the overwhelming majority of people I met just wanted a better life. In the pursuit of that for themselves and their families I witnessed bravery and determination that left me in awe.

I have often been asked in the ensuing years whether I enjoyed my time as the first High Representative for Foreign and Security Policy/ First Vice President of the Commission (yes, the longest job title in history, so from now on HRVP for short). The answer was no. There were moments of deep satisfaction, even joy, and I made some of the best and closest friends of my life. But it was relentless. There was no time to be complacent – always another problem to try to solve. I was admired and hated in equal measure every day, and the hate got to me much more than the admiration. I dreaded the press, feared the news, worried about my diplomats all over the world, hoped for good news that seldom came. I visited some of the worst places on earth, saw children living in terrible misery, heard the stories of destruction, cried alongside the bereaved and injured from earthquake or war and wondered at our capacity for evil. I saw acts of bravery and kindness in unlikely places and watched the infinite willingness of children to learn in dusty, crumbling school rooms or tents in refugee camps. I did everything I could to help, knowing it was never going to be enough, and worried that a better person than I could have done much more.

There were moments of success like the Iran Nuclear Deal, or the Serbia–Kosovo agreement. They seem fleeting now, not nailed down when they should have been. Failures still loom large: unresolved tragedy in Syria, the chaos of Libya, the horror of war in Ukraine. In between there were times when life got a bit easier for some, and sparks of hope flashed on the horizon.

This book has taken a long time to compile. My initial determination to put the past behind me gave way to curiosity about the way things had been. I found that people asked me to tell my stories and, when I did, urged me to write them down. I wanted to describe what it was really like to be in the middle of events as an ordinary person given an extra-ordinary role to play. Each chapter is based on interviews my husband Peter Kellner conducted with me at the time. I would sit in his study in my jeans and talk about the weeks that had gone before. Peter would ask questions, helping to tease out the details – what did I say? what did the place look like? how was the mood? – that colour in the black-and-white outline that press reports provide. Transcribing them took me back to those places and times. I was surprised at the level of detail I had forgotten in the meantime and felt exhausted just thinking of the thousands of miles I travelled every week. I have chosen only a few of these stories for this book and they are not in any way comprehensive histories of the time. There are many better analysts and historians who can do justice to this period in ways I never could. But I hope my memories shed some light on the complexities of diplomacy in the twenty-first century and remind us that what I wrote on my pencil case over half a century ago remains true today.

INTRODUCTION

The word 'diplomacy' conjures up a range of images, from palatial buildings filled with cocktail-sipping occupants in black tie and ballgowns to earnest discussions around paper-strewn tables, or exhausted people emerging from grubby hideaways after weeks of negotiation. These three comprise the most obvious elements of diplomatic activity: representing a nation or organisation, managing international relations, and preventing or resolving conflict. It is often described as an art form, one that relies on the skills and commitment of individuals backed by the determination of the people they represent.

There is no certain path to success for a diplomat. Most of the time they work quietly, keeping relations steady, but crises can spring seemingly out of nowhere, changing dramatically in the course of hours or days and engulfing communities and sometimes countries. Some solutions require long-term, patient action, building coalitions and working through existing structures. Others need immediate attention, despite the information available being at best sketchy and incomplete.

In any event, solutions rely on the same range of personal skills, tact, sensitivity, determination and, most of all, judgement. They rely on the same essential tools to achieve change: dialogue and negotiation with incentives. Even when diplomacy fails and situations descend into chaos, or become frozen in conflict, ultimately the only way out is diplomacy. It is, in my view, the ultimate 'weapon' in the arsenal of international relations – and it is underrated and undervalued.

The European Union (EU) was not a conventional power like the USA, Russia or China. Its decision to create a new foreign policy service – the European External Action Service (EEAS) – brought together the resources of the Commission and Council in a new hybrid structure, strengthening its common foreign policy, and using its economic clout as a soft power tool.

During the years that I led European foreign policy efforts, I learnt that some common elements improved the chances of a successful outcome. I also came face to face with some of the real dilemmas of foreign policy – above all that decisions are rarely clear-cut and easy to take. So often there is no perfect solution. I have tried to capture something of what it was like to be there and how small pieces of history are made. Every week was different, usually involving thousands of miles of travel in a relentless, exhausting schedule. My ability to withstand jet lag successfully was in part because the time of day meant very little. I slept when it was dark and worked when it was light.

During hundreds of visits to countries around the world, I stepped inside magnificent palaces and visited the poorest neighbourhoods. I saw for myself the skyline of tents for refugees fleeing war and the beauty of buildings newly restored after years of conflict. I had the chance to use all my senses – taste the air; smell the decay and neglect; hold the frightened child; hear the noise of those giving excuses or shifting the blame elsewhere; see the devastation of earthquake and disaster. Most of all I met people face to face, to try to better understand what was happening and why, and to look for answers. To sit down with people with whom one has little in common, or worse where there exists a deep distrust and bitter anger, provides the chance to find ways to – at the very least – stop things deteriorating. If we could achieve that, there was hope that we could move on to looking for longer-term answers.

Diplomacy is not an easy subject for journalists to cover. It is often painstakingly slow, requires everyone to remain tight-lipped, and mostly happens behind closed doors. It was not so unusual to read a story of what was happening in a place in which I was standing and not recognise anything of what was being reported. But while some reporters drove us quietly nuts, others took the time to get facts right and to offer an independent perspective rather than an editorial bias.

In each chapter of this book I have tried to bring out what worked, what didn't, and what could have made a difference. Diplomacy has no clear-cut end points; even when an agreement is reached, outside forces, political changes or simply just 'events' can blow it off course. It requires vigilance and nurture. Hindsight should never be the only reckoning – although it has its part to play. Some of my observations and conclusions may seem naive and badly misplaced, or suggest a certainty I did not feel at the time. I include them here rather than edit them out because that is the reality of the job. I learnt a great deal from the best in the business, from diplomats, activists, politicians, aid workers, military and civilian missions; and I learnt a lot more from the people who worked tirelessly for a better life for themselves, their families and their countries. I also learnt from the actions of the despicable, willing to cause chaos and destruction, wrecking the lives of others in pursuit of their own entirely selfish gains. Overall, it was staggering to see what we are prepared to do for people we have hardly met, and terrifying to witness what we are able to do to those we have lived beside for generations.

Sometimes I was frustrated by leaders who simply preferred to do nothing, passing the problem on to their successors or ignoring it altogether. For others, I recognised the agony of their choices – to compromise risked losing office or worse, with no guarantees that their efforts would be respected by those who followed. Why risk it all for something that might not work? Some were the creators of chaos, prepared to put personal gain ahead of any interest in lessening the plight of their people. I sat down with them all, shook their hands, posed for the photo. My job was not to like them but to work with them to find a way forward. Ultimately, the point of diplomacy is to bring people together and keep them in the room until you get somewhere.

There are broader lessons, too. For every challenge, the number of immediate responses is limited – negotiation, mediation, military intervention, sanctions, monitoring missions, pressure and so on. These options form the basis of the 'diplomatic tool kit'. As time went by we sought better, nuanced and longer-lasting solutions without forgetting some of the basic lessons about what works.

Some believe it is not the job of individual nations to sort out underlying problems elsewhere. Their argument is that each nation's responsibility is to protect its own interests, no further. If you seek a monument to that lack of vision, you need simply look around: countries scarred by years of neglect, dying infrastructure where it exists at all, corrupt governance and lack of opportunities. Failing to tackle these problems is to risk their spread. Crises suck up energy and resources like wildfire: left unresolved, they return with the roar of newly invigorated flames, hotter and more toxic, engulfing everything in their path. Preventing them or stopping them is an imperative that should be at the top of every political agenda. Collaborating with others to achieve this should be the number-one tool in the tool kit.

There is no issue we face today that we can tackle alone. Even powerful nations cannot unilaterally cope with challenges such as climate change, terrorism or disruptive technologies. The spread of Covid-19 demonstrates the speed with which danger can arrive at everyone's shore, wrecking lives and economies in weeks. We act as if these are unexpected crises, even if they have long been anticipated by many. In extreme crises we may even pretend they are manufactured or unreal problems, which makes doing nothing sound like a plan.

In the real world, if we want to protect ourselves, we do not have the option of doing nothing. We must actively anticipate and prepare for problems. Helping people to get the most out of life means cooperating too. Being able to enjoy a holiday abroad, recruiting staff from overseas to work in the health sector, bringing in students to universities, organising strong trade agreements to generate wealth for a country – all of these are achieved through collaboration with others. The first obligation of government – keeping people safe – is built on global networks of like-minded people ready to stand together to deflect danger, to create security and to offer opportunity.

The more effort that is put into pulling together, the better the chances of resolving the problem. Simple in theory, a challenge in practice. At best, leaders disagree about what is important; at worst, they are downright hostile to each other. But using times of relative calm to prepare for future storms makes sense. In an era when plenty argue for going it alone, this is a truth we need to hang on to.

Working with and for twenty-eight countries and different EU institutions was not easy. Their histories, economic interests, fears and experiences were not left at the door when they sat together. Geography also played its part. Countries close to Russia worried more about what was happening in Ukraine in 2014, and less about the problems of Egypt, and vice versa. Nevertheless, somehow, we always got to a position that gave me something positive to work with.

But not everything works best through formal organisations like the EU, North Atlantic Treaty Organization (NATO) or the United Nations (UN). Sometimes a less structured approach works better. I drew many lessons from being part of more informal coalitions brought together to try to resolve or mitigate a crisis. My stories demonstrate this over and over, especially when our collaborations included our most important partner, the USA. Sometimes, as with the mediation between Serbia and Kosovo, their role was a quiet one, hidden for the most part but vital, nonetheless. At other times they strode across the stage, making it hard for us to keep up but rarely going in a direction we disagreed with.

We moaned about each other too – as an intercepted phone call from US Assistant Secretary of State Victoria Nuland once embarrassingly revealed. Frustrated that we were not moving fast enough in support of Ukraine, she said 'Fuck the EU'. But such incidences reflected the mutterings of disgruntled family members rather than the fracturing of relations. She was swift to apologise, and the EU was swift to put it aside.

Many people complained during his tenure that President Obama was less interested in Europe than former US presidents had been. Yet the fellowship of the Obama administration and his secretaries of state,

Hillary Clinton and John Kerry, together with the support he gave to me personally, was extraordinary. But he believed, as did I, that Europe was capable of more and wanted us to be less reliant on the USA. He was not wrong and, as we have seen, his methods were significantly wiser and kinder than those of his immediate successor.

Some collaborations were more unusual. The E3 (France, Germany and the UK), with the remaining permanent members of the UN Security Council (Russia, the USA and China), formed the E3 plus 3 (also known as P5 plus 1 to denote the five permanent UN Security Council members plus Germany) to focus on the single issue of Iran's nuclear programme. The EU was asked to chair and lead the negotiations. That focus on one issue meant that even when relations became strained and hostile over Russia's invasion of Ukraine in 2014, we were able to continue working as a team. We kept at it – in my case for over four years – but our future hopes were dashed by President Trump's withdrawal from the nuclear agreement we had reached, a move that was categorised by some as an act of pique at anything Obama did, and by others as reflecting a view that an unforeseen by-product of our success was an emboldened Iran. Others just thought it a bad deal, though many could not articulate why, and much negative, ill-informed media coverage at the time did not help. An American colleague asked each person who called to complain about the deal to describe a uranium centrifuge and what it was used for. Most failed. He suggested they call back when they knew.

The format of the E3 plus 3 raises questions about what I term the 'formal' and the 'informal' structures of international cooperation. 'Formal' groupings of countries like the UN, EU, NATO and the World Trade Organization (WTO) require nations to sign on the line, often to complex rules and regulations, with shared principles of democracy and human rights as a requirement of membership. How to turn acceptance into enforcement has proved difficult, as we see in struggles to uphold press freedom and judicial independence across parts of the EU. But 'formal' relationships support depth, longevity and stability, allowing policies to develop over time. Over my five years at the helm of the EEAS

I became good at knowing where each nation would stand on any given issue, although occasional dramatic changes in government make-up added an element of unpredictability to the mix.

The 'informal' groupings like Friends of Syria and the Libya Contact Group became increasingly common. Created to tackle one issue, they brought together countries that might otherwise have had little in common. Rather than seeking out only those with shared values, the focus was on breadth of support for a solution and a willingness to take quick action. In the wake of threats made by Libyan dictator Gaddafi against his own people, the coalition that President Sarkozy convened in Paris was an example of how different countries could come together to act quickly in response to a specific danger. In time NATO took the lead, but the initial interventions stemmed from the Paris meeting. I have tried to capture how decisions were made in the build-up to military action, and what happened after that.

But the future of Libya will not be decided in any single capital, least of all Tripoli. It will require agreement among many to a solution, and the support of all to a specific plan. Iran's nuclear future will not be resolved by any single nation either, especially when animosity and mistrust make even the beginnings of a conversation impossible. Serbia and Kosovo need the prize of EU membership to be real and they require the support of others, not least the USA, to make that happen.

I often used to ask colleagues the question 'And then what?', to get us thinking beyond the immediate crisis. It was very difficult to see what might happen, but unless we defined our commitment as extending beyond the short term and planned accordingly, the chances of longer-term success were significantly lessened. Somalia's piracy crisis could not be solved in isolation from the country's wider structural problems. Young men with few options were enticed into piracy, causing havoc across a huge stretch of ocean and crippling the passage of the 30,000 ships that normally traversed Somalia's coastline each year. It required thinking well beyond the immediate crisis. As the British admiral in charge of the EU military mission to tackle the problem pointed out, the solution to the problems at sea would be found on the land.

So too for Haiti in the aftermath of the 2010 earthquake that killed over 200,000 people in under a minute. Nations and aid organisations made concerted efforts to provide emergency shelter, food and water, and medical services. But in a country that had received aid for half a century, there were huge challenges beyond the immediate crisis. To build a functioning political system and civil society is a long-term and often difficult process. But without such ongoing commitment, a generation of girls will not get to school, businesses will not thrive, government will not work effectively, nor will people be able to return home.

I was never alone. The EEAS was created by diplomats and experts from all over Europe, willing to leave home and come to serve their nation in this collective adventure. Every move, every decision, every choice was made with them, and Europe owes them a huge debt. They brought hard work, extraordinary talent and lashings of good humour to bear on the most intransigent of problems. And they put up with me. I can never thank them enough. For each mentioned in these chapters, there are many more, including the wonderful officials and foreign ministers who worked tirelessly and supported my efforts. Some I remain closely in touch with, others have moved on to new adventures. Wherever they are, I have not forgotten. My debt is the same either way.

In writing this book I was struck by how often democracy was at the centre of my narrative – the erosion of democracy, aspirations for democracy and the challenges of building democracy. During what became known as the Arab Spring, across the Middle East and North Africa (MENA) I witnessed the cheering crowds full of passion, hope and determination. 'We want what you have – democracy as a way of life,' said a young man in Libya, believing in the endless possibilities for a better future. Too often I watched that fervour of possibility disappear from their faces as optimism faded.

It is vital that those who believe in democracy and are fortunate to live in one help those who want it as a way of life. Freedom of the press, an independent judiciary, a police force that works for the people, strong non-governmental organisations (NGOs) and civil society need help to take root, flower and grow strong. These are the essential components of what I call deep democracy, enabling elections to take place in free and fair circumstances, and people to make genuine choices, free from fear. This is the best – arguably the only – answer to those who fear that the overthrow of tyranny will lead to the populism of anti-Western extremism. Europe's experience tells us that true democracy is the necessary foundation of tolerance, peace and prosperity. In those parts of the world where democracy has yet to flourish, we will not reach that destination quickly, nor do so without setbacks. But deep democracy is the only way we will get there at all.

I

THE JOURNEY
TO BRUSSELS

My phone rang again. I hit decline for the fifth time while trying to persuade my reluctant muscles to cooperate with instructions from the fitness instructor.

Afterwards, walking home from the gym, I checked the caller ID. It was a senior BBC journalist. Odd. Early October before Parliament returned was usually quiet, especially for the leader of the House of Lords. I opened the front door to be greeted by my husband, Peter: 'Come in here, quick. Has your phone been ringing? Mine has for the last hour.' The living-room TV – and the Sky News ticker tape – told me that Peter Mandelson, the EU Trade Commissioner, was returning from Brussels a year early for a position in Prime Minister Gordon Brown's government, and I was the name in the frame to succeed him. The news moved across the screen on a loop.

'Has Gordon rung you?' Peter asked. I shook my head and rolled my eyes. Number 10 seemed to have briefed the media but not the person. For now, it was all speculation, and would remain so until Gordon either called me or someone else was given the job. I was irritated; my future was being decided and I was not party to it.

The Lords were about to return after the summer recess and I had lunch planned with Lord Strathclyde, Tom, my opposite number from the Conservatives, which would undoubtedly be fun. Our aim was to agree on what upcoming legislation was controversial and would be challenged by the opposition. Members of the Lords were loyal, but many were elderly. Using their time well was important. Both of us knew that the agreement would hold for most of the legislation – but not all. It was Tom's job to defeat me, and mine to anticipate and be ready for his attempts. It was always good to share a joke with him outside the Chamber, but foolish to underestimate his ability to turn you into the joke inside it.

My car arrived and I shouted goodbye to Peter. 'Good luck!' he said. 'Let me know when you hear anything.'

'Is it true?' asked Leon, my driver, as I got in.

'If you don't know, Leon, then it can't be,' I smiled.

Whenever ministers got moved, drivers knew first. A promotion meant a better car; moving departments a change of driver; and departures meant the car disappeared. So the drivers had to know first. But Leon knew nothing.

My journey was punctuated by a series of calls and messages that I ignored. 'Congratulations!' 'Is it true?' 'Call me!' and so on. Until Gordon rang, I officially knew nothing and to admit that would make me look stupid.

Morning in the office passed with something bordering on normality as I continued to avoid questions and joked with my special advisors that Downing Street seemed incapable of getting its act together. Meanwhile my name continued its travels along the bottom of all the TV news channels.

Tom was pleasantly surprised I hadn't cancelled lunch and had a bottle of champagne chilling in a bucket.

'I've heard nothing,' I announced as I sat down.

Gales of laughter from Tom: 'Nothing unusual in that. Same problem when we were in office.'

'But it's four hours since I first saw it on the news,' I said. 'You'd think someone might've noticed by now.'

An hour and the bottle of champagne later, my phone rang. It was Downing Street.

'Can you get the next train to Brussels?' Gordon Brown asked. 'You need to get there tonight to make sure we keep trade as the British portfolio.'

'So, I am going then?'

There was a confused pause. Had nobody rung me? I explained that only he could send me; no one else could do this on his behalf. Brown was apologetic, but insisted I needed to get the train. There was no point in telling him my passport was in St Albans, 40 kilometres outside London, where I lived. No point in mentioning that he was asking me to leave my home and move abroad with no notice, no preparation, discussion or choice. Later I discovered that my interest in Europe had been taken to mean that I would happily work there for Britain. It was true, but a day or two to prepare would have been nice. I wondered later how they would've explained my answer if I'd said no. Nobody told me where I would stay that night, where I would live in Brussels, or when I would be home again. I quickly realised I was on my own.

As I was no longer a minister, the car, email address and red box had vanished, and it took a contact of Peter's to find me a seat on a sold-out Eurostar train. There I found Kim Darroch,* our EU ambassador. An old hand at the madness of government and rarely ever ruffled, Kim advised a glass of wine for both of us. He used his fantastic combination of charm and affability to great effect and was already working on making things go smoothly. I relaxed a bit, reassured by his presence. He and his wife Vanessa would continue to reassure me through my years in Brussels.

On arrival Kim and I headed to the UK ambassador's residence, a beautiful, terraced palace. Its grand appearance was a creaking veneer of ostentatious wealth concealing failing heating and aged electrics. From time to time Treasury officials assessed selling it and moving the

---

* Now Lord Darroch, Kim's career would later draw to its conclusion when his ambassadorial telegrams on the Trump administration splashed across tabloids, causing his departure from Washington DC a few months earlier than planned. His reputation, however, remained wholly and rightly intact.

ambassador to somewhere more modest, but then the prime minister
du jour would arrive, along with other ministers, and declare it should
be kept. Kim and Vanessa lived in a small apartment at the top of the
grand staircases, itself in need of updating. Vanessa greeted me warmly,
understanding immediately how weird my day had already been. It was
great to be with them, but even more so to find James Morrison already
there. A fellow Lancastrian, he and I worked together in the House of
Lords, where James had managed the Lisbon Treaty legislation for the
Foreign Office. We made a good team. He was clever, funny and a serious
problem solver whom I trusted completely. So it was wonderful to find
him in Brussels, preparing to take over the job of chef de cabinet (head
of office) of the next British commissioner, who turned out to be me.

Kim and I were soon summoned to see José Manuel Barroso, the
Portuguese president of the European Commission. Like all members of
the Commission, he was appointed for five years, and his job included
deciding which country got which portfolio or area of responsibility for
the five-year term – including financial services, energy, trade and justice.
Brown wanted Britain to keep the trade portfolio for the remaining year
of the current term, though many other countries would have liked it.
Barroso wanted to increase the number of women in the Commission
and had told Brown that if Britain sent a woman, and quickly, it would
help.

Barroso and I had twice seen each other recently. While I was taking
the Lisbon Treaty* through the Lords, Brown had asked me to fly to
Peru for a meeting between European and Latin American/Caribbean
countries, leaving on Thursday to return the following Monday. At the
formal dinner in Lima, Barroso and I were seated next to each other, and

---

* The Lisbon Treaty revised existing EU treaties. Amongst other things, it created the new
roles of President of the European Council and High Representative/Vice President as well
as the basis for the EEAS. Formally coming into effect on 1 December 2009, it incorporated
many elements of the previously rejected Constitutional Treaty, which had attempted to
create a constitution for the EU. Bringing it into being was not particularly straightforward
since it required the parliaments of all member states to ratify it.

he asked how the treaty was doing. Exhaustion and a couple of pisco sours added to my willingness to bore him with details and reassure him we'd get the Bill through. It was a reassurance he remembered, and turned out to be correct, but I fear it was born of Peru's favourite drink rather than certainty on my part.

The second time was, bizarrely, only the previous week. I'd been in Brussels to toast the successful conclusion of the Lisbon Treaty and had seen both Barroso and Mandelson while I was there. In our meeting Mandelson told me he was interested in getting back to the UK, and I expressed an interest in possibly serving in Brussels in the future, an idea put to me while attending justice and home affairs meetings on behalf the UK government. But neither of us had known what was about to happen. The press, believing my visit was no coincidence, assumed otherwise: how could two people who were about to move have been sitting together in an office in Brussels, meeting all the key people who would be involved and not have known? But it was genuinely coincidental. I'd planned my visit to Brussels with my team in the Lords. Even if Mandelson had an inkling, I'd had no idea at all.

Barroso's room in the Berlaymont building that housed the European Commission headquarters was rather stylish. He was a serious art lover and the walls reflected that. He said he was willing to allow the UK to continue to have the trade portfolio but wanted to know what my style would be like. I smiled to myself. Mandelson was a strong personality and was sure to have ruffled some feathers. I told him I worked in my own way. It seemed enough, and I returned to the residence having become both the first British woman to be a European commissioner and the first woman to hold the trade portfolio in the EU. I had, of course, no idea that within the year I would become the first HRVP of the European Commission. Nor did I have a clue that the job would claim the next six years of my life. Just as well – it had been a difficult enough day.

Commissioner for trade was a great job if you liked travel, difficult and complex discussions, and working with really smart people. The Brussels trade team were fantastic. They did the grind: details of tariffs, non-tariff barriers and phytosanitary issues. I, meanwhile, learnt the language of trade and discovered I didn't suffer from jet lag. I negotiated the endgame in the South Korean trade deal, opened the Canada trade negotiations aimed at getting rid of most tariffs, or taxes, on imports in both directions, and resolved some long-term problems with the USA over beef and bananas. In Brussels I tried to be a collegiate commissioner, responding to the European Parliament and learning to view my own country (in Commission speak 'the country I know best') from an offshore position. On occasion I would try to explain UK national positions, putting the best spin on the pronouncements while making sure not to become the UK mouthpiece.

In January 2009 we faced a problem over the EU's refusal to allow hormone-treated beef into its markets, which infuriated the USA. As tensions escalated, one of the products threatened with a reciprocal ban was San Pellegrino water, a massive Italian export to the USA. While I was dealing with this during a trip to Rome, Prime Minister Berlusconi invited me for an audience. In an ornate room we sat on gilded chairs beside a small table on which lay cake from his local bakery. Small and mahogany-hued, he spoke Italian with a broad grin and flourish of his hand and joked about his strength and determination to outlive and outlast his opposition as he urged me to resolve the dispute. Then, official business done, he relaxed and showed me photographs of the new university he was in the process of putting together. I'd been warned that, no matter where the conversation started, some reference to sex would inevitably appear. Sure enough, as he told me he wanted there to be equal numbers of female and male students, he pointed to long grass and secluded spots around the buildings, saying he hoped they would find things to do there together. His officials shuffled their feet, uncertain whether he would elaborate further. Instead, he showed me the room where he met with his senior ministers, joking that he didn't let them sit so they would not linger in discussions.

At the end of January 2009, I set off for the first time to Moscow with eight other commissioners. We arrived to a temperature of minus 15.

The hotel was close to Red Square and, as a treat, the team took me on a midnight walk to see the square, the Kremlin and St Basil's Cathedral. It was Moscow as I had imagined it, snow-covered, freezing-cold and beautiful. But beneath the beauty the Russian economy was in trouble, with over 30 per cent of reserves gone in the recession. The trade minister, Elvira Nabiullina,* wanted to get Russia into the WTO so future deals could be conducted under WTO rules, which would make some negotiations easier. It was an old refrain that many European businesses hoped would become reality, though we were not hugely optimistic. I had promised to raise this with Prime Minister Putin.

Our discussions with the government were held at the Kremlin. Green-malachite stone pillars in the formal rooms stood near doors that rose to the high ceilings, which were ornately covered in gold. Portraits of past Russian leaders looked down from the walls. President Medvedev and I had spoken at a conference in Nice a few weeks before, so we had a passing acquaintance. We moved from him to where the power really lay, or, as I wrote at the time, 'oozes from him': Putin.

We sat together and ate lunch and Barroso invited me to speak first on trade and the economy, something Putin was always interested in. There is nothing more fascinating to me than sitting opposite someone who is completely different from most of the people I encounter. The first thing I do is to watch – how do they react, what their style is. Everyone has a 'tell', a way of being, that you can learn from. All these years later, whenever anyone asks what a particular leader was really like, the chances are it will be Putin. He fascinates and disturbs people – with good reason.

He looked just as he does on TV or in photos – not taller or shorter or different in size. He has noticeable blue eyes, but they're neither piercing nor shark-like as some have suggested; I am wary of the tendency to imbue certain leaders with extraordinary physical characteristics or seemingly magical powers. He rarely smiles; there is no sense of warmth.

---

* Now head of the Central Bank of Russia.

In all my meetings with Putin he gave no sign that he recognised a shared future on the European continent. For him the sense of grievance went deep: Mother Russia had been invaded, sacrificed its millions and suffered over centuries. He was not there to offer friendship. His interactions with the EU were about the usefulness of a relationship that one day – possibly soon – would not offer enough to make it of value. When that day came he would abandon it without a backward glance.

He looks intently at whatever is holding his interest. On this occasion it was the small cards he had in front of him. I imagined that each contained a potted history of the people sitting in front of him, but that was probably my flight of fancy. Most likely it was a list of who they were and a short note about what he wanted to say. When I spoke he focused on me, nodding briefly when he agreed but otherwise giving nothing away. None of that was particularly remarkable, and yet it was clear he was in charge. As I was to discover again and again, controlling the time was part of his strategy. On this occasion everything overran, and we had to race back to our plane; on other occasions we would be kept waiting for ages for the meeting to start. Rarely would he arrive on time. Whichever it was, he was in control. I encountered him many times in the years ahead on issues where our interests coincided – the Iran nuclear deal being the most consistent example – or where they sharply divided, as over Ukraine.

The trade portfolio brought me to the attention of the capitals of Europe. Any deal required the agreement of all twenty-seven states (this was before Croatia joined the EU), and each was heavily lobbied by its own business sector. Many understood the overall benefits of a thriving and growing economy, even if a particular company gained little from a new trade deal, but politically it was tough. I spent a lot of time in Berlin and Rome talking to the car industry, particularly when it came to the South Korean deal.

James had an extraordinary depth of knowledge of how the Commission worked and what member states were thinking. He also had a passion for restoring old Mini Coopers. Strangely shaped parcels were constantly arriving from eBay or a Mini collectors' club at his home in Brussels, or at our Berlaymont office. His enthusiasm for a piece of misshapen metal from a 1960s Mini was endless and infectious, and there were always at least three cars being rebuilt somewhere in a field in England. James would visit to discuss and work on the cars himself; if I ever wanted to doze in the back of the car or needed a break, asking about his latest find or purchase would elicit a detailed analysis of his progress . . .

During this year as commissioner for trade I had every expectation it was just an interlude. As autumn 2009 grew closer, I packed up, literally and emotionally, to go home. I'd managed to combine my UK life and Brussels pretty well, though most weeks involved travel outside both. The Lisbon Treaty, now successfully agreed by all twenty-seven countries, was coming into force and the search was on for the first people to take on two new positions: president of the European Council and the EU top diplomat, the HRVP.

It is difficult to understand the constant tug of war between individual countries' desire to maintain control and their willingness to invest action in the EU without also understanding three of the main EU institutions: the Commission, Council and Parliament. Members of the European Parliament (MEPs) are directly elected by voters under a system of allocation that ensures smaller member states receive more seats than if they were simply assigned according to population size. Overall there are 705 MEPs, including the president of the Parliament. The Parliament has legislative and budgetary control as well as power over who is appointed to the Commission. It can require commissioners to attend its plenary sessions and committees. Established in 1962 and still immature in character, it had not yet developed the tools to keep parliamentarians from behaving badly in the Chamber or making 'hit-and-run' accusatory speeches to the hapless commissioner forced to reply to their debates, and then promptly departing to brief the press rather than waiting for a reply. Thanks to a 'gentleman's agreement' on non-scrutiny with the Council, it never disclosed its own expenditure details, though it had a rabid interest in everything the Commission did.

The Commission consisted of a president, appointed by the member states and ratified by Parliament, and one commissioner from each of the other member states. Each commissioner was allocated a portfolio determined by the president. A great deal of lobbying went on behind the scenes as member states attempted to get the most important, or most relevant, portfolios or to keep them out of the hands of another country. Once allocations were finally made, each commissioner had a few weeks to learn their portfolio before being scrutinised by a committee of the Parliament. These meetings were often brutal. Parliament had the power to veto the whole Commission, so any commissioner who failed to impress would be dropped and another would take their place. For Parliament the hearings were an opportunity to extract promises for the future, in the hope that desperate candidates would agree to anything to ward off difficult questions. Commission officials devoted large amounts of time to explaining to candidates that, despite the temptations, under no circumstances must they commit to anything that gave MEPs more power or more oversight.

The European Council was made up of the leaders of the twenty-seven member states, who met quarterly. Before the Lisbon Treaty came into force, each country took the rotating presidency of the Council, including chairing the European Council, for six months, bringing their own priorities to bear as well as continuing with existing work. So, for example, during Vladimir Putin's first eight years as president of Russia, the biannual summits with Russia were chaired by sixteen different EU Council presidents. Each time the EU's issues, priorities and style would change, as would Russia's relationship with the presidency country. It was messy.

Following the Lisbon Treaty, the newly appointed president of the European Council, chosen by the member states, would chair European Council meetings, represent all member states internationally, work with the president of the Commission and provide direction and continuity to the EU's agenda for up to five years (two terms of two and a half years). At ministerial level, other formations of the Council, such as justice and home affairs or finance, would continue to meet under the chairmanship of the rotating presidency, giving each country a chance to take the lead on a particular policy area for six months. The exception was foreign affairs, which, post-Lisbon, would be chaired by the HRVP for a term of five years. Foreign ministers would also no longer attend the meetings of the European Council alongside their leaders. Instead the HRVP would represent the views of the Foreign Affairs Council.

The HRVP role brought together three distinct jobs: the chair of the Foreign Affairs Council (and chair of Defence and Development Ministers' Councils, who met less frequently as a subset of Foreign Affairs); the high representative for the Council, essentially a full-time job managing foreign policy on behalf of the member states; and the external relations commissioner, responsible for the Commission's work across the world – especially important in terms of relations with Turkey, the Middle East and the Balkan countries.

It was a challenging role. The job was, uniquely, half Commission and half Council. Each half had different rules and different areas of 'competence'. The Commission side was responsible directly to the European Parliament, which was eager for more say and control. The Commission had authority stemming from its powers to propose initiatives. But, in Foreign Affairs, it relied on member states giving it the power to act. The Council worked purely inter-governmentally, requiring unanimity in its decision-making and without referring to the European Parliament. It had no wish to delegate to the Commission nor to involve the Parliament, especially on defence and security issues. The Commission meanwhile wanted to increase its delegated authority, believing that would support better long-term decision-making. Each side viewed the other with suspicion. On paper the HRVP was intended to be a unifying force, but would be watched closely by all three institutions for signs of favouring one camp above the other. Whoever took on this new role would be battling with themselves while fighting a war on three fronts.

If the politics of the institutions weren't tricky enough, there was also the party politics of Europe to contend with. There were three main groupings, roughly translatable to UK politics as conservative (EPP), liberal (ALDE) and labour/socialist (PES). Depending on who came out on top during the European elections, the assumption was that the winning political grouping would take the top jobs. In other words, the winning group would choose the president of both Council and Commission, and the HRVP job would go to the next-largest party. The role of president of the Parliament, also up for grabs, was increasingly shared between the two biggest groups for half a term each.

Alongside party politics was the hierarchy of EU countries. The founding six members – Belgium, Luxembourg, France, Germany, Italy and the Netherlands – expected to claim one of the big roles. Smaller nations like Portugal or Ireland wanted to be represented, while Eastern European countries also wanted a stake, knowing that if they didn't get a top job this time they could expect it next time, as happened when Donald Tusk, former prime minister of Poland, became president of the European Council in 2014. It was a careful balancing act between size, geographical location and political group, with occasional mention of the need for gender balance.

Following the 2009 European elections, which the conservative EPP won, the puzzle was pieced together. Barroso would remain Commission president for his expected second term (conservative, Portugal, South, small country). Jerzy Buzek became the first of two presidents of the Parliament (conservative, Poland, big country, Eastern new member state) followed by Martin Schulz in 2012 (socialist, Germany, big country, founding member).

Meanwhile, discussions were quietly under way as to who should fill the new job of president of the European Council. Most assumed that it would go to one of the small founding countries – Belgium, the Netherlands and Luxembourg – in part a reflection that the key part of the job was to chair proceedings, while national leaders, especially from the bigger countries, retained their authority. The European Council met to make its decision on 19 November 2009 and appointed the Belgian conservative Herman Van Rompuy as its first permanent president. As prime minister of Belgium, the cerebral Van Rompuy was highly respected and well used to finding creative solutions for a country with a population divided between French- and Flemish-speaking communities. His capacity to reconcile conflicting positions was an important key personal quality, especially as the financial crisis started to take its toll across the EU. Both Commission and member states were worried about Greece in particular. Given his deep interest in economics, Van Rompuy's appointment signalled that member states saw the new presidential role above all as chair and coordinator of their political and economic debates.

Although based in Brussels, NATO is a completely separate institution, but its next secretary general appointment was also factored into the 'top jobs' equation. NATO has a separate membership that includes the USA and Canada and excludes a number of EU member states. By tradition the secretary general has always been a European, and the choice was made at roughly the same time – August 2009 – as the other European jobs. The former prime minister of Denmark, Anders Fogh Rasmussen, was appointed to the position (conservative, Scandinavian, small country).

The role of HRVP was a different rank – foreign minister-level – and so came at the end of the list of considerations, by which point certain elements of the choice were already in place. First, the other roles were all taken by men – there had been no serious female contenders for the top jobs once Chancellor Angela Merkel made clear she was not interested in being president of either Commission or Council. This made the pressure to appoint a woman as HRVP quite strong. Second, all the other positions had been taken by conservatives (apart from the second half of the European Parliament presidency from 2012). The socialist group, which had done very well in the European elections, therefore felt the role should be theirs. As a strong third party, the liberals (ALDE) also felt they should get a major role, but the other two were not interested in sharing. Lastly the British, having thought for a while that Tony Blair might be appointed president of the European Council with the strong support of France, now had none of the 'top jobs'. There was quite a lot of support for the UK to have something, provided the candidate was right. The push for a woman to be appointed was meanwhile gaining momentum.

At a meeting in India some weeks before the decision was taken, President Barroso asked to see me in his hotel room and came straight to the point. 'For the HRVP job we need a Brit and a woman from left-of-centre politics.' He smiled. 'Those deciding across Europe will not know many – but they will know you.' I laughed – it seemed utterly ridiculous to me; there was nothing from Downing Street suggesting I was in the running, and I didn't think I had the right background for the job.

But Barroso continued to pursue the idea. He didn't want the Commission to be forgotten in the new role, and my experience as a commissioner would help. He also felt a strong affinity to the UK and saw the logic of having the new External Action Service set up by a Brit: the 'maths' added up – the job was seen as needing to go to one of the big countries, and the UK wanted a role. It was generally regarded as having a strong record on international diplomacy and would likely be well placed in terms of relations with the USA, a key partner. Over the following weeks I could tell which EU countries Barroso visited by the press stories citing me as a possible candidate. But back in Britain there were different ideas. Prime Minister Gordon Brown had wanted an economic portfolio to pursue British interests. But as decisions got closer he decided it was more important for the UK to get one of the top jobs, and that meant the HRVP.

David Miliband was an instant and popular choice, but his ambitions lay in domestic politics (and his eventual, unsuccessful, bid for the leadership of the Labour Party) so he ruled himself out. Later he asked me whether I thought he should have done it. He would have been terrific, but his family life would have been non-existent. With two small children he made the right choice, and International Rescue – if not British politics – was the clear winner.

It became clear that there were two serious UK-based candidates: Lord Mandelson, to all intents and purposes deputy prime minister, and Geoff Hoon, the chief whip and previously both defence secretary and a former MEP. Brown made it clear to EU socialist leaders that he would propose candidates for their consideration as they would be expected to put forward a nomination if this job was to go to the socialist group – a likelihood, as the presidency and other roles had gone to conservatives. Spanish Prime Minister José Luis Zapatero, coordinating the socialist leaders' choice, advised Brown to put forward a woman. My name was added to his list. Others can tell the story of how it happened, but, for whatever reasons, my name emerged as the unanimous choice of the socialist leaders. Stewart Wood,* Gordon Brown's advisor and a good friend, rang to congratulate me, sounding a little overwhelmed. I had mixed feelings. On the one hand I too felt overwhelmed, however much I understood that this was a compromise option. On the other, I couldn't resist saying it would be nice if someone had asked me if I wanted the job. He was sympathetic, but clearly knew that he could not go back into a room where this was now a done deal and raise any suggestion that I might not want it.

Gordon called to congratulate me. I was sure his preferred candidate would have been Peter Mandelson, and I offered to turn it down so he could put his name forward again. He said no. James nearly fell off his chair when he heard me make the offer. I am sure there were plenty of times later when he wished I had.

Although I had the socialist leaders' support, I still thought I wouldn't be appointed. I assumed that many countries would suggest candidates – foreign ministers who would be more obvious choices. Before the European Council began a couple of hours later, a number of bilateral meetings took place. Gordon Brown sought support from Merkel,

---

* Subsequently Lord Wood of Anfield.

Sarkozy and Berlusconi for my appointment. Martin Schulz from the European Parliament rang to say the socialist group in the Parliament was in favour. It became clear that I might find myself in the frame.

The meeting began in the Council building, opposite the Commission. Assuming it would take many hours for the decisions to be taken, and would not involve me, I had planned on a long weekend at home. But as I sat in my office with my suitcase it dawned on me that being on a Eurostar midway between Brussels and London while the discussions were going on was not a good idea. James and I opened a can or two of beer, sat down and waited. The news started to filter through – I even saw a report that I was in my office drinking beer. The press really did know every move I made. (Later they would report on how I liked to sit when I was talking to my team, legs curled underneath me. I stopped doing it.)

In the European Council meeting across the road, President Barroso nominated me, Gordon Brown seconded, and Chancellor Merkel came in to support. Others nodded assent and that was that. I got a text from President Barroso's Chef de Cabinet, João Vale de Almeida, now the EU ambassador to London, congratulating me. People started to appear in the office to wish me luck – some meaning it more than others. James got a call to say we should come over to the Council building and meet the leaders. I dug out the least creased jacket from my packed suitcase and we set off.

There was an air of excitement in the Council building, along with deep relief. What many feared would be a drawn-out process had been completed in an hour. I was congratulated by several prime ministers. Chancellor Merkel told me that she supported me today and would do so every day. Throughout five years of ups and downs she was true to her word.

At that time the Swedes held the rotating presidency of the Council so were responsible for managing the announcements. Their prime minister, Fredrik Reinfeldt, calmly brought us together in his role as president: Barroso, reconfirmed as president of the Commission, Herman

Van Rompuy and me. We walked into a crowded press room and Herman produced a sheaf of paper from his pocket. Clearly his appointment had been long in the making – understandably, as he had to resign as prime minister of Belgium. I, on the other hand, had to wing it.

In their questioning the press were relatively kind, though obviously unimpressed. They didn't see Herman and me as big beasts but rather as conciliators at best and compromise candidates at worst. While hugely important for member states and institutions, the art of compromise is often sneered at by the media, who prefer to see strong figures and conflict. For some the smoothness of the appointments was a big disappointment.

After the press conference we all walked to the local pub – called Kitty O'Shea's – where I had a beer. It was the first and last time I ever went there. My life as far as Brussels was concerned more or less ended then – and I never went out in the evenings except on the rare occasions I had a dinner. To be seen enjoying myself would have been a disaster, press-wise.

From there I went (as always seemed to be the case in times of trouble) to the home of the UK ambassador. Having assumed I was going home, I had given up my apartment, and until I found a new place to live they let me stay with them. That night Kim, Vanessa, James and I ate pasta and drank champagne in the kitchen – while I tried to come to terms with the future.

Later, unable to sleep, I thought about the journey that had led me here. Twice I had been asked to take on roles I had not looked for or expected and, despite strong reservations, twice I had said yes. Why? Partly because the prime minister had asked me to, and I believed in public service – as simple as that. That remained just as true when the government changed. And partly because in each case by the time I realised what was happening, my appointment was effectively a done deal that would have been difficult to get out of. But also because I wanted to do it. Throughout my career there have not been many opportunities for women in public life, and in both these cases I would be the first woman to hold the post. Yet personally I felt no exhilaration at the prospect of taking up this new job. I was more aware than anyone that I came with few obvious credentials and lukewarm support – if that – from many quarters, even in my own country.

Years later I asked James what he remembered about that first year. 'Perpetual rain,' he said. Apart from representing the EU across the world, chairing the ministerial meetings and dealing with whatever crises came our way, we also had to set up a diplomatic service from scratch. James carried a huge part of the burden of getting this under way, repelling all boarders who came with their own ideas or interests. We had to assume responsibility for thousands of staff, as well as military and civilian missions, and convert commission delegations into the EEAS embassies in over 100 locations. We staggered under the weight of attempting to build this new European institution while also doing the day job and balancing the wants and needs of member states, the Commission and the Parliament. In the UK and across Europe the press were harsh, following me across the globe to ask when I would resign. The misery it caused me was slightly alleviated when I read that being good at negotiating required a higher level of sensitivity. I channelled my anxiety into that thought and worked harder.

Finally, after a year, as James put it, 'the sun came out', as we got the proper resources to hire staff, find offices and create a functioning European External Action Service. From then on there were others to share the task, bringing their expertise and experience to lead areas of work. It was never easy – I described it as trying to fly a plane through turbulence while bolting the wings on at the same time – but at last we had a European diplomatic and foreign policy body, and the journey began.

All this lay in the future. For now, I tried to get some sleep and prepare for the first day of a new chapter.

2

SOMALIA AND
21ST-CENTURY PIRATES

Somalia sits at the midway point between Europe and Asia, easily recognisable as the pointed end of the Horn of Africa. When, in 1869, the Suez Canal linked the Mediterranean Sea and the Indian Ocean, the 3,000 kilometres of Somali coastline became strategically important for ships moving to and from the canal. Finally gaining full independence in 1960, its fragile democracy was quickly shattered nine years later by President Siad Barre's brutal dictatorship.

After years of unrest, Barre's government was finally overthrown in January 1991. The civil war that followed raged across the country: tens of thousands of Somalians died as local militias fought for control of different regions. Farming communities were displaced, with famine and drought leading to the loss of hundreds of thousands more lives. In the chaos the Somali navy was disbanded, leaving communities along Africa's longest coastline vulnerable to foreign boats fishing illegally and destroying the livelihoods of local fishermen.

Since the 1980s, there had been reports of toxic waste being dumped off Somalia's coast, highlighted when the strength of the 2004 tsunami lifted rusting tanks of unidentified material from the seabed, throwing them on to the coastline, where ecosystems collapsed and people fell ill. Ships bringing the waste were reported leaving with holds full of fish, making life even more difficult for local fishermen. With the support of their communities, fishermen banded together to protect their fishing grounds and deter foreign boats. Increasingly armed, some started to hold on to captured illegal boats, demanding a ransom as a means of compensation. They gave their groups names like 'National Volunteer Coast Guard'. Others joined with local militias who offered work to unemployed young men, and started to attack commercial vessels crossing the vast Indian Ocean.

Between the end of Barre's regime and 2003, multiple attempts to form some kind of government failed and Somalia sank further into chaos. In 2008, the UN Security Council approved military action to deter the pirates and support the delivery of food and aid. By this time over 1 million Somali people had fled, many of them to Kenya, Yemen and Ethiopia, and all in need of help.

Under the UN mandate, the EU created Operation Atalanta to protect World Food Programme ships delivering aid to those in desperate need and to deter pirates operating between the Suez Canal and the Indian Ocean. During my mandate, Atalanta was headquartered in the UK and led by a senior British military commander. The first I was to encounter was Rear-Admiral Peter Hudson, who managed a team assembled from within the EU and as far away as New Zealand. Peter dealt with all using great charm and grace, turning each nation's sometimes vague promises into real assets – ships, planes, people, and a willingness to prosecute and imprison pirates. Dressed immaculately in his white short-sleeved shirt and carrying a small briefcase, he would calmly set out to all the EU ambassadors the reasons why they should engage, then tour the nations most affected by piracy, all the while listening carefully to their views and ideas and gaining their respect and support.

The morning after my appointment as the first HRVP, and still feeling rather shell-shocked, there were two sharp knocks on my door. In walked Lieutenant-General David Leakey, then head of the European Union Military Staff, whose bearing and voice gave away his Sandhurst background immediately. He explained the military missions that fell into my portfolio, focusing my attention on Operation Atalanta.

I doubt he realised how astonished I was to discover this side of the job. It was my own fault – the 'just in case the unthinkable happens' principle had passed me by and, never thinking I would be chosen for the job, I had not done my homework. But Atalanta was to prove a real achievement, involving at various times up to twelve member states of the EU both at headquarters and at sea as part of an international effort across the world. Other more complicated and terrible issues would command greater attention in the future, but when I took office, this was the number-one security threat.

Many of the pirates were young men, some merely teenagers, enticed by the offer of thousands of dollars. There were few alternatives in Somalia's wrecked economy. When David walked into my office, over a thousand of them had been detained, raising many questions about what to do with them. Under the UN Convention on the Law of the Sea, piracy took place on the 'high seas' and the responsibility for prosecution lay with the country of the ship that intercepted the pirates. But there was a reluctance for overstretched judicial systems in faraway countries to take on the prosecution of young men, far from home, without family or support. So the UN and EU looked for more local solutions, proposing courts in areas of Somalia such as Puntland, investigating building facilities to house the pirates, or striking agreements with neighbouring countries to take them. But there were not many solutions. This growing challenge landed on my desk close to the Christmas of 2009. A Dutch ship with the Atalanta mission had been holding a group of pirates for two weeks, looking for a country willing to take them. They had been unsuccessful, and the crew were due to head home at the end of their tour of duty. I was contacted to be told that their only choice was to release the pirates, recognising that this sent a bad message that could embolden others, giving them a greater sense of security, which influenced my approach to action later.

The problem grew worse over the next year with the use of more sophisticated equipment. In 2010 pirates attempted 127 attacks on ships, succeeding forty-seven times. They boarded the ships, took control of the vessel and cargo, holding the crew at gunpoint. In some cases, they extorted ransoms for all three. By the end of the year, 400 people were being held to ransom. Crews were held on average for five months, but some remained captive for up to three years. By the next year, 5,000 pirates were operating in what was now a booming business that earned them $146 million, nearly $5 million per ship. Criminal gangs and militants became more involved, as lucrative ransom payments led to a major expansion of activity. Some attacks were within 400 kilometres of the coast of India. No longer linked to the fishing trade, heavily armed men in boats searched for prey. With little knowledge of the sea and inadequate food and shelter, a hijacked ship might be the pirates' only certain way of getting back to land. Violent attacks increased as ransom demands spiralled. Despite success in ensuring that no World Food Programme ships were attacked, we were losing the fight to keep the sea open and safe.

We knew we had to think differently. After twenty years of civil war the rise of al-Shabaab, originally a militant youth group and now affiliated openly to al-Qaeda, added to the lawlessness and destruction. Twenty thousand African Union troops tried to restore law and order and suffered many casualties, but people's basic needs were not being met. There was little chance of success at sea if we didn't have solutions on the land. Without alternative ways for young men to thrive, nothing would improve.

Despite a number of development projects in Somalia, there was no overarching vision for the country. Coordination between institutions is always a difficult problem, as anyone who has ever worked in government knows; but I was still surprised to discover that, until I brought them together, the commanders of Atalanta and the development team in Brussels had never met. From different traditions, each was mandated to take the lead in their area, keeping resources separate. Silos existed where networks should have been.

All plans needed to consider military, civilian, deterrence, development and justice requirements. Seizing the assets of those who organised the piracy was just as important as disrupting the pirates at sea.

I flew out to visit the ships in the Atalanta mission and talk about their tactics. An area of 8.3 million square kilometres, the Somali Basin is vast and difficult to police. An operation to protect each of the 30,000 vessels that crossed it each year was impossible, but with the help of the International Maritime Organization, NATO and countries in the region, an 'Internationally Recommended Transit Corridor' was established, which reduced attacks from twenty-one a month to a maximum five a month.

I also wanted to know how best to support the countries most affected. The small nation of Seychelles relied heavily on tourism for its income and on supplies being brought in by sea. Piracy had destroyed its cruise-ship tourism completely, and it once came within days of running out of fuel because of hijacked supplies. It had tried to fight back – 30 per cent of its prison population were Somali pirates – but limited resources made it hard to patrol its large number of small islands, and it was in danger of being overwhelmed. At their President Michel's request, we found and supplied fuel, keeping the story out of the press to avoid alarm.

I wanted to better coordinate our efforts and, after discussions with leaders in the region, convened a conference in Seychelles' capital city, Victoria, in May 2010. It was the logical place to show both the devastating effect of piracy and the commitment of a government to dealing with the problem. Ministers came from Djibouti, Kenya, Mauritius, Mozambique and South Africa together with the African Union, COMESA (Common Market for Eastern and Southern Africa) and the IOC (Indian Ocean Commission). INTERPOL and the UN Office on Drugs and Crime joined us.

I flew over Mahé island in a helicopter to Victoria, my only opportunity to see the country for myself. I decided that for my term as HRVP no press camera would ever catch me walking on a beach or swimming in a pool. Throughout the five years I stuck to my decision, sometimes looking longingly at people enjoying a cool swim, especially at the end of long meetings on hot days. The first time I walked on a beach after I left office was with Secretary of State John Kerry as we mulled over the final pieces of the Iran deal while strolling along the shore in Muscat, Oman. The sand under my toes felt like freedom.

The conference was the first concerted effort to join forces and put African leadership at the forefront. As at other international meetings, the commitment was captured in a dry final communiqué that put deterring and capturing pirates as the immediate priority and strengthening the capacity of the region to prosecute and imprison them as the medium-term goal. Most importantly, it said a solution could only be achieved by addressing the security challenges and development causes that created and sustained it. That gave us the mandate to work together. From Brussels we launched a Regional Maritime Strategy so EU countries would join forces to tackle piracy; African nations in the region did the same. Mauritius offered to join Kenya, Tanzania and Seychelles in prosecuting and imprisoning pirates and to host a follow-up meeting on 7 October 2010.

By the summer we had ten ships and 1,200 people operating in the area. Informal collaborations with NATO and other countries, including Japan, China, India and South Korea, worked well, making sure we did not duplicate or waste resources. All were linked through the EU's innovative network, named Mercury, sharing information and tactics across the different operations. If a ship was targeted, others could avoid the area and the military vessels could move in; simple but effective. Vessels were made harder to hijack with high-pressure water hoses and nets strung across bows, sometimes with razor wire. More controversially, some companies hired private armed security teams, which created a lot of debate about the level of force they could or should use. It was a debate that ship owners were prepared to have. The costs to shipping in 2011, when action against piracy was often successful, was $6.9 billion. Eventually a code of conduct combined with effective training helped to allay some of the concerns.

Pirates were afraid of the armed guards, and as their numbers increased and overall coordination became more effective, the number of successful attacks declined. But action at sea alone was not going to be enough. On 15 May 2012 we conducted our first and only attack on land. European helicopter gunships opened fire on a pirate base on the Somali coast, destroying the boats on the beach. It lasted just minutes, with a helicopter crew launching from a ship just offshore and raking beached and unmanned pirate speedboats – known as 'skiffs' – with machine-gun fire, destroying fuel stores and equipment. There were no 'boots on the ground' and, most importantly, no casualties.

This simple one-off mission took months of planning. The operation commanders knew that destroying the boats before they put out to sea would stall the pirates for a whole season. But the mandate given to them by the EU member states was limited – deter and disrupt at sea, but certainly not military action of this kind.

Rear-Admiral Duncan Potts had taken over command the previous autumn. He understood very well that attacking the pirates' boats directly, and on land, took EU action to a new level. A particular worry was that young boys might be asleep in the boats at night to guard them or for want of anywhere else to go. Duncan was clear he would only give the order when he was as sure as he could be that the mission could be achieved without loss of life. But he and I knew it was a risk.

I gave the political green light to get the member states on board. This was done through a committee of ambassadors called the Political and Security Committee, with responsibility that ranged from agendas for the Foreign Affairs Council to the civilian and military missions across the world. They were the eyes and ears of their governments, and Duncan needed everyone's agreement to his proposal; foreign policy issues required unanimity, and any country could choose to hold back their agreement. It was not going to be easy, but Duncan was exactly the man to do it. He expressed himself calmly, rationally and with humour and listened carefully to concerns from historically neutral countries like Ireland and other states willing to act but not wanting to lead the deployed forces when it happened – a classic response of yes but 'not on my watch'. It took time. Eventually, after (in my view) far too much deliberation, the decision was taken. We had moved to when, not if.

Duncan called me on the evening of 14 May to confirm that reconnaissance suggested there was nobody at the boats and it was his plan to go ahead. He did not need my permission, but he did need to know that politically I stood with him. This was my final opportunity to pull the plug. If it went wrong, it would be my political failure and I would have to bear the consequences. I had never been anywhere near a decision like this and I didn't sleep much. In the early hours I got a message to say it was done. Then I waited anxiously for what might happen next.

One of the risks we had considered carefully was retaliation. Pirates held more than 300 hostages of different nationalities and, so far, had refrained from harming them. Immediately after the attack the pirates responded by threatening to kill hostages if they were attacked again – something we had no plans to do. Somalia's government spokesman Abdirahman Osman said publicly that the government was aware of and had backed the strike and even encouraged further attacks. That mattered a lot. Although Somalia was still largely lawless, it was important that we respected what government did exist there. There was a noticeable impact on pirate attacks during the following months as they scrambled to find new boats. It also sapped their morale. The combination of our willingness to use force on the land combined with a less tolerant attitude within Somalia itself and the deterrents at sea caused piracy to dwindle.

I visited Somalia in August 2012. It was not an easy place to reach and security was a massive issue in Mogadishu – then frequently labelled the most dangerous city on earth – but I wanted to show Europe's commitment to the country's future, and I was worried about possible delays in getting the presidential elections under way.

I had no plane and there were no commercial flights. We couldn't hire a small plane in a war zone – it was impossible to get insurance even if a crew was prepared to fly and an owner willing to risk their plane. We found a UN aid cargo flight leaving Nairobi whose crew were willing to give me and my small team a ride both ways – there was no way to spend a night there. I flew to Nairobi and got ready to go. I had a black trouser suit with a red top – smart enough to meet the president, but loose enough to be comfortable on a cargo plane – and shoes I could run in. For once my security team were very clear. I was to do what they said when they said it and they apologised in advance if that meant they physically threw me into a car or on to the ground. I was very happy to be thrown if that kept me safe.

It was not always easy to be out and about in dangerous places, keeping the smile going and looking relaxed. I was nervous as we boarded, my heart pumping as I looked for the best spot to sit. I breathed easier when we took off, conscious that I was lucky to be able to leave. The plane was uncomfortable, but the UN crew could not have been more welcoming on the two-hour flight. We crossed the Kenyan border not knowing what to expect. Out of the window I saw lush farmland and a stunning shoreline, waves crashing onto golden sands – a surfer's paradise. Inland was entirely green with crops, trees and shrubs stretching as far as I could see: a bread basket for this part of Africa if farmers could get their crops to market. It was beautiful.

The airport was the only secure place for meetings in the country. The government only fully controlled just over 2 square kilometres of land from the airfield in a country nearly the size of France, so my meetings with the political leaders took place in the terminal buildings. I met with Hassan Sheikh Mohamud, who less than a month later would be elected president. A softly spoken man in his fifties, he had been a teacher before the civil war and worked with UNICEF among other NGOs before becoming an MP. He, along with the other leaders, made it clear that they were determined to end the twenty-year crisis. It was a massive task, but I was in awe of this group of men and women in a small room in an airport prepared to try, knowing it would make them a target.

To my delight, we were going to open our 'embassy' during my visit. It consisted of a corrugated-iron hut complete with bed, bedside table, table and chair and not much else. It was initially put within the secure perimeter, looking out to the ocean, and would be a temporary home for our Horn of Africa representative Alex Rondos, who happily laid

on the bed for photos. Outside we managed to get a flagpole and pull
up the EU flag of blue with gold stars. It fluttered in the breeze as we
solemnly declared our mission open. A small gesture, but a signal that
we were there to stay.

I really wanted to see more of Mogadishu, and I asked our dynamic
Italian head of crisis planning, Agostino Miozzo, to see what could
be done. Enthusiastic about the way the city was coming back to life,
he told me that at this time of day local people, especially the women,
would be sitting in cafes drinking coffee and visiting shops and it would
be a great way to meet them. I mentioned this to my security team, and
for the first and only time in my five years they put their foot down
and said no. They would put up with my request to drive around the
area, but under no circumstances was I getting out of the vehicle. Seeing
them with bullet-proof vests, helmets and large guns (an unusual experience) I was in no doubt they were serious. It was simple – unless I agreed
to do as they said I was going nowhere. I agreed.

The Somali government had purchased old armoured vehicles from
South Africa – notorious because they had been used to attack groups of
black protestors in Soweto and elsewhere – and repainted them to look a
little less menacing. Still, it was in some ways horrible to climb into the
back of one. Set high above the normal level of a car with huge wheels
ready for rough terrain, the inside consisted of two leather benches running along the sides and small windows with glass so thick it distorted
the outside view. The driver and aide sat in the front with a glass window
between them and those of us sitting in the back. I could imagine the
heavily armed South African police sitting where I now was. My team,
even inside these monsters of steel and reinforced glass, wore full body
armour. It was too hot for me, so I took mine off – nobody argued with
me. I had discovered how heavy and uncomfortable it was in Afghanistan
when I wore it to travel by military plane across the country.

We drove around looking at the city, dusty and ruined, the effects of
a twenty-year-old civil war clear in shattered neighbourhoods and the
entrails of what were once beautiful stately buildings. Even with all the

destruction it was possible to imagine what it must have been like, and even more what it could become. No matter how many times I saw terrible destruction, it never failed to anger and depress me: behind every destroyed building were the destroyed lives of hundreds of people. But there were also signs of a new life. People were sitting in makeshift cafes drinking coffee and not looking nervously around. Some new buildings were going up as Somalis or enterprising others rebuilt or invested in what they thought could be a brighter future. It felt like a city coming back to life – as far as I could tell through the thickened glass as we drove by.

When we returned through the gates of the airport my security team were visibly relieved. This had been a particularly challenging 'ask' on my part. I said goodbye to the people we had met and headed back to the cargo plane. We flew over a gradually darkening terrain. Nowhere does a sunset of gold, orange and red look like it does in this part of Africa. I watched as the light faded to darkness, listening to the loud hum of the cargo plane and the chatter of the pilots.

A few weeks later, Hassan Sheikh Mohamud was elected president and the transitional government disappeared in favour of the federation that is the Federal Republic of Somalia, and the hope of the international community turned to him and his team. The president, despite many attempts on his life, including one shortly after my visit, made progress. But as I flew from Nairobi to the next visit in a never-ending travel schedule, I knew his new government would need massive international aid and support. Together we had managed to curb piracy and the 20,000 African Union troops had had some success in pushing al-Shabaab back from their strongholds. For the first time in my memory, it seemed like it might be possible to turn a failed state around.

In Somalia and Brussels, with a new mandate to work together, the teams began to formulate a genuinely comprehensive approach to Somalia's many challenges. We had successful missions at sea, and development projects in Somalia itself. Now we needed to make sure these were not individual projects sitting side by side but interwoven comprehensive plans that addressed all the country's needs, from health care to food production, job creation to policing.

The UN Office on Drugs and Crime worked up a new programme to detain and transfer convicted pirates back to Somalia. They renovated or built prisons to international standards and offered training and education to give convicts opportunities when they had finished their prison sentences. We wanted to help countries tackle piracy themselves and in July set up an EU maritime mission to help Djibouti, Somalia, Seychelles, Kenya and Tanzania patrol and protect their own coastlines, capture and convict pirates and, importantly, offer rehabilitation and the prospect of a new life on release. The real solutions lay on the land.

As al-Shabaab was pushed back, obvious needs became clear. Many communities lacked water, food supplies and health care. Life expectancy for men was fifty-four, for women fifty-seven. Establishing good health and maternity services was vital, as was education, crucial to give the next generation opportunities, especially those recruited into al-Shabaab or into piracy. The president invested in a programme he called 'Give up your guns and go to school', persuading young people that the war was over and they should come home. I had seen plenty of research that showed being in school was a key factor in dealing with trauma in war-torn communities and preventing a return to conflict as a way of life.

In September 2013 I launched a New Deal for Somalia at a conference President Hassan Sheikh Mohamud and I jointly chaired in Brussels. All EU member states attended, along with the countries across Africa most affected by the conflict in Somalia and many others who had suffered at the hands of piracy. The Deal gave long-term sustained support that Somalia could rely on: investment in police services, courts, education, small business and so on, to be matched by firm commitments from Somalia to tackle corruption, fight crime, build the economy and treat people fairly.

After surviving attacks on his life, Hassan Sheikh Mohamud lost the 2017 presidential election and peacefully handed over power to the victor, Mohamed Abdullahi Mohamed. Holding an election across the country proved impossible – the levels of violence and insecurity were still too great. Instead the new president was chosen by the parliament, voting in an aircraft hangar in Mogadishu airport.*

As I read the news I thought back to Mogadishu and the extraordinary people I had met there, especially some of the women community leaders who had expressed their determination to end the conflict. Instead of displaying the weariness of endless conflict, they showed the fire of determination to bring about change. As so often is the case, they were more impressive than the men. As the prime minister of Somalia, speaking at the UN in New York, had said two years earlier:

> Our women – mothers, daughters, sisters – also deserve limitless praise for enduring the worst of our brutal conflict. The survival instinct of the Somali people is most evident in women: raising families whilst their homes are being bombed, walking miles without water in search of safety and burying their children whilst continuing to work to feed the rest of their family.

Even so, I knew these women would find it harder to get their hands on the resources to effect change. But there was hope. The new constitution stipulated that at least 30 per cent of MPs had to be women.

Across the world I was to meet thousands of women prepared to brave terror, violence and destruction to make their communities safer and more prosperous. They did so at great personal risk, not least because in many places they were expected to remain uneducated and silent. But in Somalia I heard and saw them, and they did indeed deserve 'limitless praise'.

Somalia has a long way to go still. Turning a failed state around is a complicated, long-term undertaking. It requires the investment and determination of many organisations and countries, all working

---

* Hassan Sheikh Mohamud was re-elected in 2022 as president.

effectively together, tackling each part of the problem for years to come. It means committing resources for decades to build strong foundations for institutions and communities, with generations growing up in peace and security. It is a big ask. But what is the alternative? The economic costs of piracy have been estimated at billions of dollars each year. Investing some of that money in Somalia's reconstruction and security over a long period would be more cost-effective for everyone involved. More importantly, it would save lives. If ever there was an example of why collaboration between nations and a comprehensive approach to solutions should be part of the twenty-first-century diplomatic tool kit, then Somalia is it.

3

NATURAL DISASTERS: HAITI AND JAPAN

No matter how developed a nation is, or how used to earthquakes, floods or fires, when disasters hit, any country can be overwhelmed. Recent fires in Australia and the USA; floods in Germany, Indonesia and the UK; earthquakes in Turkey, China, Iran and across the Caribbean have devastated regions and traumatised peoples. Some countries have managed with their own resources, while others have needed support for basic needs or specialist advice and equipment. Immediately after disaster strikes, the priority is to save lives, treat the wounded, shelter the homeless and provide food and clean water. But getting planes, ships, helicopters, equipment, food and water to disaster areas is a monumental challenge. Because disasters are rarely single events, continuing aftershocks, rainfall and fast-moving fires can hamper rescue efforts, and where disaster is piled on top of instability or conflict, rescuers may need protection from armed gangs or looters. However quickly help arrives, it can seem slow to the desperate. As events are captured and broadcast in real time, demands for action in response have taken on a new urgency.

I witnessed all of these challenges, particularly after the 2010 earthquake in Haiti and the 2012 earthquake and tsunami in Japan. Both victims of geology, their differences were obvious from the outset. Japan, a wealthy nation, was able to mobilise its resources to help its people – though it was nonetheless quick to ask for specific help from the international community. But Haiti, the Western Hemisphere's poorest nation, immediately found itself struggling. A catastrophic death rate, a lack of sanitation and food insecurity meant that, despite the willingness of its people to reach out and feed friends and strangers, it needed everything from the very beginning.

I was in Haiti a month after the earthquake and in Japan eight months after the earthquake and tsunami. In Haiti I went to see what more could be done to rebuild a shattered country in ways that would give it long-term resilience. In Japan it was to see how our support had made a difference. In both it was to hear people's stories, to show they were not forgotten, and to offer more help. In both countries I witnessed the resilience of the human spirit and the mind-numbing shock that in a matter of seconds life as people had known it was gone.

Haiti

On 12 January 2010 I went to bed, tired from a day at the European Parliament. I had appeared before a committee, as all aspiring commissioners must do, where my knowledge of foreign policy issues was tested. Sleep was welcome after such a day, but around 3 a.m. my phone rang, dragging me back to a sort of waking state. It was the EU Situation Centre – a twenty-four-hour monitoring room that watched the news and kept in touch with EU missions and delegations all over the world. Four hours earlier, at 4.53 p.m. local time, Haiti had suffered a massive earthquake and the next thirty-five seconds left 230,000 dead.

Haiti sits on a fault line between the North American and Caribbean tectonic plates and has a long history of earthquakes. But it had been 200 years since a major quake had hit, and the impoverished country was ill prepared. The quake was a 7.0 magnitude and, unlike many earthquakes that happen deep underground, was only a few miles under the earth, causing more devastation. The government lost most of its senior personnel. The National Assembly building, presidential palace and cathedral were all destroyed, along with 250,000 homes. The archbishop died in the cathedral.

The Centre could not account for all our staff there. Later that day I was told that Pilar Juárez Boal, a talented Spanish diplomat serving as our deputy head of mission, had perished when the annex to the UN building collapsed. She had been attending a meeting with the UN chief of mission Hédi Annabi and his deputy Luiz Carlos da Costa, along with advisors and administrative staff, to discuss how to get more aid to Haiti. Everyone present died.

But the vast majority of casualties were ordinary Haitians – men, women and children going about their day, crushed in the devastation. On top of the death toll, over 300,000 were injured and millions traumatised. Failing infrastructure made everything worse as telephone networks collapsed, hospitals were destroyed, roads were impassable and the airport was badly damaged.

In Brussels I briefed the commissioners, who met every Wednesday morning. I arrived early so I could convene a meeting of officials I thought could help, including military personnel from different member states, working in the nearby Council. Humanitarian aid staff told me they could not be seen sitting down and working with the military. They feared it would put their neutrality at risk: that neutrality kept them safe. I could see their point, but they had completely missed mine. The military knew what ships in the area could provide medical help, earth-moving equipment, helicopter support, food, supplies and so on. I would do nothing to compromise them – I just needed them to work together in Brussels so we knew what we had available and used it.

Their mutual wariness was a hangover that the Lisbon Treaty sought to resolve. In bringing together the different strands of the EU's 'external action' programme, it was expected that different parts of the machinery would collaborate more effectively. But at this point, although only across the street from each other, military and humanitarian staff were miles apart.

I asked Barroso, president of the Commission, to help. He reassured his staff and, trusting his judgement, they reluctantly agreed to cooperate.

Nevertheless, the humanitarian team from DG ECHO (the Commission department responsible for providing emergency aid around the world in the wake of natural disasters and other crises) sat with folded arms radiating a frosty hostility, while the military staff, in full uniform, looked equally uncomfortable. I started talking about the crisis and asked the military representatives what they could offer. When they disclosed the number of hospital ships in the area and explained how to get heavy-lifting gear to the island using boats, the ice started to melt. Given the chance to work together, they would – as long as such cooperation did not compromise the neutrality of our aid workers. I made a mental note that joint planning and regular meetings would help. It was just one example of the need to bring different parts of the institutions together and the difficulties I would encounter in doing so.

The priority in any natural disaster is to get aid there fast. But to provide aid and support rapidly I needed to deal with a huge, complex set of issues, from the bureaucracy and decision-making of the institutions to the politics of the member states.

I had only been in post for days at this point. In fact, I was only half in post: the Commission vice president part of my role still had to be confirmed by a vote in the European Parliament (a Parliament that contained members who despised the EU, thought the new Foreign Service should never be created and that my post should be abolished). Until the vote, I was not supposed to take any initiatives since I did not have the dual role. As a result, half the EU wanted to get me to Haiti immediately; the other half was quick to remind me I had no authority to operate.

In the high representative part of my job, I had been confirmed by heads of state and government in November – and in that capacity I could mobilise member states to provide aid and other forms of support. But I had no team or budget, and only limited access to people scattered across eight buildings and three institutions who would at some point become part of a new service. It would all take time – but Haiti couldn't wait.

At this point we were still trying to work out the responsibilities and parameters of my new role. Commissioner Kristalina Georgieva, later head of the International Monetary Fund (IMF), was designated to deal with crises: our roles overlapped so we had to find a way to work effectively. Anything that happened within Europe was Kristalina's responsibility, while anything outside was split between us. She had access to large amounts of Commission money to help NGOs and get support on the ground. I could coordinate member states' efforts. Our collaboration often worked smoothly, but occasionally a problem would arise. Kristalina stood her ground, firmly but with good humour, while making sure I understood and accepted her position.

If working out our relationship had been the only challenge, it would have been easy. But every issue brought one or more of the twenty-eight countries centre stage. Here it was France, which had a long and historically complicated relationship with Haiti, its former colony, leaving a legacy that included a common language. Spain held the rotating EU presidency, which meant it was responsible for supporting EU nationals in Haiti.

Commission staff got on with providing resources to NGOs operating in Haiti and getting help there. The badly damaged airport in the capital, Port au Prince, had only one working runway; the main airport building had collapsed while the second had huge cracks in it and was quickly declared unsafe. Elsewhere the port lay in ruins and the only other way in was a long drive from the Dominican Republic, which was deemed unsafe following reports of violent attacks from bandits. That meant prioritising supplies into the country and ensuring that everything they needed was covered. This was a big coordination job, involving talking to each member state, finding out what they could offer and who could transport what and when. But it made our contribution even more effective, working closely with the ECHO team, who were busy helping the NGOs on the ground.

I called Ban Ki-Moon, secretary general of the UN, whom I had not yet met. In his first term, and widely regarded as steady if not inspirational, he faced the same problems I did but magnified: all the world's major powers were telling him what they believed the UN should do. Where possible, they chose their secretary generals to be consensus builders who listened to the member states and didn't take an independent stance too often. Ban Ki-Moon fitted that mould well.

When we spoke, he was grieving the 102 UN people lost in the earthquake. I asked him if there was any benefit to the Haitians in my visiting quickly. His answer was clear: please go at some point but not now. That message was repeated to me by every UN agency I spoke to. Planes were stacking in the air for five or six hours before landing. Others never got in at all and had to find somewhere to refuel. Everyone wanted to help, but without wider coordination or planning, the consequences of just sending supplies were damaging. When I talked to Hillary Clinton about the disaster, her view was the same. The Clintons had a long history with Haiti, from the time President Bill Clinton sent troops to restore its first democratically elected president in 1994. The former president was now the UN special envoy for Haiti. Unsurprisingly, the Haitian president asked Hillary to visit but she did so reluctantly, not because she resisted helping – far from it – but because she knew her visit would require efforts that were needed elsewhere. She went and stayed at the airport, met the president, did a press conference and left causing the minimum disruption.

I thought it obvious that, when a disaster happens, the first responders should be those who could provide practical assistance – generally not politicians. But the pressure to visit, to be seen there was tremendous – as I was to discover. The expectations from all sides – politicians, press, public – that ministers would arrive to show their support publicly, in front of the cameras, made it hard to stay away. Over the years I was to recognise the value of being seen to do something, to demonstrate commitment and solidarity through a well-placed image or soundbite, but I was really confused in this case. I felt strongly that my job was to work the phones and organise as much help as possible.

A couple of French bloggers reported that the French commissioner, Michel Barnier (later Brexit negotiator), had said in my position he would have gone. This reignited the ever-simmering rivalry between France and Britain and the British media happily joined in. Barnier later found me and apologised; he'd meant that as a French minister, given France's connections with Haiti, he would have gone. Indeed, the French foreign and development ministers went a couple of weeks later. But I felt sure of my ground on this. When Joseph Daul, the leader of the conservative European People's Party, told Parliament I should have gone, I countered that I was not a doctor, nor trained in clearing rubble and would never want to stop supplies getting in while my plane landed. I challenged the Parliament to say what point there would be in my arriving at this early stage in the crisis. The UN were clear that the priority was to keep the runway open for essential traffic only and VIPs were already clogging up the airfield and needing escorts all over the place. I saw my priority as coordinating the supply of European aid: water, food, shelter, medical equipment, clearing debris and rebuilding. I stood by my view despite the noise that swirled around me, but the purpose of visibility gave me pause for thought. Those who can help should go first, but showing publicly that the EU was present and involved was important too. I was to return to that dilemma again.

I arrived in Haiti a month after the earthquake when the dead had been buried, the injured treated and supplies had arrived. The Spanish minister for development offered me a lift in a very small Spanish air force plane, which bounced around in the turbulence before arriving in Port au Prince. The airport terminal had huge cracks running through its middle. By the time we left, the airport lounge ceiling had collapsed.

A convoy of UN vehicles arrived and our acting head of delegation waved from one of them. I got in with my host, the Spanish ambassador, who'd arrived a few weeks before to take over from Spain's previous permanent ambassador to Haiti, who had been pulled from the rubble and was now in hospital. The Spanish diplomatic residence was destroyed, so we headed to a newly acquired house further up in the hills where there was less damage.

The evening was warm and humid, and we passed people on street corners selling basic foods and clothes. Bar the remains of one or two government buildings, there were few signs of affluence. But the damage this disaster had wrought on an already impoverished country was devastating. As we passed rows of houses, there would be three or four intact, then one that looked as if someone had picked it up and turned it upside down, then four or five flipped over, followed by a row of houses that looked fine, and then several totally destroyed. I sat silently gazing at the scale of this tragedy.

We arrived at the relative calm of the temporary Spanish residence. Sitting outside over dinner with the ambassadors from the US, Germany, France and Brazil, I listened to stories of near-escapes and lost colleagues. During the night, aftershocks rocked my bed and found their way into my dreams. I woke early and headed for the EU delegation building which, though still standing, was badly damaged and needed to be demolished. Everyone had a story to tell. A colleague showed his leg, hit by falling masonry; another had driven his partner, badly injured with a broken back, leg and skull, to the Dominican Republic for treatment. I talked to local staff who'd lost sisters, parents, friends. Most had seen their homes destroyed and were sleeping in tents on the streets or in parks. They were frightened of the strong aftershocks that regularly shook the already fragile buildings. I offered what practical support I could: money to get extra supplies or safe places to stay.

I set off for an established project set up to ensure that babies and young children received the nourishment they needed. With every second house we passed either badly damaged or a pile of rubble, the project was now in a hot and stuffy tent, full of women and babies and a few men sitting around.

The Irish staff were busy weighing babies and chatting to the mothers as I gave out the playmats, toys and equipment we had brought. Parents showed us their babies. A small boy of about three clung to me and buried his head in my shoulder for a long time. He and his older sister were happy to be distracted by this woman who'd brought toys to play with. The moment was captured in a photo that appeared in newspapers across Europe. A few weeks later, Joseph Daul waved it at me in the Parliament with a big smile on his face. 'This is MY high representative,' he said. I smiled back. I understood.

Behind the tent was a small camp, built to support some of the 1 million people made homeless by the disaster. I walked through it, talking to some of the inhabitants about what had happened. Children surrounded us, holding my hand and guiding me through. There were no schools. Most had collapsed and many children had been buried in the rubble. An older woman, in a wraparound bright yellow and red skirt and top, was stirring a huge *pot au feu* of meat and vegetables, the delicious aroma wafting through the air. I asked her how many she would feed and she laughed, pointing to the people gathered around her: she would feed whoever needed it. Supplies had reached the area, but relied on the kindness of people to turn them into the delicious fare in front of me. A small girl with solemn eyes and a dimpled smile stayed with me for the tour of the camp and I asked her what she wanted most. Hairbands, she told me. Remarkably, a little later on I found a woman selling bits and pieces including a bag of green hair scrunchies – the only pack I saw in the entire trip. I bought them and took them back to the little girl. She smiled and raced away to show her friends.

I left the camp and headed for a meeting with President Préval and Prime Minister Bellerive. Their offices had collapsed and what was left of the Haitian government was meeting in a police station. That building too was mostly rubble, but one room had survived and the table in the middle of it was where the government met. President Préval looked to be in a state of shock while Prime Minister Bellerive seemed impressively in control, though the grim expression etched on his face gave away the magnitude of what he knew lay ahead. Over the weeks the two leaders would sit at this table and talk to prime ministers, foreign ministers, aid specialists and parliamentarians from every part of the world about the future and the challenges of reconstruction within a broader economic and social context that had existed long before the earthquake. There were many offers of help, but those required decisions. Decisions seemed very hard for both men: the scale of what they faced was overwhelming. Soon the calm warm weather would turn to torrential rain and high winds, and finding shelter for everyone had to be their urgent priority. Everywhere they looked they were confronted by poverty and a lack of opportunity. But what struck me that day was the intimate scale of suffering. Here were two men sitting in a half-destroyed building, clearly traumatised, undoubtedly having lost people, trying to figure out what to do first on a seemingly endless list of problems.

I hugged them both as I left to take the first of two helicopter flights to another part of Port au Prince. The helicopter teams were invaluable because they could reach places impassable by road, but it was dangerous work. Tragically, one of the Spanish helicopters crashed a week later, killing the team on board. From the helicopter I could trace the path of the earthquake. A metal roof from a school was bent into the shape of a giant wave, showing the way the earthquake had moved across the ground leaving half metre wide cracks, as if someone had furrowed the ground. We landed and were immediately surrounded by children who led us, as they smiled and waved, to where an Italian team, newly experienced from the tragedy of the 2009 L'Aquila earthquake in central Italy, were clearing rubble and rebuilding the school. Two hundred children had died when the old building collapsed. Italian teams of firefighters, NGO staff, builders, civil protection staff and many others had cleared the site and buried the children.

I flew further towards the coastal area, 25 kilometres from the capital, where the epicentre had been. I was told that 95 per cent of the buildings were destroyed. I couldn't find the 5 per cent that weren't. On landing I transferred to a jeep and we drove through smaller towns, dodging rubble, avoiding bits of walls still standing at awkward angles, and passing a church with its walls half demolished.

The driver pointed to a site that had been cleared and was mostly empty. It had been the Christopher Hotel, the UN headquarters, and its collapse killed many of the staff. The grey dust lodged in my hair and mouth and made a monochrome canvas on which occasional flashes of colour were painted. We turned a corner into the ruins of a church. I jumped out and greeted several indefatigable Italian doctors busy vaccinating hundreds of people, offering everyone a smile and the smaller children a hug. All day long people queued quietly, patiently, waiting with their children to make sure they got their jabs.

In Cité Soleil – a sprawling shanty town of Haiti's capital – I visited a well-organised camp run by European volunteers. The children sang and took my hands to show me where they were living and playing. I asked a nine-year-old boy who had chosen to walk very close to me where he was staying. He frowned then said, 'Avec Maman . . . Papa . . . Je ne sais pas.' He hadn't seen his father since the earthquake. I held his hand for the rest of the visit knowing I brought little comfort and wondering how these children would bear this trauma.

Towards the end of the day I met Edmond Mulet, head of the UN mission, at their airport camp. The armoured vehicles and machine guns would not have looked out of place in a war zone. Bathrooms were few – one sign said showers only between 8 p.m. and midnight. Mulet was there to mourn his colleagues who had died, before picking up the pieces and getting on with the job. A Guatemalan and old hand in Haiti, he was an interesting and clever man. He pointed out that the first aid mission was in 1955 and since then the international community had propped up the country, which was still grappling with a complicated colonial legacy and the effects of a brutal dictatorship that ended in 1986. Instead of long-term nation-building, corruption and political paralysis had flourished, leaving its infrastructure crumbling and its people in poverty. 'If you fly over the Dominican Republic – which shares the island with Haiti – you see wonderful woodland. When you cross the border to Haiti there are no trees anywhere. They have cut all of them down and burnt them for fuel.'

Eighty-five per cent of Haitians who stayed in education until the age of sixteen then left the country and didn't return. For 65 per cent of MPs, being elected also meant receiving an official pay packet for the

first time in their lives. This meant that well over half the members of
the Haitian parliament had never earned any money – at least formally
– before taking on the responsibility of being an MP. Many countries
try to entice successful émigrés to return home – or at least invest in
the country. But dual nationality is forbidden, and legal protection of
property ownership rights impossible – less than 5 per cent of land is
officially accounted for.

Small examples illustrating the scale of the challenge abounded. A
beautiful country, especially in the north, Haiti was an obvious tourist
destination, but it wasn't always able to capitalise on that. One American
cruise ship, for example, visited regularly and docked in Haiti at 4 p.m.,
but the shops closed at 3.30 p.m. and there were no restaurants in that
part of the island. So tourists came ashore with money but nowhere to
spend it. Nobody seemed to know either how to ensure that the ship
docked earlier or to keep the shops open longer.

Haiti also produced fabulous mangos, but the export of perisha-
ble fruits provided few jobs. A product like mango chutney could have
increased the number of jobs dramatically – producing, packaging, mar-
keting, transporting it and so on – but there was no industry to make
it. Over the years there had been many proposals to reconstruct and
develop Haiti's economy, and there would be many more. Mulet and I
talked for a long time with no shortage of ideas before we grew quiet,
lost in thought. Whatever happened, it would be a long process.

Night was beginning to fall as I said goodbye, but the day was not yet
over. I flew by helicopter to the European hospital ships anchored off the
coast, landing on an Italian navy ship, its bright lights in sharp contrast
to the darkness on the land. The crew lined up to pipe me aboard and
somewhere in the distance the captain was waiting. 'What do I do now?'
I said to nobody in particular. Fortunately, my colleague was ex-British
military. 'Just look towards the captain, walk straight down between the
lines. They will salute you – for God's sake don't salute them back!' I did
exactly what he said and somehow passed the test. I ate dinner with the
crew, and the others who'd come to help: NGO staff, doctors, nurses,

construction workers, firefighters, army, navy and helicopter personnel, ferrying the injured to the hospitals. They sat down exhausted by the horrors they'd seen and wondered how to help Haitians build something substantial from this tragedy.

The Italians had learnt a lot through bitter experience in the wake of the L'Aquila earthquake, when more than 300 people died and thousands of homes were destroyed. They had brought a dentist, knowing that teeth get broken in earthquakes, as well as psychiatrists specialising in trauma. They had workers from Operation Smile, a charity for children born with cleft lips and cleft palates, and medical volunteers from six continents providing specialised care for babies and children. One told me that volunteers clearing rubble had noticed a boy of about eight years old being bullied by other children, not because of anything to do with the earthquake but because he had deformed ears. The boy and his father were persuaded to come to the ship where surgeons from Operation Smile fixed the problem. I went to see him, bandaged and grinning from ear to ear on his hospital bed. 'He has never smiled before,' said his father.

The hospital ship where the boy was being treated was completely full and I went to see each patient. The oldest was an eighty-eight-year-old woman whose foot had been saved from amputation. A little girl arrived so badly burnt that her chin was glued to her neck. One young man told me he had been at the university when it collapsed on him; his forearm was now amputated as a result. The ship had an oxygenation tank, intended for divers suffering from 'the bends' but also helpful to those suffering from burns or crushed limbs. They had saved four children that week who otherwise would have lost limbs by giving them massive doses of oxygen. The youngest victim I saw was a tiny two-year-old boy found in the rubble of Port au Prince. They had no idea who or where his family was, or what he might have seen. They had found someone to foster him for the time being, but his cries and sobs were unbearable and nobody could calm him, the nurse told me with tears in her eyes, especially when evening fell.

Back at the Spanish ambassador's residence, mentally and physically exhausted, I crawled into my allotted camp bed and immediately fell asleep. Aftershocks continued through the night, occasionally strong enough to make me sit up and wonder if I should move outside. Every now and then the ambassador, keeping watch, would tap on the door to see if I was OK.

Thanking everyone and saying goodbye was hard. Our staff were working in half-destroyed and unsafe spaces where regular, violent aftershocks threatened to finish the job. At the airport I sat in a line with the team who were leaving with me, on schoolroom chairs along the runway waiting for the plane, thinking about the enormous task that lay in front of an exhausted and traumatised people.

In March 2010 a conference hosted at the UN in New York pledged $5.3 billion in support for Haiti. I was there to give the EU's €1.2 billion contribution and to talk about long-term development. Despite the pledges, by the summer of 2010 there were demonstrations in the streets of Port au Prince at the slow progress of rebuilding. The earthquake left 16,000 civil servants dead and thousands of land records destroyed, making it impossible to establish ownership before rebuilding could start. The lack of coordination by aid agencies had been exacerbated by the absence of a national reconstruction plan to galvanise support from foreign governments wary of Haiti's inability to handle the relief effort.

Throughout its history Haiti has suffered cyclones, hurricanes, tropical storms, torrential rains, floods and earthquakes. It remains one of the poorest nations on earth, rife with corruption and a lack of leadership. Money keeps people alive, but there is little investment. Haiti has inadequate roads, water systems, medical care and schools. Violence and the lack of any rule of law creates even greater instability. Since my visit there have been thirteen prime ministers, the longest-serving for two years and seven months. July 2021 saw the assassination of President Jovenel Moïse in his private residence in Port au Prince. With the capital under siege by gangs and a collapsing economy, the few elected leaders left in the country sparred for control, hindering normality, let alone development. In August 2021 another major earthquake killed 2,000 people and destroyed over 50,000 homes. A quarter of a million children need basic support as a result. In a population of just over 10.5 million, 6 million live below the poverty line. Two-thirds of adults do not have formal jobs, in part because only half of the children ever go to school.

But there are small pockets of development and individual success stories. Within three years of the earthquake the EU money had provided homes for 500,000 people. The resilience of a people suffering from extreme poverty, political instability and natural disaster is not in doubt, even if years later it still seems there is everything to do.

Japan

I'd hoped never again to see such devastation as Haiti's, but fourteen months later, on 11 March 2011 at 2.46 p.m., an earthquake measuring 9.1 on the Richter scale struck the north-east part of Honshu, the main island of Japan, over 350 kilometres from Tokyo. Lasting six minutes, the fourth most powerful quake in the history of seismology knocked the Earth 17 centimetres off its axis and moved Japan closer to the USA. It was followed by a tsunami – a Japanese word, *tsu* meaning harbour and *nami* meaning wave. Hokusai's *Great Wave*, the iconic, evocative woodblock synonymous with Japan, illustrated the perils of a country of 6,852 islands (430 are inhabited) on the Pacific Ring of Fire where tectonic plates meet and move. The devastation of that day was captured forever on an endless loop of documentary footage as water forced its way into buildings, tossing cars and boats around as if they were miniatures made of plastic.

The Meteorological Agency had issued a warning, advising people on the north-east coast to evacuate the area. Some sought higher ground, others didn't. With waves reaching 40 metres at speeds of up to 700 kilometres per hour, the tsunami travelled ten kilometres inland and over 16,000 people died, most of them by drowning; more than 2,500 others were never found.

The EU offered help from the outset, both collectively and as separate nations. Coordinated by Commission staff working with the External Action Service teams and our Tokyo delegation, the first of seven shipments containing 70 tonnes of aid from Lithuania, Denmark and the Netherlands was flown in free by Lufthansa. It contained blankets, sleeping bags and water. It was followed by shipments from France, Denmark and the UK with either Lufthansa, UPS and others offering free transport or the Commission paying the costs.

There were no historical ties linking Japan with European nations, as had been the case with France and Haiti, so there was little pressure on me to visit Japan at the beginning. I went there eight months after the earthquake to follow up on how European aid had been used and report back on what more might be needed.

The Fukushima nuclear plant, 65 kilometres from Sendai city, was badly damaged by the tsunami. Japan has an extraordinary safety record, and the nuclear plant survived the earthquake itself despite its severity, the reactors shutting down automatically and emergency generators keeping coolant pumping around the hot cores. But the 14 metre-high tsunami knocked out the generators and the nuclear fuel started to overheat, causing the cores to partly melt. Nuclear experts held their breath as 150,000 people were evacuated. The Fukushima facility was eventually declared stable, but clean-up efforts are still continuing today.

Unlike in Haiti, buildings were constructed to withstand earthquakes and its people were well drilled. Rescue services and emergency aid were available, and good communications both inside and outside the country meant that aid and rescue was coordinated quickly. Japan was a rich, well-organised country able to get on with its initial rescue efforts and ask for help as it needed to. While it welcomed immediate support from the international community Japan gave every indication that – beyond the ongoing crisis of Fukushima – it would recover quickly. As it mourned its dead, the country was also focused on clearing and rebuilding for the future.

I took the bullet train from Tokyo to Sendai, a large city in Japan and the most damaged. The mayor greeted me on a cold, bright day and I watched the local fete in the square. Children danced and there was grateful applause for the EU's help. Many people came and thanked me for the efforts made to help them get through those first weeks, when large quantities of blankets, clothing, food and water were needed. Having visited many places damaged by conflict or chaos, I felt it was a rare opportunity to see what kind of recovery was possible, albeit in an exceptionally organised and wealthy nation.

From Sendai I took the boat to Matsushima Bay. Regarded as one of the most beautiful parts of Japan, its name comes from the Japanese for pine and island. We passed breathtaking scenery amid bright-blue water studded with 260 tiny islands. Seagulls followed the boats and swooped down to take titbits of food from our fingers. Each island was unique, some too small to stand on, some big enough to have vegetation and rock formations. Some of the smallest islands had disappeared with the earthquake. After docking we walked to a 400-year-old tea house overlooking a calm sea. My sense was that Japan had weathered the terrible events of March and I was enjoying the day in this stunningly beautiful country.

A shady, pine-tree-lined narrow road leads to the entrance of Zuiganji Temple. Founded in the ninth century, its pitched tiled roof rose in the familiar upturned V shape. As we reached the temple building our guide pointed to a line on the ground and explained that the tsunami water had stopped just short of the structure. We took off our shoes and sat cross-legged to have tea, the view out to sea framed by painted sliding screens in gold and green. I could have stayed all day enjoying the peace and watching the sea. It seemed impossible to imagine that an earthquake and a tsunami had wreaked their havoc so close by and so recently.

We drove out to the villages that had been most affected and from the car window I saw signs of what had happened: every now and then a telegraph pole was bent at a strange angle, then piles of debris pulled together, like a scrap-metal yard with a thousand cars bent and twisted and piled high. The car turned a corner into a strange landscape with familiar objects in unfamiliar places. A boat sat in the middle of a field. I counted four more, all marooned on the flat agricultural land. From a distance the faint hum of diggers broke the otherwise eerie silence.

This area, the local guides told me, was one of the biggest in Japan for rice production and fishing. The local village was a community of around 2,000 people and as we drove in I could see neat rows of houses reduced to their foundations. These were solid-brick structures almost completely destroyed by the water. As we got closer, I saw through a gaping hole in one house a man's suit hanging inside a wardrobe, gently swaying in the breeze. In the kitchen of another house pans and dishes lay scattered all over the floor where the waves had left them. The air was damp and cold and I thought I was at the coast, but the deep water in front of me was floodwater. The guides said that around twenty people, and some houses, had simply disappeared. It would take five years before the water receded enough for them to be found: all anyone searching for them could do was wait. I looked down to where a child's bicycle and a bright-blue and red pedal car were just visible under the water.

We met a group of volunteers who said that some places still hadn't been reached and no one wanted to move things that survivors might one day reclaim. I pointed to the cooking pots, and they nodded. Across the landscape I realised there were cooking pots everywhere, hundreds of them, scattered as far as I could see.

Further on, two volunteers spread their maps on our car and showed us the difference between the area as it was before and now. A new so-called Disaster Map had been created because so much of the coast-line had disappeared or changed. Around 2,000 people had died on this stretch of coastline. It was terrible in a different way to Haiti. There the earthquake's effects were visible; here it was about the wave. The only structure still standing upright near me was a telegraph pole. I asked the volunteers how high the wave would have been at this point. Twice that height they said: up to 9 metres – the height of a three-storey house

– with the force of the water behind it. But that wasn't the worst hit area. Further down the coast the wave had been over 35 metres high. I looked down at the water as a suitcase, a pair of children's white trainers poking out, floated past me.

The second wave came twenty minutes after the first, when people thought it was over and had returned, only to be swept away. One of the volunteers had lost his daughter in the tsunami. He spoke calmly but the anguish was there: he hadn't found her body. At the local school three more volunteers met us, two of them young people who had given up their jobs in Tokyo to help, the third a high-school teacher who came every weekend despite living far away. They'd worked for six months and were proud of what they had managed to achieve – especially rebuilding the school hall.

I was invited to have a look. I'd seen many school halls as an education minister, and this felt very familiar with its wooden floor, high ceilings, stage for productions or prize-giving and balcony for people to watch the performances. In one corner stood a table with a few bunches of flowers on it.

The volunteers explained that Japan had a system of meeting points at which to gather after an earthquake. This hall was the village meeting point. When the earthquake stopped and all seemed quiet, the villagers made their way to the hall. Many put their youngest children on the balcony where they would be able to see and not be squashed by the adults below. Then the wave came. It took 200 people from the hall immediately. All the adults perished as the children above watched. I asked how high the wave was here and they pointed to a faint mark on the plaster, just a few inches under the balcony where the children were standing.

It had been very cold that day in March and it got dark quickly. The children didn't know if the wave was going to come back; many were in shock and didn't dare to move. One little girl called out that they had to fight to stay alive and they all began to shout. That was how the rescuers found them – shouting had kept them warmer, and their voices had carried to those looking for survivors. The volunteers thought that might have saved their lives. I asked what time this happened, and the volunteers pointed to the round school clock by the side of the stage. When the earthquake hit, the clock stopped at eleven minutes to three. The man who'd lost his daughter quietly left the room. She had been taken from the hall by the wave.

I felt totally overwhelmed, unable to speak, struggling to grasp the horror of that moment: to reach a place of safety with your family and then watch them being swept away.

Someone touched my elbow. It was time to move on. A few miles further inland we reached a makeshift village made up of tiny, neat, prefabricated houses where the elderly mayor came to meet me. Together with his wife he invited me into their new home. The door opened straight into a kitchen, neatly furnished with oven and fridge – small but functional. Two other small rooms led off the kitchen, a bedroom and a sitting room, then a bathroom with a tiny bathtub. They shared the house with a friend. We sat and smiled at each other, then suddenly they began to cry. I asked could I do anything, and the mayor said they were very moved that someone had come all this way to see their tiny village.

They showed me a poster made up of letters offering sympathy and good wishes. The translator explained that the Red Cross told them the donations for their kitchen came from Denmark, and they wanted me to pass on their thanks. I promised I would.

There were 350 families in this block – largely involved in fishing or rice-growing. Most had lost close relatives, friends and neighbours. All had lost their homes and livelihoods. Few had gone back to retrieve possessions. They shook their heads at the thought of visiting the remains of their past lives.

The new village was unusually designed for a Japanese community. The original plans had the doors positioned to the side, offering privacy from their neighbours opposite. But the people said no. They wanted to face each other and feel their community being together. The design was changed.

There were thousands of these communities all over Japan. They were finished in August, just five months after the earthquake, and the expectation was that they would be needed for a couple of years or so. Nobody quite knew where to build permanent houses – with so much industry lost, people needed new livelihoods. The temporary village I visited was about twenty minutes' drive from where its residents used to live. They couldn't be any closer because too much water had seeped into the land to make it safe for building on. This was the nearest available site with space for the housing needed and a small shop.

What would happen to the area where they used to live, I asked? It was too expensive, the local guides explained, to build a barrier against the waves. It would have to be very long and very high and would be difficult to build. And whether that was a priority for funding was questionable. So the land has been ceded to nature – cold, damp, bleak and eerie.

A group of small children ran towards us laughing as they blew bubbles on soapy wooden sticks, eager to show the foreigners how their bubble sticks worked. The carers supporting them told me they were either orphans or living with extended family, often in cramped conditions. The coming winter would be especially hard on these traumatised children, they feared.

I thanked the mayor and his wife and wished them well, waving goodbye to the children. I travelled back to Tokyo in silence.

I thought again about the importance of travelling to places devastated by disaster and the value of pictures in saying much more than any words can – the photograph of me holding the child in the hot, stuffy tent in Haiti; the image of the clock in the school hall stuck at the moment of the earthquake in Japan. While I remained steadfast in my belief that the first responders should always be those who can offer practical help, I understood better the need to be seen and the opportunity it gives to capture the scene to understand what is needed and to show the survivors they are not forgotten.

Nothing exposes the differences between countries more than how they deal with a natural disaster. The contrast between Haiti and Japan was stark. Haiti was, and remains, heavily reliant on outside aid; Japan could draw on its own resources. While Japan builds for the future, Haiti struggles to manage the present.

But the people suffer wherever they are. Their loss is unimaginable, their sorrow the same. Visiting the aftermath of a natural disaster is to feel helpless in the face of awesome power – its effects scarring and transforming landscapes and whole populations in moments. The value of immediate aid was obvious to me in both situations; the importance of long-term development blindingly clear. In the wake of disaster there are many things we can do. Tackling climate change, better early-warning systems, buildings constructed to withstand earthquakes or hurricanes, well-prepared short-term aid supplies – all of these make a difference. But most of all we have to find ways in which to offer a future to those who have lost so much.

4

THE ARAB SPRING I:
EGYPT AND THE FALL
OF MORSI

'Don't call it the Arab Spring,' my Egyptian companion said, shaking his head. Tahrir Square, normally a scrum of cars navigating the Cairo traffic, was roiling with people shouting and wielding placards demanding change. 'Spring in Egypt brings sandstorms that last for days carried on the hot sirocco winds. They cause chaos and destruction. It is not like in Europe: spring is different here.'

I thought about that later as the protests grew, forcing out leaders in Tunisia and Egypt and enveloping Libya in chaos. The truth was, we had no idea then where the dramatic changes might end, even as we understood where they had begun – with a desperate man in a small town in Tunisia.

In December 2010 Mohamed Bouazizi, who sold fruit and vegetables in the street in Sidi Bouzid because he could not find full-time work, doused himself in petrol and set himself alight after police confiscated his stock because he did not have the necessary permit. He died from his injuries a few weeks later. Mourning and outrage, especially among the young, led to a popular uprising. Within days, after twenty-three years as Tunisia's president, his regime rife with corruption, Ben Ali fled the country. From Brussels we froze all of his assets held in Europe.

The process by which to do that was complicated and it could often take weeks to get all EU countries to agree. This time we did it in four days. The money belonged to the people of Tunisia and we wanted to return it to them.

The demonstrations rippled across Jordan and Lebanon, sparks spreading from Morocco to Yemen. Protestors wanted an end to corruption and abuse, free and fair elections, human rights and a better economic future. They wanted what we had.

In the early weeks of 2011, a million Egyptians took to the streets of Cairo, with a million more in the surrounding towns and villages, under the rallying cry 'Bread, freedom and social justice'. 'This is a revolution,' said the Egyptian ambassador, who had discreetly come to see me. 'I know it because there are people out on the streets who would never be on the streets in any other situation.' She picked out judges in the Cairo crowd. One of my Polish colleagues was puzzled, though. 'There is no stage set up, no microphone. If this was in Eastern Europe you would see speeches, hear rock songs. They would have it organised. There would be leaders. There is none of that here.' She was right. It was a mass crowd with nobody in charge.

By this point, President Mubarak had been in power for twenty-nine years and was heavily criticised for failing to deal with the underlying problems of rife corruption, crumbling infrastructure and poverty. His apparent grooming of his son to take over from him was widely resisted. He greeted the demonstrations with armed police, who fired on the crowds. In two days in late January seventy-four people died. Eventually the number would grow to over 800.

Statements from the Obama White House, from European capitals and from Brussels calling for restraint had little effect. Media across the EU and the USA were pushing hard for us all to say that Mubarak should go immediately. Worried, I wrote myself a note: 'The only organised group in Egypt is the Muslim Brotherhood, who are obviously waiting.' Founded in 1928 the Brotherhood, a Sunni religious and political movement with millions of members, advocated Sharia law. It was banned in

Egypt and elsewhere in the Arab world. But it had garnered support in many communities across Egypt, providing hospitals and medical care as well as schools and job-training programmes. In a country undergoing dramatic change it was well placed to gain support in elections held before alternative political parties were established.

Mubarak clung on, sacking his entire government and pledging not to run for re-election. In response the White House at first sent veteran diplomat Frank Wisner to help salvage the situation, but quickly relayed a clear message that the transition needed to begin immediately. Mubarak was shocked, as were other Arab nations. Mubarak had close links to the USA, had engaged with the Middle East peace process and was seen as an ally to the West. That he could be cast aside so quickly, as they saw it, troubled them. Hillary Clinton worried that it could take generations to bring about the stability and democracy we all wanted to see in Egypt and beyond. 'Tread carefully,' she urged. None of us knew what would come next. Mubarak finally conceded defeat and resigned on 11 February.

My office became a rolling news centre, the TV tuned into whichever channel had the best view of Tahrir Square. Making decisions about what to do and say meant gathering as much intelligence as possible. A constant stream of officials and military personnel from the EEAS and across the EU arrived with news from discussions with Egyptian military leaders. We called everyone we knew, urging them to stay calm and listen to the people. I had a busy week at the UN in New York in early February followed by a trip to Tunisia, Jerusalem and Ramallah, before going to Amman, Jordan for consultations and finally ending up in Lebanon. I wrote to the EU foreign ministers: 'I believe we face our most significant challenge. A new foreign policy service that is five weeks old, with many staff not in post, must move from its traditional role of responding to events to working through a proactive approach to our relationship not just with Egypt and Tunisia but the whole region.'

I flew to Cairo as soon as the demonstrations had calmed down and headed for Tahrir Square. A huge space with a grass-covered central traffic island, where roads feed into it from different angles, it is far from a typical square. The Egyptian Museum and other large, imposing buildings surround the space, which is normally packed with traffic and filled with the sound of tooting horns. On this day there were no cars – instead it was full of people, smiling and waving flags, literally jumping for joy. 'This is a revolution,' said a young man to me, while others crowded around nodding, 'we are just not sure that the system has realised it yet.' People rushed up to announce they were forming a new political party or preparing to stand for election. Their enthusiasm was catching, and I happily returned their smiles, handshakes and occasional hugs as they whirled around the square. 'But it isn't going to stay like this,' I muttered to myself: 'the system' was clearly struggling to come to terms with the scale of change that would be needed.

I went to see the prime minister, Ahmed Shafik. A former air force general and a Mubarak appointee, he had only been in office a couple of weeks. Outside the large windows the sounds of people celebrating rose and fell as I urged him not to rush to the elections: 'Prime Minister, elections are the cherry on the icing on the cake of democracy. On their own they won't deliver a democratic country. You have to prepare carefully for them and bake the cake first.' Either he wasn't listening or he didn't believe he could afford to wait. He stayed in office only thirty-three days before resigning. He re-emerged as the presidential candidate who narrowly lost to Mohamed Morsi in 2012. It might have been different if he had won.

I repeated the message to his successor, Prime Minister Essam Sharaf, on my next visit to Cairo. He stayed in office for a total of 279 days, leaving at the end of the year. Again, the problems of moving too quickly were ignored by nervous acting ministers who wanted to get to some form of legitimate change as quickly as possible. It was clear that the demand for elections needed to be met.

Back in Brussels, the European Council had to decide what the EU could offer. UK Prime Minister David Cameron proposed making support for Egypt conditional on progress towards democracy and respect for human rights. Chancellor Merkel pointed out that taking such a position, if applied to other countries, would result in aid to Afghanistan being halted. Cameron recognised that we had to get aid flowing quickly and came up with new language which allowed that to happen while not forgetting the need for progress on human rights and democracy. The outcome of the meeting was that I had a mandate to try to help the people of Egypt. I could work with that.

Egypt was a priority leading up to the presidential elections in June 2012, when the key candidates were Mohamed Morsi, standing for the newly formed Freedom and Justice Party representing the Muslim Brotherhood, and Ahmed Shafik, the former prime minister. Shafik stood on a platform of continuity from Mubarak, gaining support in some rural areas where security and order were key issues. These two were the most polarising candidates. Other, more moderate candidates, including Amr Moussa, the highly respected secretary general of the Arab League, had been defeated in the first round.

Morsi was not the first choice for the Freedom and Justice Party. Their original candidate, Khairat el-Shater, had been deemed ineligible to stand. He had only left prison a year earlier after serving twelve years for his association with the Muslim Brotherhood, and the rules required a six-year gap between finishing a sentence and running for office. Morsi had an interesting background. He had an engineering PhD from the University of Southern California, had worked for NASA on engine development for the Space Shuttle and on returning to Egypt had been professor of engineering at Zagazig University. Rising up the ranks of the Brotherhood, he was elected to the People's Assembly in 2000 (as an independent, the Muslim Brotherhood being formally banned), before serving on its highest body, the Guidance Bureau, and becoming chairman of the newly formed Freedom and Justice Party.

After the second round Morsi was declared the winner over Shafik, with a million more votes. Observation missions, including a European delegation, said the process seemed fair. Morsi became president of Egypt, taking office on 30 June 2012. The 52–48 per cent result, although decisive, was close enough to demonstrate the importance of reaching out beyond his supporters to the rest of the country.

Much of the focus in Brussels was on the Egyptian economy. Infrastructure was creaking or non-existent and too many young people had no jobs and few prospects. Many European businesses were interested, but unsure their investment was, or would be, safe. As we had done in Tunisia, and would do later in Jordan, we brought the European Investment Bank and the European Bank for Reconstruction and Development (EBRD) into Cairo in what we called a task force. The Italian EU commissioner, Antonio Tajani, did a magnificent job in convincing over a hundred major European companies to travel to Cairo as well. Overall, the task force pledged a potential 5.5 billion euros of investment for Egypt, along with political support from the EU.

I arrived on a warm November day to lead the event, which was put together by two diplomats, Bernardino León and Christian Berger. I had met Bernardino when he was working with José Luis Zapatero, the Spanish prime minister, and had appointed him as EU special representative for the Southern Mediterranean. Christian, an Austrian diplomat with extensive Middle East experience, was our director for the region. I was fortunate to have their skills and experience alongside those of Jim Moran, who, having headed our work in Libya, was the obvious choice to lead our delegation in Egypt. With Jim in situ and Bernardino and Christian in Brussels and across the region, it was a formidable combination.

I loved being in Cairo and November was a good time to visit. The smell of the Nile, petrol fumes and constant noises from the traffic all merged together, not so much pleasant as distinct. I knew I was in Egypt. The scorching heat of summer had subsided, leaving pleasant European summer temperatures. Walking down the steps from the small plane we had hired, I was greeted by the Egyptian Foreign Ministry and protocol team. I knew the routine. The airport bus sped us to a small building designated as a VIP area, where men lounged drinking coffee and chatting, acknowledging me as I walked past them into a lounge full of red-velvet sofas where tea was immediately offered and gratefully accepted. While the passport formalities were done the team showed me the *Egyptian Gazette* headline 'EU stands side by side with Egypt', heralding the meeting the next morning. I was pleased with the message.

Then it was on to a vast room in the Conrad Hotel where hundreds of people sat in rows twenty across. At the front on a large dais were four armchairs. Behind, written across a sky-blue backdrop, were the words 'EU–Egypt Task Force Meeting' with the EU gold stars and the Egyptian flag. Commissioner Tajani and I sat together next to the latest prime minister, Hesham Kandil. He was joined by Mohamed Amr, an experienced diplomat, now deputy prime minister and foreign minister. Both would resign the next summer, though in very different circumstances.

Waiting for me at the hotel was a replica of Tutankhamun's tomb. For three years a team from Factum Arte in Madrid had been working to process the highest-resolution large-scale facsimile project ever undertaken at that time. Their painstaking efforts had produced a replica so exact that it was impossible to distinguish between it and the real thing. I had been asked to formally hand over the finished work to the people of Egypt, and the announcement of the task force seemed a good occasion on which to do it. The replica now rests in the Valley of the Kings – an entrance sign declaring it officially opened by me – next to the house of Howard Carter, the man who discovered it. It was a rare moment to savour before getting back to business.

I opened with a short speech about getting Egypt's economy back on track by reviving tourism, creating new jobs and encouraging investment. As Egypt's main trading partner and the biggest source of aid and investment, the EU had a key role to play. I also made it clear that some things were non-negotiable: 'It is vital that this transition continues to ensure the full respect of human rights for all, not least women, who played such a key role in the events of spring 2011.'

We negotiated a tough statement on human rights – Egypt had never before made such serious concessions to an outside body, at least on paper – but I was under no illusion. The Morsi government was already showing signs that it was not inclined in that direction. A conversation with Morsi's human rights advisor ended abruptly when I asked for legislation on gay rights. Still, I hoped their commitments might give them pause for thought when they needed EU aid. After the speeches I drove to the presidential palace, with a group of foreign ministers and business leaders. Recent government pronouncements had worried some that contracts would not be honoured; others needed reassurances before considering investing.

Morsi received us in a vast, stunning room with walls of patterned inlaid wood and arched windows with floral wood carving. Doorways framed by large rectangular wood surrounds led into the room on all sides, dwarfed despite their grandeur by the huge space within. On the ceiling were more carved designs. Even the floor was covered in patterns, albeit of a more subtle geometric style. Green plants sat in the centre of a gleaming wooden table that easily accommodated the forty people gathered there.

On one side was an arched inset where a large golden Egyptian eagle hung with the Egyptian flag, its head turned to the right. Below sat Morsi, who beckoned me to his left, while Mohamed Amr sat to his right. The rest – foreign ministers interspersed with Egyptian officials and business leaders – found their places opposite Morsi, who, with short greying hair, beard and glasses, still looked like a professor. It was easy to mistake his laid-back manner for calm introspection. The truth was that he was not in charge nor capable of dealing with any of the real issues that Egypt faced. Nonetheless he did his best to reassure businesses that their contracts were safe, dismissing concern about government statements that had worried some around the table as being just the rhetoric of politicians. He gave a good impression, the attendees murmured to me as we left the room, but it was going to take a lot more action to really persuade them.

In late November the first battle between Morsi's presidency and the institutions of state began. Morsi issued a declaration that effectively gave himself unlimited power, including the right to make laws without judicial oversight. He argued that the establishment, including the judiciary, was loyal to Mubarak and still regarded the Muslim Brotherhood as a terrorist organisation. In practice it meant the proposed new constitution would be put to a referendum before the Constitutional Court could rule whether the assembly that drew it up was itself constitutional. In the run-up to the referendum, large demonstrations across Egypt focused attention on problems such as women's rights, freedom of the press and religious freedom.

The USA and Europe urged Morsi to change direction. I visited the presidential palace and told him we wanted to stay engaged with Egypt but needed to see movement towards democratic accountability. Morsi rescinded a decree that would have given him greater power, but fears remained. Former presidential candidates Mohamed ElBaradei, Amr Moussa and Hamdeen Sabahi formed the National Salvation Front (NSF) as a direct response, bringing much of the key opposition together. Morsi should have reached out to them – but he didn't.

The referendum on the constitution went ahead in December but was boycotted by the opposition parties, leaving only Morsi supporters taking part. Despite their decreasing numbers it passed easily on a low turnout of 32 per cent. Protests and criticism grew louder, from politicians and especially young people, and Tahrir Square started to fill up once more. In January 2013 Bernardino, back in Cairo for one of many visits, met with all the political parties who expressed strong criticism of Morsi and the steps he was taking.

By February we were getting messages, via Bernardino, that more engagement from us would be welcome. Even the army discreetly let us know they would be content for us to engage.

The people were fed up. Poverty still stalked the country, and even those prepared to give Morsi and the Muslim Brotherhood a chance were worried by the creeping repression. In early April I was back in Cairo, where the atmosphere was now very tense. On the way to meet the opposition leaders I could see small demonstrations everywhere and tanks parked in side streets with young soldiers sitting around them. 'Key

Morsi–Ashton talks today' read the newspaper headlines, but before I met Morsi, Bernardino and Jim wanted me to hear what the opposition leaders were demanding. From the NSF, ElBaradei, Moussa and Sabahi, whom we visited in his campaign headquarters, wanted Morsi to make changes, starting with the prime minister. They wanted the prosecutor general, removed by Morsi, reinstated. The appeal court had already ordered this but Morsi had not complied, angering the judiciary, who saw it as an attack on their authority. Moussa wanted an inclusive national economic conference. ElBaradei, worried by government economic incompetence, agreed. All feared the economy was collapsing. I talked with them, other politicians, journalists and young activists late into the night. Bernardino, Christian and Jim spoke separately to individual groups in different rooms in the hope of putting together a plan.

The next day with Bernardino I got into the UK embassy car, put at my disposal because it was armoured, and we set off through the dense Cairo traffic to the presidential palace. Discussions the night before had been grim, but there was still a chance to find a way through if Morsi understood what had to be done.

The high walls of the presidential palace stood out against a hazy sky. Spring in Cairo is always full of dust, but this was worse than usual because of the tanks positioned every few yards around the palace walls. He's under siege, I thought, not in control of anything beyond these walls. On the streets outside the tension in the atmosphere was palpable: this was a powder keg about to blow up. The newly increased security greeted us and took us to the room in which he had received us many times before.

Morsi was sitting as usual in a high-backed chair beside a long coffee table away from the windows. He greeted us enthusiastically and we exchanged pleasantries until tea had been served. I asked him bluntly what he was going to do. He said everyone outside the palace was his friend and supporter. We pushed back hard. I pointed to the demonstrations, the opposition, the decision of the courts. I repeated over and over that he had to act, had to show that attacks would not be tolerated, work with political groups other than the FJP, and most of all he had to show leadership. I laid out the key demands – changes in government, the prosecutor general. The meeting was intended to be his opportunity to put forward ideas. Instead his mood darkened, and he seemed to switch off. It was clear he had no control over the government, no control over events. I turned to Bernardino and mouthed that we should leave. We said goodbye, angry and dismayed.

We drove to the pyramids as dusk descended. I had been many times before, day and night, marvelling to touch and feel those ancient, beautiful monuments. I climbed up and sat looking over the city, this time in tears. Egypt seemed to be descending into civil war and the president was in denial. Back at the hotel I watched from my window as four fires raged across Cairo. I knew one was at the Coptic Church. I rang Morsi's advisor, Essam el-Haddad, who assured me Cairo was calm. 'So how come I am looking at fires?' I asked. He had no answer. I slammed the phone down and left Cairo the next day.

Tensions continued to grow. Every day I received reports from Jim and the team. Bernardino continued to travel to Cairo regularly; Christian coordinated the EU response. Morsi reshuffled the government on 7 May. He removed the entire economic team but not ministers dealing with political issues – the key demand from opposition groups. Instead of widening the government, he increased the number of Muslim Brotherhood members in the executive.

Bernardino wrote to me in early June: 'We are in an interim period of the interim period.' There was no activity on the streets, but no real calm. The economy was still in desperate straits. The European Commission was reluctant to pour resources into the country while there was no progress and little support was getting through to the poorest people.

Young activists started a petition calling on Morsi to resign. It gathered 20 million signatures. On the anniversary of Morsi taking office, mass demonstrations rocked Cairo and cities across the country. The country teetered on the brink. Morsi did nothing, staying behind the high walls of the presidential palace. Bernardino went to see Mohamed

Khairat el-Shater, the Muslim Brotherhood leader barred from running as president. Bernardino later described the scene. On the table was a bowl of fruit. Bernardino lifted most of the fruit from the bowl. 'You used to have all of this support, now you only have what is left here.' Nothing changed. Morsi was frozen, unable or unwilling to act.

I travelled to Bahrain for a meeting of the Gulf States, and then on to Brunei to chair a meeting of European ministers and their Asian counterparts. Not for the first or last time, I felt I was in the wrong place.

On 1 July the army issued an ultimatum to Morsi. He had to respond to the crisis within forty-eight hours or face their intervention. The following day, Morsi made a defiant midnight speech calling for his supporters to remain firm rather than offering ways to move forward: 'If the price for safeguarding legitimacy is my blood, then I am prepared to sacrifice my blood.'

Suddenly everything changed. On 3 July a group led by the head of the army, Abdel Fattah el-Sisi, removed Morsi from office. He disappeared and Tahrir Square erupted with throngs of cheering Egyptians. Many were happy to see el-Sisi, together with ElBaradei representing the National Salvation Front, the Nour Party (the second-largest Islamist organisation), the Grand Imam, the Coptic Pope and others standing together. The Coptic Pope, Tawadros II, told the press: 'We are gathered under the Egyptian flag.' It was a coalition of politics, the military and faith.

El-Sisi was hugely popular in the country, with many believing he had saved Egypt from chaos. Posters everywhere depicted him in military uniform, the 'Saviour of the Fatherland'. But others were nervous, fearing a military takeover, and Jim reported clashes between Muslim Brotherhood supporters and the army. A stand-off developed at the presidential palace, where infantry and armour were heavily deployed and highly visible.

By 7 July I was working the phones, talking to ElBaradei, Amr Moussa, Mohamed Amr and Nabil Elaraby, the new head of the Arab League, working out what to recommend to the Foreign Affairs Council. The dramatic change of leadership needed to be discussed, and decisions taken on what the EU would say. Christian, Jim and Bernardino were clear that we should continue to pursue a democratic transition and offer our help. Getting all member states to agree that the removal of Morsi was part of this process needed to be handled carefully – not everyone had been watching events as closely as we had. We also had to decide how closely to align with the USA. There was a lot of anti-US sentiment in Cairo including against their ambassador, Anne Patterson, a skilful, highly respected diplomat. Some argued the USA had been too close to the Brotherhood and so reluctant to oppose their actions. Posters across the city showed Obama with a long white beard, as if he were a member of the Brotherhood, and Anne Patterson's image crossed out with the caption 'Witch go home'. Behind the scenes Jim was working hard to persuade those acting against the USA to stop.

I called the interim president, Adly Mansour. Mansour had been appointed as chief justice of the Supreme Constitutional Court in May and been persuaded to act as president until a solution could be found. I told him we were following the situation closely and wanted a return to a legitimate government as quickly as possible, making clear Egypt's importance to Europe. Mansour said they were busy forming a government, which would take a few more days, then they would amend the constitution, hold a referendum, and have parliamentary and presidential elections – all within six or seven months. He was clearly worried about the economy and hoped we would support them. He said nobody would be arrested without reason and that Morsi was in a safe place, being treated well in line with other former presidents. I wondered about that – the only former president I could think of was Mubarak, who was in prison. He invited me to visit Egypt soon.

My next call was to General Abdel Fattah el-Sisi, who at this point was defence minister. He explained, eloquently, that the army's intervention had been a response to the people's desire for change. The army had contributed to that change by the appointment of an interim president and government. Believing we might have some influence with the Muslim Brotherhood, who had so far refused to participate in interim government discussions, he asked whether we could help bring them back into the political discourse. He pointed out that public opinion was against them, and fair elections would only give them 10–15 per cent of the vote. He too said that Morsi was safe, but agreed with Mansour that releasing him would spark violence and increase tension.

I returned to Egypt the following week, on 17 July. Jim met me at the airport and gave me a rundown on the ever-changing picture. I went first to the presidential palace, where I met Mansour in a different room to the one used by Morsi. It was strange to be back there with a new group of people in charge. Mansour was sworn in on 4 July but never seemed to be happy in the role of president. A grey-haired man in his late sixties, he had the solemnity of a judge. He was calm, measured and unpolitical, and I could see why they had chosen him as a figurehead. He made it clear that the Muslim Brotherhood had to understand there was no way back. The coalition of interests was a response to the desire of the people. If they accepted this, they could be part of Egyptian life, and nobody would be pursued except for those who had committed crimes. Mansour said Morsi had not followed the rules of democracy and he and his close advisors had been detained 'to protect their lives, and to prevent more violence'. He expressed his concern for the economy, adding that they were busy looking at the constitution and elections. But, he stressed, the army had no role in this. 'This was not a coup,' he said, 'but a correction.'

Christian and I took a brief break from meetings and went to Khan el-Khalili, a market that had been in existence since the fourteenth century. I liked to go there and meet people. At first we were greeted with standing ovations from people in the coffee shops, but quickly a crowd carrying posters of el-Sisi formed around us chanting 'Sisi good; Morsi bad'. The tension rose and our security team decided we had to leave. With difficulty our cars manoeuvred their way back to the main streets.

I went on to meet ElBaradei, and later the youth movement that had organised the petition, who I urged to get involved in mainstream political life. We worried that their idea of urging people all over the country to write down what they wanted in the constitution would be a challenge to those who preferred an orderly, more traditional approach. I saw representatives of the FJP, the party of the Muslim Brotherhood, and Kandil, the former prime minister; dazed and confused about recent developments, they wondered what would happen next.

The main event was my first meeting with el-Sisi at the military headquarters in the centre of Cairo. He arrived promptly, impeccably dressed in his uniform. He greeted me warmly and indicated where I should sit before taking his place in a large chair. I told him I'd come to show our continued support for Egypt and recognised how challenging the last weeks had been. He listened carefully as I asked him how he saw the immediate future.

He spoke about the challenges Egypt faced, making it clear they welcomed assistance but not interference. He said the military had worked hard on compromise and reconciliation, but Morsi never listened. At the end Morsi had offered the army whatever it wanted, but el-Sisi had refused all favours for the sake of the country. In the end they had no choice but to set a one-week and then a forty-eight-hour deadline. 'What else could I have done?' he asked. He talked at length, as many leaders do, but was more philosophical and detailed than I expected. He was concerned about the plight of young people and the economy. He understood the serious security issues to be tackled but pointed out that without jobs and a future there would be greater problems in the longer term. When I asked about Morsi, he said only that he was safe. I suggested that I might see him later, to make sure he was being treated well. El-Sisi said they would see what could be done.

Not on this visit – I had to return to Brussels to chair the Foreign Affairs Council with one question in mind: was what happened in Egypt a coup? If EU ministers decided it was, then should we demand reinstatement of Morsi? It was clear to me that this was not in the interests of the country, and we should not position ourselves against the coalition that had taken control. But if it was a coup, should we continue to fund projects and support the government or refuse to give any more money? That did not seem right at all. But if it was not a coup, what was it?

Ministers arrived with different views. Those who'd followed events closely felt some relief; others were concerned that the army was in control. All wanted new elections as quickly as possible and in the end the word 'coup' did not appear in our published conclusions. Instead, we agreed that the armed forces 'must accept and respect the constitutional authority of civilian power as a basic principle of democratic governance. It is now of utmost importance that Egypt embarks on a transition, allowing a transfer of power to a civilian-led and democratically elected government.' I was relieved. It was a united position that I could work with, and we could continue to offer support. It was enough for now.

By the end of July, I needed a break. There was no question of a holiday somewhere. Time at home in London seemed ideal. I arrived back on Friday evening, the 26th, with a few free days ahead. Hillary Clinton told me that clearing out closets and cupboards was her antidote to the stresses of political life. My equivalent was writing a 'to do' list of domestic chores and ticking off each one with relish. On Saturday morning I had my list ready and was about to put the first washing load on when the phone rang.

It was John Kerry, now secretary of state, having taken over from Hillary Clinton for Obama's second term. A long-term senator, he'd been chair of the Senate Foreign Relations Committee before taking up this post and there wasn't much he didn't know about foreign relations or American politics. He was earnest and to the point, though always warm, making you feel you were the only person he wanted to speak to that day. He and I had worked closely together on the Iran talks and the Middle East peace process and I knew his call meant something was up. The situation in Egypt was very fragile. The non-coup and removal of Mohamed Morsi had gone as well as could be expected, but counter-demonstrations, especially outside Cairo, were big and growing, as was the violence. There was unease at the crackdown by the army, and the numbers of dead and injured were increasing. Kerry had consulted with people in Egypt; Mohamed ElBaradei, now vice president, told him he was worried. He would be held to account by those who saw him as a moderate, a true democrat and a man who abhorred violence. He couldn't afford to become the acceptable face of an unacceptable situation, however much he agreed with the decision to remove Morsi.

Kerry had also spoken with Arab leaders, especially in Qatar and the UAE, about what should happen. The UAE and Saudi Arabia were generally relieved that Morsi had gone, but all worried that Egypt was in danger of falling into civil war. Kerry urged me to go back to Egypt as soon as possible – preferably that day. He listened in disbelief as I explained I had to find a flight, get a ticket booked in Brussels and so on. Won't the British fly you there? he asked. No chance, I told him. More importantly, Egypt had to invite me, and if I was to convince the EU that I should be there, working for a peaceful solution, I would need to see Morsi and show he was alive and well, wherever they had taken him. Kerry thought that was possible, and rang off the line to make contact again with Egypt.

ElBaradei rang next. He was clearly unhappy about 'these guys', the hardliners who didn't want a solution; he feared they would simply send in forces and kill the Morsi followers – there had already been about 200 deaths – and he couldn't be part of that. He invited me to Egypt and I agreed, with the proviso that I could see whom I wanted, and that this must include Morsi. He called back later with the news that el-Sisi had agreed that I could see Morsi on this visit. I was confident that el-Sisi would keep his word and also that Morsi was alive.

With Bernardino away, I arranged to meet with Christian and Jim in Cairo the next night.

My last call of the day was from Sheikh Abdullah bin Zayed Al Nahyan, minister of foreign affairs of the UAE. He thanked me for going and I was touched by his courtesy. His concern was clear – if Egypt collapsed there was no telling what would happen next in a region where chaos had taken hold.

I put another washing load in the machine and added 'pack for Egypt' to my list for the day. Peter, ever supportive, pointed out that I had been asked to do this: 'You have to go. You can sleep later.' I laughed

and went upstairs to pack my hand luggage bag. (I never travelled with
luggage in the hold, however long the trip. Given my travel schedule, if
it got lost it would never catch up with me again.)

I arrived the following evening – Sunday, 28 July. Cairo was hot, even
at night. The plane was delayed and I was late, but ElBaradei was still
eager to meet. The UK armoured car met me off the plane, and the driver
managed the Cairo traffic like nobody else – and nowhere else is like
Cairo traffic. Different authorities had responsibility for keeping traffic
flowing but had little contact with each other, which meant that even
traffic lights were not synchronised, roads were permanently blocked,
U-turns in impossible places common, and a sense of mayhem prevailed.
Short journeys could take hours. Somehow my amazing driver managed
to nudge his way through, taking shortcuts down alleys adorned with
goods for sale followed by U-turns across central reservations, and got
me to ElBaradei.

We met alone in his small office in a darkened building for over an
hour, before Jim and Christian and some of ElBaradei's advisors joined
us. He spoke softly but quickly, wrinkling his forehead as he emphasised
his points. Glasses and a small moustache gave him a distinguished look,
compatible with his scholarly reputation. He was deeply distressed by
the violence. The day before, security forces had clashed with demonstrators in Cairo and at least 120 Morsi supporters were killed. Tens of
thousands of Morsi supporters were now camped in squares across the
city, and it was hard to see how this would end peacefully. I had a sense
that members of the interim government were becoming increasingly
uncomfortable with the security forces' role. I listened carefully and
watched his discomfort. A way through had to be found, ideally with the
Muslim Brotherhood allowed to remain a political force. But the Morsi
presidency was over – on that he was categoric. This was inevitably a
very hard sell to the Brotherhood, which had won the presidency in an
election we had all declared fair.

ElBaradei was worried that 'hardliners', as he saw them, wanted to
take Egypt back to where it had been, or worse, under Mubarak and

he wasn't sure where el-Sisi stood on all this. He wanted everything to calm down and we discussed what is known in diplomatic parlance as 'confidence-building measures', including safe exits from the squares, denouncements of violence and a road map to a civilian government. He wanted the EU to be a facilitator and guarantor of these measures and asked me to stay as long as possible to achieve this.

Christian, Jim and I were quiet on the drive to the Conrad Hotel, lost in thought on how we might engage and with whom. The hotel manager, an affable Frenchman who'd made Cairo his home, greeted me warmly despite it being past midnight. He told me the hotel occupancy rate was 5 per cent and I wasn't surprised. Egypt was never a place where I felt afraid – though I did in plenty of other places in my time – but there was chaos in the streets and travellers from overseas had been warned of uncertainty. The manager insisted that I stay in the largest suite, stretching across the front of the hotel with a great view of the city. I stood on the balcony eating fruit, feeling the breeze on my face and watching the city below. The next day was going to be long and probably difficult, but sleep did not come easily. Eventually I grabbed a few hours before going down to breakfast around 7.30 a.m. wearing my traditional dark trousers and low-heeled shoes, plus a cream embroidered-silk jacket made for me in Beijing by a talented Chinese tailor I had been very pleased to meet.

The staff at the Conrad were always delightful, and it was like greeting old friends. They brought all my favourite Middle Eastern mezze foods, and Christian, Jim and I tucked in to as much as possible as they brought me up to speed. It was Ramadan, which meant nobody was eating or drinking until the evening. Visitors were excused this, but I abstained after breakfast and throughout my meetings. By the time it was dark, in the Cairo summer heat, I was very thirsty and quite hungry.

Efforts were under way to start a national reconciliation dialogue with all sides, but the Muslim Brotherhood refused to attend. There had been violent attacks on military and police institutions in Sinai, with a bomb detonating at a police station. Acting President Mansour had

called on pro-Morsi supporters to leave the squares, saying they would
not be harmed. The army gave the Muslim Brotherhood an ultimatum:
they had to sign up to the political reconciliation by Saturday afternoon.
The Brotherhood had already called for demonstrations on Friday to
show support for Morsi. Then el-Sisi asked for nationwide rallies on
Friday to give him a mandate to 'confront terrorism'. Millions turned
out for both sides. There were clashes in Alexandria and eight people
died, but the worst death toll seemed to be in Nasr City near a pro-Morsi
sit-in, where the number of dead was estimated between 80 and 120. It
was pretty grim.

We left the hotel and I headed to the Ministry of Foreign Affairs to
meet Nabil Fahmy, the new, US-born foreign minister. His father had
been foreign minister to Anwar Sadat, and Fahmy had served a long
stint as Egyptian ambassador to the USA. Across the table Fahmy, a no-
nonsense politician, made it clear that Egypt was set on a course, and
that although our help was welcome, he was not there to be told what
to do. Security had to be addressed urgently, but Egypt was not solely
the image of violent demonstrations shown on TV. He did not like the
Muslim Brotherhood ideology, but it had its place in Egyptian politics
and the country was facing increasing polarisation, with high expectations on the government. He was honest about the challenges they faced
but determined to face them. I liked him immediately.

The most important meeting that day was with Defence Minister
General el-Sisi. We met in the same room as last time, where he greeted
me warmly and seated me beside him, his advisors and military staff
scattered around the room. I told him previously that I thought of him
as a philosopher general – a term he liked – not to flatter him but to
recognise his breadth of thinking. I had not expected the then minister
of defence to focus so much on the problems of youth unemployment,
or Egypt's popular image on TV. Now he spoke in earnest, his words
(at least in translation) precise. He too questioned the perception of
Egypt that the international media was broadcasting, saying that this
was an internal fight and that in the twenty-five days since Morsi was

removed, people had become aware that the Brotherhood's objective had been to take control and impose their ideology. He recognised the need for a proper political process and that international observers were key to this, insisting it was not a coup but a move to tackle a bad regime. Egyptians, he said, did not want a dictatorship and they rejected violence – but disillusioned young people demanded new choices. He was worried things could spin out of control, escalated by Brotherhood supporters, of whom he thought there were now about 1.5 million. The army would be needed to play a part over what he thought would be a six-to-seven-month time frame to get everything in place as Egypt moved to a civilian government, but he insisted that would not interfere with the people's right to choose a new leader: 'The army does not rule – and does not want to rule.'

I made the same points to el-Sisi that I made to everyone else I spoke to that day: this was for Egypt to resolve, but we wanted to help. I didn't believe the situation was out of control – yet – but it needed to calm down, and fast. Security was not going to be achieved by locking everyone up, but rather by showing that Egyptian politics could find room for a broad set of opinions. Those facing criminal charges should be properly dealt with, but dropping charges where there was no criminality might help send a message of conciliation.

Next was Acting President Mansour. He'd convened a reconciliation meeting that the Muslim Brotherhood had refused to attend. So had the Salafists, who numbered about 5 million in Egypt, were conservative in outlook but covered a spectrum of opinion. They were recognisable in many photos of the time by their long beards – the representatives I met were always men. Mansour was clear that there should be no more politics under the 'cloak of religion', declaring that civilians not the military were in charge. He insisted over and over that his invitation for dialogue was sincere and open-minded, but for all the reconciliatory talk it was obvious that this country was deeply split.

The Brotherhood, in no mood to respond to the overtures, had declined the reconciliation meeting partly, I supposed, in fear of being arrested if they turned up. They were genuinely outraged that their elected president had been removed and had disappeared. They refused to talk with anyone.

The Tamarod, Egypt's 'revolt' movement, formed to register opposition to Morsi, were clear that they expected Europe to respect his removal from office. They bluntly told me they did not expect to hear calls for his reinstatement. There was no danger of that from me, but I feared the opportunity to move forward could be lost.

I saw the Islamic coalition, which included the al-Wasat (translated as Centre) Party, and the Muslim Brotherhood. Hesham Kandil, prime minister under Morsi, joined us. I knew that people were occupying squares across Cairo, particularly the al-Nahda and the larger Rabaa al-Adawiya, and was fearful that the army would move in. Could they be persuaded to go home? The Brotherhood said the people had been there for weeks and were not leaving without anything in return. I asked what they hoped to achieve and they said they would be prepared to talk but wanted detainees released and the hate campaign against them stopped.

Kandil had returned to Egypt from the Africa Development Bank in 2011 to help rebuild the country. His first job had been minister of water and irrigation. After that he became prime minister, despite not being part of any political party. He stayed in post after Morsi was removed but resigned five days later after fifty-one demonstrators were killed in Cairo. I could see the stress of the situation on his face. He had no idea what would happen to him. He was arrested at the end of the year, but on appeal was released in July 2014.

That day I met, and listened to, every group or political party we knew. At this point the EU's greatest strength was that we had open channels of communication with everyone, and they trusted us. Everyone maintained they wanted peace but said they didn't trust others and wondered about what the army would do. Some wanted Morsi back to stay, others wanted him back so that he could resign. Many didn't want him back at all. We talked for hours about detainees, the constitution, how the EU could influence the debate, whether independent people going to the occupied squares would help. Kandil asked whether Human Rights Watch could visit the squares and talk to the demonstrators. As always, rumours were everywhere, especially that those in the squares were stockpiling weapons, which could provoke an attack by security forces. Everyone claimed to be ready to negotiate, but their starting points or preconditions were starkly different. As the evening arrived and people could break their fast, food and drink arrived in our meetings. I waited for a message from el-Sisi about seeing Morsi.

In a break during one of our discussions, Christian said the message had arrived. I would see Morsi that evening. I'd been told it would only be possible at night, which I presumed was because it was easier to slip me into wherever he was held and out again in the dark. I didn't argue. The meeting wound up just before 8 p.m. as a car arrived. Christian agreed to be the one person allowed to accompany me. The rules of the trip were explained before we set off. We could take nothing with us – phones, passports, money, any possessions must be left behind, and no bags of any kind. They were to be no photos or recordings of the meeting. We were driven to the Almaza air base in Heliopolis in the centre of Cairo, which was a huge site but carefully tucked away, and it took a few attempts to find the right gate. The building was reminiscent of an airport VIP lounge, with ornate chairs and uniformed men with spotless white gloves who offered me tea, which I politely declined.

The Egyptian team who greeted us explained to Jim and my security team what would happen. There would be a fifteen-minute helicopter flight and Christian and I would have a half-hour meeting with Morsi before returning. It was 8.20 p.m. and they anticipated I would be back around 9.30 p.m. That made sense. El-Sisi had told me that Morsi was being held on a military base, which I interpreted to mean he was in living quarters there. I asked to set up a meeting with ElBaradei for 10 p.m. so I could brief him on what I found.

I was beckoned to the far corner of the room, where double doors opened to reveal a Black Hawk VIP helicopter sitting on the tarmac, its dark paintwork lit up by spotlights and shining against a night sky. As Christian and I walked towards it, I felt like I was on a movie set – all we lacked was rousing music. Once aboard, the pilots started the engines and we rose into the Cairo night. The fifteen-minute ride stretched to forty-five minutes. I had no idea where we were, having no sense of direction, especially on a dark night in a foreign land, but Christian was an old hand at the geography of Egypt and told me we were heading north.

The officials who briefed us had said that we would not be told where Morsi was being held and that Morsi himself did not know. This was for our protection and for Morsi's, he explained. I agreed not to say anything about the location, in part because I did not want the responsibility of him being moved to somewhere where conditions might be worse.

After nearly an hour we landed at a small, disused airport and were taken to a very old, very dirty airport lounge. Waiting for us were six or seven military staff who insisted we walk through metal detectors and asked again if we were carrying anything. They were polite but insistent. We were clearly on a large military base of some kind.

As we were led out of the building, the colonel in charge asked yet again if we had anything with us – like a camera, he suggested. We shook our heads. By the kerb were two dusty old dented cars. The colonel pointed to a battered Toyota Corolla; the back and side windows were taped over with black bin bags and cardboard and he asked us to get into the back. Two young soldiers wearing jeans and T-shirts and carrying machine guns got into the front. The colonel leant in, said goodbye, and reminded me not to ask where we were. I looked up. Across the top of the airport building was a huge unlit sign with the word 'Alexandria' written on it. A bit late for that, I thought, but I nodded assent. The doors closed and a quick test confirmed that they did not open from the inside.

I assumed this would be a short journey to another part of the base, but the car in front of us led us out into the traffic. This was a very poor, neglected part of Egypt, with piles of rubbish everywhere. Deep potholes made the journey a bone-shaker, and sometimes brought us to a halt. We drove at walking pace on stretches, avoiding rubbish, packs of dogs, people on donkeys and carts and at one point a small lake caused by a broken main water pipe. It lasted over an hour – though it felt longer.

I half joked to Christian that if the car did finally topple over, nobody would know who we were or why we were there. The two young soldiers up front thought we were from the Red Cross, there to inspect Morsi's conditions, and wanted us to know they did the best they could under difficult circumstances and hoped we would report that. They made an effort to be nice and passed us bottles of water, which we accepted happily. I sipped carefully, aware that a bathroom stop was highly unlikely. I have been asked many times since whether I was afraid of getting in the car that night. The answer was no. I was nervous about how bad the roads were but never about the people we were with. I was confident that the Egyptian army would get us there and back safely. But it still felt like the closest experience to a kidnap I ever want to get.

After an hour we turned off the makeshift road on to a desert highway for a few minutes and then into a large military base. It lay in pitch darkness, but through the front window I could make out ghostly shapes of different buildings and every now and then odd signs of activity. The soldier in the passenger seat turned and said Morsi had agreed to meet us (he had refused to meet others). Too right, I said, after all this effort to get here. There was no way I was going back without seeing him. We drove through the base to a corner building at the far end and our doors were opened. There was no light, but I could just make out cylindrical shapes made of concrete and iron, like huge storage facilities. The door was corrugated-iron, like a hangar door big enough for large vehicles. Cut into it was a smaller door for people to go in and out. It was obviously for some industrial purpose, and we found out later that it was a repair workshop for small submarines. Through the darkness I glimpsed soldiers standing around the building.

The colonel in charge – it did not escape us that the badge on his uniform said 'Presidential Guard' – introduced himself to us as the door opened and light flooded out. As we walked in, I remembered how both President Mansour and General el-Sisi had told me that Morsi was being cared for as I would expect for a former president. I had not anticipated that this meant he and two advisors were living in a workshop.

I looked around the shed, getting used to the harsh neon lights. The building was a rectangle nearly 20 metres long, with concrete walls and a concrete floor. In a corner by the door was a table with a kettle on it so they could make tea. Down one side was a row of offices, half brick wall and half window. On the opposite side was a small bathroom marked WC. Inside a shower head hung from the wall but there was no bath underneath. I tried the sink taps; only one worked. The first office contained a large fridge-freezer full of takeaway food next to lockers. I saw no oven or microwave; presumably they took food away to heat it and brought it back. There was a makeshift bedroom with three camp beds in it – no tables or lamps. At the end of the building the tools for the workshop were still evident. If Morsi or either of his team walked towards that end, they were sharply told to come back by the ever-present military.

Sitting in the middle of the room on a brown-leather sofa flanked by two leather chairs was Morsi. In front of him was a coffee table on a patterned carpet. A sudden buzzing sound made me notice a mosquito trap on the wall, like a small electric fire but with purple glowing bars. Every now and then it zapped to denote the destruction of a pest. Our driver had said they had air conditioning – Egypt is very hot in July – but this turned out to be two large fans that sat on opposite edges of the carpet. Behind the sofa were two prayer mats. The only light was the neon glare of the workshop lamps.

I was stunned. The last time I had seen Morsi, just weeks before, had been in the presidential palace in Cairo with all the trappings of office. Now both he and his advisors were wearing grey tracksuits with brand-new gleaming white trainers. They were pristine. These men had probably been inside for weeks.

Morsi smiled and invited me to take a seat on the sofa. He moved to the chair, sat down and, leaning forward, said: 'I don't know where I am, do you? I wasn't allowed to see. I think I am near Alexandria because I can smell the sea.' I murmured that I didn't know, not least because directly behind Morsi, so close he was touching the chair, stood the colonel with a gun. He stayed there throughout. Another of his men remained in the room too, closer to the door. Several times Morsi invited the colonel to sit down but he refused – whether to intimidate or because he considered it inappropriate, I couldn't tell. The colonel never spoke or engaged with us, but his presence made it harder to talk freely. I sensed his wariness of us as the first people to come into contact with Morsi since his removal from office.

Morsi seemed genuinely pleased to see me. He focused first on Cairo, asking me how things were in the capital. I told him that he was not going to like my answer and explained that, though some of his supporters were out protesting in the squares, most of Cairo felt as normal. He asked me if I remembered our last conversation in the palace and what I had said. 'Vividly,' I said, quoting myself back to him: 'It isn't enough to be elected, Mr President, it is what you do with it that matters and your country is in deep trouble.' He nodded and started to talk about the possibility of coming back to put right his mistakes. Christian and I shook our heads. I said bluntly that was impossible. He thought for a moment, then suggested he come back to formally resign. His supporters would find that easier. I shook my head again. That too was impossible. Nobody would trust him, and if he reappeared it might inflame an already difficult situation. He became agitated – he was the properly elected president, and as the constitution had not been suspended before he was removed, there had been a coup.

I went through the breadth of the coalition of leaders who'd supported his removal and told him he needed to accept the new reality for the sake of Egypt. He rejected this as ridiculous. He did not believe this would solve the country's problems. This was a deteriorating situation and tensions between his supporters and the security forces would worsen after Ramadan, especially in Sinai. As he grew calmer he admitted there had been mistakes, due to his governmental inexperience, but he also blamed the previous regime for resisting his plans. One advisor was more strident. He said the Muslim Brotherhood had 'support from the masses, but not the elites who had worked against them and especially against Morsi'. The 'deep state' had never accepted the regime and had pre-staged the coup, fixing dates in advance. He thought resistance to the army ruling Egypt would grow.

Morsi claimed that under his presidency there had been no arbitrary arrests and no TV stations closed. He said how sad he was that more than 200 people had died since he left and said he should be allowed to talk with his party. He urged me to talk to everyone and come up with a proposal that all sides could accept.

I pushed back and reminded him that the country had been running out of time – that he as president had been running out of time. The situation now was complex, not clear-cut. What we could all agree on was trying to find a way to stop more people dying in the short term and help democracy flourish in the future. 'I am keen to help,' I said, 'but I won't interfere. The solution has to be an Egyptian solution.'

But he still didn't understand that there was no going back. The coalition that had deposed him represented a massive part of Egyptian society. He had alienated or failed far too many people to be welcomed back, other than by his most ardent followers. Looking around at his situation, I saw no point in trying to drive home what should have been obvious. This part of our conversation was over.

I asked how he got his news and he showed me a 1960s-style TV set with a small rounded screen and an aerial that sat on the top. It showed state TV channels, very snowy images, when he turned it on. To my consternation, the news was about my meeting President Mansour earlier that day. I said I really hadn't wanted him to see that. He shook his head, it didn't matter to him, it was what I should do. I asked if this was his only news and he showed me two newspapers he received each day.

There was no sign of ill-treatment. Morsi underlined several times that he was treated well and receiving what he needed. They had food, drink, medicines and somewhere to sit and sleep. But that was the extent of it. Christian said later that it showed the contempt they held him in.

One of the points I had made to el-Sisi was how interested European foreign ministers would be in the conditions in which Morsi was held.

Just before 12.30 a.m., it was clear that it was time to go. We had spent two hours together. Morsi joked that he hadn't spoken this much English in a long time. I told him I would make sure his family knew he was safe and well; they had had no contact for twenty-six days. When I said goodbye, I told him I would try to see him again. But I knew this was probably unlikely and wondered what his fate would be. I had spent a lot of time with him as president, discussing his country, which I had come to love. Clearly a man of intellect, he had sometimes given me hope, then dashed that hope by his actions or, just as often, his inaction. I had pleaded with him, got frustrated and sometimes plain angry at his complacency and I thought him a very bad president. But I was still shocked at where he was now and concerned that his situation would get worse.

We got back into the car with our soldiers and started the long journey back to Cairo. A security officer from the site came to the airfield to see us off, again anxiously insisting that they were treating Morsi well within the means they had at their disposal. He reminded us again of the need for secrecy and I reassured him, thanking him for allowing the visit to take place.

It had been a long day, but our minds were working overtime. Until we were back in our own space we said nothing, lost in thought and not wanting to be overheard. Our helicopter touched down in the Cairo base, and we were once again greeted by white-gloved staff who led us across a red carpet laid for our arrival. I joked with the one security team member there to meet us that, considering I had been missing, so to speak, for hours, he looked very calm. He smiled and said he knew the Egyptian army would look after me.

As Christian and I headed back to the Conrad, we discussed whether we should tweet that I had seen Morsi. Walking through the hotel earlier, on our way out, a number of journalists had been waiting in reception. 'Is it true you are seeing Morsi?' a few shouted. Cairo was a rumour mill and nothing remained secret, but I didn't respond. We contacted his family to tell them he was safe and well. I didn't want his wife to see that on a tweet. It was 3 a.m. but we knew that our press team would still be up, waiting for our return. We decided to say something simple, then agonised about how to describe Morsi, finally deciding on Mohamed Morsi, no 'former president' or any other title. Our short tweet went viral almost immediately, creating headlines the next morning. We drove back to the hotel, ran upstairs away from any waiting journalists, and slept. Some weeks later a TV channel claimed to have received a readout of our meeting. I was upset until I actually read it. It was pure invention for media attention. Nothing further was ever said about our discussions that night.

We continued to seek solutions to the violence and to help Egypt move forward. With Bill Burns,* then US deputy secretary of state, Bernardino and Christian worked with ministers from the region and people across Egyptian political life in search of compromises. Bernardino went to the occupied squares with assurances that no force would be used, and that a few prominent Islamist leaders would be released, provided – as a first step – no more protestors would join, gradually leading to a peaceful dispersal. But many Morsi supporters still refused to accept that he was no longer president and continued to demand his reinstatement – even if only so that he could resign immediately afterwards. The other side, meanwhile, were not prepared to risk Morsi reappearing and igniting matters further.

On 8 August John Kerry and I issued a joint statement expressing our deep commitment 'to a strong, democratic, inclusive and prosperous Egypt . . . these are the choices only Egyptians can make and there is nothing neat or easy about any of them.' We were disappointed that the government and opposition had not found a way to break a dangerous stalemate, and deeply worried about what could happen with tensions continuing to rise every hour.

---

* Now director of the CIA.

I spoke with ElBaradei, reiterating our willingness to help and our concerns that security forces might move into the still-occupied squares. I made ten visits to Egypt, worked with talented and diligent diplomats plus a united group of member states, but in the end all our efforts failed.

On 14 August hundreds of protestors were killed when security forces moved to clear the squares. The same day, ElBaradei resigned as vice president: we understood his predicament though tried over long conversations to convince him to stay. Kerry and I coordinated our response. This was a needless tragedy that should have been avoided. My public statement read: 'With dismay and great concern I have followed the events in Egypt in the last few days. The toll of death and injury is shocking . . . Responsibility for this tragedy weighs heavily on the interim government, as well as on the wider political leadership in the country . . . I again call on all sides to end violence . . . and keep the possibility open for a political process that will lead Egypt back on the path to democracy and heal the wounds inflicted on Egyptian society.'

On 21 August I convened a Foreign Affairs Council meeting to discuss what was happening. After a lengthy debate we agreed a statement that emphasised our 'long and close relationship with the Egyptian people', and that we stood by them in their 'ongoing search for democracy, respect for human rights, dignity, social justice and security'. At my insistence we emphasised the EU's need to continue socio-economic support.

El-Sisi ran in the May 2014 presidential elections, for which we prepared an EU election observation mission. It was difficult – for some, that represented an endorsement of Morsi's removal. Although Egypt had asked us for the mission, the logistics proved a real challenge. For Christian and Jim it took hours of meetings and phone calls to sort out.

In a three-hour meeting with el-Sisi – for once dressed in civilian clothes – he explained to me his vision for Egypt. It was obvious he would win, given his huge popularity. People saw him as a key player in the coalition that had removed Morsi and promised a better future. The military was a strong force in the country, deeply engaged with the economy and seen as able to bring stability out of chaos. I hoped he would focus on Egypt's younger generation, an extraordinary pool of talent and energy who deserved a brighter future. 'Any advice?' he asked me at one point. 'Make sure you eventually resign,' I said. 'In the entire history of Egypt it has never had a president who has resigned and handed over power. Please be the first.'

As I was preparing to leave office I got to open the new EU delegation premises. I had inherited buildings all over the world when we set up the EEAS and took over Commission delegations. Some were in shocking conditions, and the Cairo offices were a case in point. Rats had eaten through wiring, and using the lift came with a 50 per cent chance that it would break down before you got to the right floor – if it worked at all. It was a pleasure to witness the team's delight as I cut the ribbon on their new home, and an equal pleasure to see a meeting room with my name over the door. I sent a farewell letter to President el-Sisi. He sent a gracious reply, in which he repeated his desire for a better future for 'our children and peace and stability for the region'. He renewed his invitation to come back to 'your second home, Egypt'.

Morsi remained in prison until his death in June 2019. President el-Sisi won a second landslide victory, despite growing concerns about deteriorating human rights in Egypt. In 2019 he extended presidential limits that could allow him to remain in power until 2030. While he argues that his focus is on stability and security, criticism of his repression of peaceful opposition grows.

It remains my ambition to return to Egypt.

5

THE ARAB SPRING II:
THE COLLAPSE OF LIBYA

As the plane circled down into Benghazi airport, I could see yellow-ish, grey-stone buildings below me. Every now and then a building was missing, destroyed by precision 'flattening', which left those on either side intact. As I was being driven from the airport, I saw posters with the words 'I have a dream' scrawled in large letters and others proudly declaring Benghazi part of the new, free Libya. Amid the piles of rubble spilling into the streets, people went about their daily lives, the roads were busy and the shops were open as men wandered by with guns slung casually over their shoulders. Just beyond the city limits the fighting was intense.

It was May 2011, and Libya was in the throes of a crisis; Benghazi lay at the heart of the turmoil. It was home to the 'rebel stronghold', as it was known in the media, a symbol of resistance to Colonel Gaddafi and his oppressive regime.

When I walked through the freshly named Freedom Square, full of the debris of demonstrations, people recognised me. 'Welcome Cathy, welcome Europe – thank you for visiting us!' A huge EU flag flew over the courthouse. Some Libyans had cried, I was told, when it was hauled up and unfurled. One man on a bicycle had a French flag sticking out of the handlebars. 'Sarkozy had promised to defend us,' he told me happily, 'and he has!' Everywhere the headiness of liberation and a slightly anarchic feeling of people doing exactly what they wanted had taken over. People shouted and fired off guns at will. This was new – Gaddafi, Libya's autocratic ruler, did not allow ordinary Libyans to carry guns. But in Benghazi the old rules were gone.

Gaddafi came to power in a coup in 1969 and dominated the country, suppressing reforms, creating divisions and stamping out dissent. Like many autocrats he claimed he was ensuring stability, and that his actions were necessary. Libya was a rich country, able to take care of everyone, but Gaddafi had deliberately starved some areas of funding to punish them for any opposition. His rule meant the country stood still instead of moving forward, with democracy a distant dream. But such suppression had also created a pressure cooker, ready to explode, and the dramatic events across the Middle East – what would become known as the Arab Spring – quickly spilled over to Libya.

In February 2011 demonstrations erupted, mainly in Benghazi. Security forces fired on the crowd of protestors, killing over 100, causing strong condemnation across the world. The UN Security Council froze Gaddafi's assets, but he rallied his forces and pushed eastwards towards Benghazi.

In response, President Sarkozy of France proposed to UK Prime Minister Cameron the creation of a 'no-fly zone' to protect the people of Benghazi. It quickly became the preferred option of the UK and France and gathered support from other countries looking for a response that did not include 'boots on the ground'. This idea gained traction, but with very different ideas of what it meant. The Brussels military staff pointed out that it carried the responsibility to act, including being prepared to shoot down aircraft or taking pre-emptive action to destroy airfields and disrupt radar, even going so far as to destroy a country's air defence systems. As the term 'no-fly zone' was tossed into conversations by leaders, commentators and NGOs, it became clear that some thought it merely a declaration or a benign patrolling of the airspace, while even those who understood that it was military action differed in their interpretation of what it meant.

In Libya, some of Gaddafi's opponents formed the National Transitional Council (NTC). They were invited to the European Parliament in Strasbourg where, encouraged by the removal of President Ben Ali in Tunisia and the recent resignation of President Mubarak of Egypt, Mahmoud Jibril – the soft-spoken representative of the NTC who had served in Gaddafi's government – put forward the case for European support. But the NTC was unknown, and many countries were wary of who its members were and, more importantly, whom they represented. They might wish to lead their country, but it was far from clear at this stage if the country would follow them. Moreover, I was unsure that I could get all the EU countries to a common position. The leader of the NTC, Mustafa Abdul Jalil, was Gaddafi's former minister of justice and had been responsible for charging five Bulgarian nurses in 1999 with deliberately infecting over 400 children with HIV. Their initial death sentences were commuted to life imprisonment, but they spent eight years in prison before returning to Bulgaria, where they were pardoned. The Bulgarians were inevitably wary of Jalil. More broadly, the thirty-one representatives of the NTC were largely unknown to us. Embracing them simply because they were not Gaddafi only took us so far.

From Strasbourg the NTC went to Paris, where President Sarkozy assured Jibril of his support. This sent a strong message across the EU, and Libya, that Europe was prepared to work with the NTC if the people were behind Jalil and his colleagues.

On 10 March, NATO convened a meeting of defence ministers. A short journey across Brussels got me to the then NATO headquarters, a strange building originally designed as a hospital, which explained the extremely wide corridors and door openings. NATO is mostly made up of EU member states, but the big difference is the leadership of the USA – the heart of the alliance, with the biggest military. I sat next to US Defense Secretary Robert Gates, who had served both President G. W. Bush and now President Obama. He was the one most had come to hear. To some surprise, he was non-committal about US engagement in any action in Libya. I assumed that discussions were still ongoing between the White House, State Department and the Pentagon, so Secretary Gates was simply fudging while they worked it out. The effect was two-fold. While it gave prominence to France and the UK and the prospect of a no-fly zone, it also made it harder to get countries to coalesce around a common position without clear US leadership.

The next day, Friday, we held an extraordinary European Council for only the third time in history, primarily to talk about Libya. I knew President Sarkozy would press for action, supported by Prime Minister Cameron, but before we got to that the Commission president, José Manuel Barroso, and I made our case for the three 'Ms': money, market access and mobility. Money would help build infrastructure; market access to the EU would boost the economy; mobility would enable young people to study in the EU, get jobs and further their careers. I left discussion of a fourth 'M' – military action – to Sarkozy and Cameron, but referred to the coordinated evacuation of 7,000 Europeans. No European plane had taken off with only its own citizens on board: every plane had taken many other EU nationals, including two UK Hercules aircraft carrying only forty British nationals but many other passengers (other Britons had already been evacuated). As it was, we only had seventy EU nationals still waiting to leave.

The meeting turned to the proposal for a no-fly zone. I pointed out that even if we agreed to go ahead, the EU did not have the capability; I suggested that this be passed to NATO. President Sarkozy and Prime Minister Cameron started shaking their heads – it was clear they had already agreed they would lead this action, outside of NATO. In that case, I said, they needed to establish lead member states in a framework to be agreed by all EU member states. It was an example of why a common EU defence policy was difficult to put in place. It was challenging enough to get agreement at NATO, whose primary purpose was defence and where the machinery existed. For now, the vital US position was still being worked out, so all eyes were on the UK and France, who were way ahead of everyone else.

Cameron pointed out to me that a no-fly zone could mean simply jamming Gaddafi's military radar. I did not disagree, but suggested we needed a common understanding of what was meant if the Council was to sign up to the action. There was little sign of that unanimity at this stage – several times the full meeting broke up into huddles of leaders trying to find a form of words that worked for everyone. Germany and Romania had serious reservations, and the frustration coming from France and the UK was obvious. The debate focused on the consequences of putting a direct reference to a no-fly zone in the text of the public Council conclusions. Chancellor Merkel asked whether a public declaration of a no-fly zone would lead to expectations that it would happen, regardless of whether in the end this was the best option. Cameron responded by pointing out the opposite: if it did not appear as a possible option, then the EU would be seen to have moved backwards and given up. There was a great deal of unhappiness with either position. Some felt bounced into agreeing with France and Britain; others worried that failure to act would make Europe seem irrelevant in the face of aggression. The discussion went on late into the night, breaking for periods of reflection and more huddles.

Meanwhile I was caught up in a small media furore. A mistake by my press team had excited the British press into thinking I opposed a no-fly zone – and Cameron – when I had simply been trying to clarify what he meant. Sarkozy and Cameron were concerned that I had set up the story, which I vehemently denied. Once we discovered the mistake we set about fixing it, but it was an uncomfortable few hours. Cameron accepted that it was just a cock-up and never referred to it again, to my relief.

We edged slowly towards a draft statement. The no-fly zone was put in, then taken out again, with passionate arguments on all sides until eventually Merkel and Cameron worked out a compromise using the phrase 'all possible means' to describe what action might be taken. While there was no direct mention of a no-fly zone, those who supported one could say it was included in 'all possible means', and those who opposed it could say as far as they were concerned it wasn't. Sometimes leaving enough room for ambiguity in the interpretation is necessary to move forward – rarely is it the last word on any subject, but it gives space for more discussion beyond the formal meeting.

Under the agreement three conditions had to be met before any action could be taken. First, there had to be a legal basis to act – for example, through a UN Security Council resolution. Second, there had to be support for any action in the region itself, particularly from the Arab League, based in Cairo and representing Arab nations. Finally, there had to be an identified need for action. It was a clear position that everyone could get behind and defend: the relief around the Council was visible. It was never easy to find consensus, either at head of state or ministerial level. For a variety of reasons countries had different positions – a combination of politics, geography and history. It made finding answers harder, but, in theory, agreed outcomes stronger. Most of all it took time.

A couple of days after the European Council meeting, the Arab League in Cairo voted for a no-fly zone, concerned for the safety of Benghazi's population. Two of the three conditions set by the European Council had now been met, and attention turned to New York and the UN Security Council discussions as I flew to Cairo to meet with the secretary general of the Arab League, Amr Moussa. Now in his mid-seventies, Moussa had led the Arab League for ten years and was a passionate advocate of democracy and human rights. No foreign minister would visit Cairo without calling on him – his knowledge and insights were invaluable.

We talked about Egypt then focused on Libya. He was forceful: 'We've done our bit. We have voted for a no-fly zone. Now we want to see it happen,' he said. Curious, I asked him whether there was a definition that all Arab League members accepted. He was clear. We should start by blocking the Libyan radar and be prepared for Gaddafi's response.

On 14 March, France hosted the G8 meeting of foreign ministers. It was an informal meeting of representatives from France, Germany, the UK, USA, Japan, Canada, Italy, and Russia, the eighth member at the time, with the EU always present. (Later Russia would be suspended indefinitely following its annexing of Crimea, and the group reverted to being the G7.) The focus of the meeting depended on which country held the rotating chairmanship: this time President Sarkozy sought to gather support for his position on Libya and put France in the lead. When I arrived, France and the UK were pushing hard for action, Russia and Germany were more cautious and the USA remained studiously silent. The US press was reporting divisions between the Defense and State Departments, as the implications of another intervention in the region, and the consequences for their ongoing operations in Iraq and Afghanistan, were considered. On the Monday evening I spoke to Hillary Clinton at the French Foreign Ministry. It was obvious she was considering the USA's options carefully. She left the meeting early, travelling back to Washington DC to continue discussions on what action to take.

At all international gatherings the final communiqué is the focus of discussion. The public statement, agreed by all, is often hard fought over. Much to the unhappiness of the French team, who had hoped for strong support for France's position, opinions were split. President Sarkozy said he wanted his presidency of the G8 to be like his presidency of the EU when, during the Russia–Georgia conflict, he had played a role in resolving the crisis. But by the time the meeting ended on Tuesday afternoon, I was still concerned that we did not have a common definition of a no-fly zone, and even less of a shared position on our role beyond intervening to stop any attack on Benghazi.

There is a long journey to be travelled from the hope that military action will lead to something better and the reality that it has. Failure to prepare for the aftermath of such action could be disastrous. We were already operating against a backdrop of violence and revolution within the region with no clarity on how that might end. Resources were stretched and ultimately finite; the sums of money being requested to help struggling economies were huge and the prospects for peaceful transitions, while encouraging in places, were far from certain. In other words, we did not know where the region would end up, who would be in control and whether the forces unleashed by the toppling of old leaders would usher in a new democratic future or a different version of oppression and corruption.

But, for now, the question was whether the UN Security Council would pass a resolution on Libya that would meet the first of the conditions laid down at the European Council. France and Britain, as two of the five permanent members of the Security Council, were drafting a resolution together with Lebanon, which held one of the two-year rotating places on the Council.

As they worked through the wording, the USA presented a tougher draft resolution that included the possibility of air strikes in support of Benghazi. I remarked to Deputy US Secretary of State Bill Burns that they had gone from 'no position to lead position' in one move. 'We like to leapfrog over everyone,' he replied. 'When we finally decide to go – we go.'

Everyone waited to see if the resolution would pass and if any of the five permanent members would use their veto. France, the UK and the USA were aligned, but Russia and China were less easy to read. Other Security Council members, elected on rotation, had no veto, but their views were important: the more votes in favour, the stronger the underpinning authority for action would be. The Brazilian foreign minister was uneasy: 'The wonderful thing is that so far not one European flag and not one American flag has been burnt in all of this unrest. We want to keep it that way. So be very careful. We, together with South Africa and India, are opposed to military action.' Behind the scenes those in favour of the resolution were working hard to persuade others to support it or to abstain during the vote. France was determined to show its leadership and sent Foreign Minister Alain Juppé to sit in the Security Council, rather than leaving matters to its ambassador.

Ultimately their efforts were successful. No country voted against military action. Germany, Brazil and India abstained, as did China and Russia, whose President Medvedev agreed with some of the analysis but not all, sufficient to abstain but not endorse. Moscow claimed later that they had done so because they were misled, especially by the USA, about the focus and scope of the action. When Vladimir Putin regained the presidency, the Libyan abstention became a touchstone for American duplicity, and Russian vetoes became much more common. At the time I thought the influence of the Arab League was more significant in Russia's decision to abstain: it valued relations with the Arab nations, and there was a strength of feeling on the part of many against Gaddafi.

At last, all three conditions that the European Council had set were met. The president of the European Council, Herman Van Rompuy, and I welcomed it with a joint statement. I wrote to Barroso: 'The challenge is upon us, with an urgency that requires us to up our game substantially . . . The economic and political challenges are substantial; the risk of chaos ever present. We have to be as ready to help those trying to reform as those who have seen revolution.' I wanted us to be very clear about our role: 'We are, and should be seen as, in this for the long haul – the partner that countries can rely on into the future.'

Unsurprisingly, President Sarkozy announced that he would host a meeting the following Saturday in Paris. Such meetings do not always transpire, especially when the invitee list is long and very high-profile. Besides, nobody was in doubt that attending the meeting was effectively signing up to action, and some were cautious about such an endorsement. A number of countries in the African Union were deeply unhappy about any attempt to confront Gaddafi. The head of the African Union, Jean Ping, announced he couldn't attend for 'political and logistical reasons', as five African leaders were travelling to Libya on a conciliation visit that same weekend.

In my office there was disquiet. Germany and France appeared to be in different places still. The prospect of having to decide whether to go to Paris or stay away, unavoidably favouring one or other of them, was my nightmare scenario. Fortunately, the two leaders came to an agreement. Chancellor Merkel would attend, but Germany would not participate directly in the action; instead it would help in other ways. 'We want our friends to win,' she said. With a sigh of relief, I left for Paris.

The meeting took place at the beautiful Élysée Palace, the formal residence of the president of France. Each participant was received with red carpets and photo opportunities, with military and diplomatic teams at the ready to assist. It was a good turnout, and nobody looked more delighted to be at the centre of this pageantry than President Sarkozy. Eleven leaders, including those of Canada, Germany, Spain, Italy and Norway, were joined by foreign ministers from the UAE, Jordan, Qatar and Morocco, together with Hillary Clinton, UN Secretary General Ban Ki-Moon and the Arab League. I joined the president of the European Council in representing the EU.

We were shown to our nameplated seats around an ornate table, and I took my place between Prime Minister Zapatero of Spain and Prime Minister Harper of Canada. President Sarkozy sat opposite Ban Ki-Moon, who was clearly nervous about the UN being associated with military action. He and I met in the margins of the meeting, sharing concerns about what would happen in the weeks and months beyond a military campaign.

President Sarkozy opened the meeting with a businesslike and brisk tone. He was not inviting discussion – he wanted to get to a conclusion. 'We are here today because there is a dire situation in Libya. We must act. It is a moral responsibility for us to do something. We have come together to see what we should do – we have the legal basis. We have regional support. Are we all united to move forward?' He invited Ban Ki-Moon to impress on everyone the importance of the UN resolution. Ban did so, emphasising the principle behind the Responsibility to Protect, endorsed by all member states of the UN. Its purpose is to protect all populations from murder, among other things, and gives the Security Council the right to act in extreme circumstances. Libya's current situation seemed to fit the requirements. Sarkozy went around the room inviting contributions. Everyone made clear their support, some in general terms and others more specifically. Italy offered the use of its military bases; Spain, Canada, Denmark and Norway, among others, offered aircraft. After ninety minutes it was done. Sarkozy took the floor again: 'Within two hours our planes will be over Libyan airspace,' he announced, to the slight alarm of those who had not anticipated action beginning immediately. France was firmly in the driving seat once again, even if everyone knew it would be down to US firepower in the end.

There were many unanswered questions. Although the European Council's three conditions had been met, ensuring unity among the EU for action, I was not sure that we would have reached a decision to begin air strikes in an open debate. That aside, there was no discussion of what might happen if Gaddafi simply moved back and waited, or how long air strikes would continue for. While the meeting was not the place for that kind of detail, the first bombs were going to fall within hours. I hoped somebody was working this out. The Arab League and the NTC in Libya were adamant that foreign soldiers would not be tolerated on Libyan soil, and there was no appetite for such a move from the Americans, British or French. So we had an agreement provided air strikes were effective, but if they proved not to be there was no consensus on how to move forward. Most strikingly, almost everyone who spoke at that meeting said Gaddafi should go. 'He has lost legitimacy' was the phrase most used. Regime change was not part of the UN resolution, yet that was the outcome expected in the end.

All EU member states appeared to be content with where Paris had ended up. Some were more engaged than others, but no country was out on a limb with a different perspective, which was as good as it was likely to get when it came to decisions about taking military action. Air strikes took place during the next few days. French planes, as Sarkozy had promised, were there first. The initial coalition of ten countries expanded to nineteen. NATO took over control of the no-fly zone on 24 March, while targeting ground units remained under the command of the coalition. By the end of March military planning was being done within a NATO framework. Overall, NATO flew 26,000 missions, including 9,700 strike sorties.

It was at the end of the initial bombing that I flew to Benghazi. Air strikes had prevented any possibility of the bloodbath that Gaddafi had threatened, but by that point, over a quarter of a million people had fled the fighting. Many had worked in the oil or food industries, and we also heard that all the Egyptian bakers had gone, leaving Libya without bread. Whatever the truth of that rumour, the departure of so many people, together with a collapsing economy, had a much wider effect. Workers were no longer sending money to their families, which created hardship in neighbouring countries like Tunisia and Egypt as well as further afield in the Philippines or India. Eventually nearly 1 million Egyptians left Libya to return to their home country during a time of unrest and instability.

One of the main reasons for my visit was to meet the NTC – to speak with those determined to bring a new future to the country. There were rumours of disunity within the NTC which I wanted to check out, but more importantly I was eager to hear their plans. The Italian air force staff who had offered to fly me in were adamant I could not stay overnight. It was just too dangerous. Instead, a pre-dawn flight out of Rome made me the highest-ranking diplomat to visit the city since the bombing stopped.

The NTC were meeting in a low-rise, flat-roofed, anonymous-looking government building – the kind that could have been anywhere in the world. A young girl called Fatima greeted me at the door, wearing traditional clothes with hammered silver jewellery on her ankles, wrists and fingers. At six years old she was tall for her age and quite shy to find herself the centre of attention. She handed me a bouquet of flowers and welcomed me to Libya. Even in these bizarre circumstances, the courtesy of greeting was not forgotten. Fatima lived with her mother and two younger brothers, under the care of her uncle as her father had died. I took her hand and she sat with me while I talked with the NTC. She embodied the future they were trying to create. When I returned to Libya later that year, I was given a letter from Fatima adorned with dried sunflowers, and photos of her and her brother.

There were thirty-one people in all, including nine women – a better ratio than in many governments I could think of – and they came from different parts of the country. Some had been in Gaddafi's government; others had returned from careers overseas. The designated minister for reconstruction had returned from a job with the World Bank to help. Their differences in background and locality added to a sense that they had the measure of what was needed for the whole of Libya, and I could see no signs of disunity among the group.

I listened to around a dozen short presentations on everything from reconstruction to health care and schools. They sounded just like a government in waiting, I said, to their delight. 'We want to do this ourselves,' they told me. 'We just need your help in some areas.'

If the NTC took over, they would have access to around $60 billion of Libyan money to use for the most pressing needs. They would have to persuade the vital oil and gas field workforces to return to get the economy moving. I asked Jalil how they proposed to manage the finances; he knew it would be a big test to get funds out to communities in ways that were transparent and inclusive, but they were a long way from getting everything in place.

One immediate concern was security. Libya's borders were now porous, and the country was becoming awash with weapons, some of them attached to mercenaries looking to fight. The NTC needed a civilian police force and border management to bring some order to the chaos. I knew we could help with this. While security was the most important issue among older people, the younger ones were more focused on establishing democracy. But none of them were under any illusions about the job before them. The fighting outside the city was brutal and Gaddafi's defeat was not certain. They all had relatives and friends on the front line, and as I sat and listened to them I could feel their tension and fear about the unknown future.

We talked for hours, then someone said food had arrived. I love Middle Eastern food and was really quite hungry by that point; it had already been a long day. What appeared was fried chicken and chips in white boxes with plastic forks, now cold from its journey to us. It was such an odd moment to be eating this in the middle of Benghazi that

we laughed about these extraordinary days, even amid the fear. I left
them, with my good wishes, and went to meet a group of twelve younger
people who had gathered in another part of town. They were running
radio stations, developing women's support networks, working in charities. Some, like Mohamed, a young man in his late twenties who was
now working for a human rights group, had been a political prisoner
for many years. Mohamed was surprisingly sanguine about the past.
'Being in prison wasn't the worst,' he told me; I found that hard to think
about. 'The biggest crime was that Gaddafi tried to kill our spirit and
our dreams.' Yezid, a former engineer now running a newspaper, nodded
in agreement. He was typical of the 'Shabab', the young pro-democracy
revolutionaries. Many of them had set up newspapers or radio stations
– there were at least fifty-five papers in Benghazi at that point. Some of
the women spoke passionately about wanting a bigger role in the future
of their country. 'We need women to believe in themselves, to understand
that they can get involved in building our democracy. We have never been
allowed to or given the chance, so we need help,' said Nada, a young
activist. Mohamed closed our meeting with the focus on democracy I
heard so often among young people. 'It's not just about elections,' he
said. 'We want what you have – democracy as a way of life.'

To work directly with the NTC, we needed to have a base in Benghazi.
Agostino Miozzo, who coordinated our crisis work, worked closely with
the Commission to provide resources on the ground. This was a big
challenge for a Foreign Service that had been in existence for less than
six months, and it meant we had to meet very different expectations to
those of our predecessor delegations. In general, those delegations would
have been recalled when conflict looked imminent. Now the Service had
to be there precisely because conflict had broken out, working the diplomatic routes to find solutions and providing support directly rather
than from a distance. Many of the people we employed were willing to
do this and I had a duty of care to look after them, but we were working
in more challenging circumstances than were ever previously envisaged.
We had to rewrite the policy to take account of the Service's new role

in such situations, while also ensuring that staff safety was never compromised. I was in awe of the passion for and dedication to Libya I saw in diplomats, development staff, security experts and so many others from all over Europe.

TV cameras captured the chaos of Libyan fighters running to engage Gaddafi's troops then turning to run back, prompting the UK and others to send in military advisors. Success for the opposition was far from certain as slowly the fighting got closer to the capital, Tripoli. Supported by NATO bombing, they moved in. In Brussels Libya became our number-one focus. An EU team arrived in Tripoli on 31 August, taking over hotel rooms as long-term planning began, including negotiating with the NTC for land on which to build a secure EU compound that could also house member states' embassies. There was a sense of urgency to move into action.

The next day, 1 September, Sarkozy hosted a 'conference in support of the new Libya'. He invited most of the countries and organisations who had met in Paris earlier in the year, as well as China, Russia and India. Nobody was surprised that the venue was Paris once again, and Cameron, to his credit, didn't argue that it should be London's turn. I expected Sarkozy and Cameron to visit Libya soon to show their support. Two weeks later they flew to Tripoli, the news crews filming them as they walked around the city, delighting in the cheers of the people who came out to welcome them.

By this point it was relatively straightforward to keep the twenty-seven countries together on Libya: for many it was a relief to focus on supporting the transition to a peaceful, democratic, successful state, where previously they had been unsure about the military campaign.

Each EU nation understood that Europe's path to twentieth-century liberal democracy had been long, bloody, painful and slow. The EU itself was born from the ashes of conflict and the horror of democracy breaking down. Even as we asserted that democracy was the necessary foundation of human progress, we needed some humility. What lay ahead was the long and complex process of building deep democracy;

people freely electing a government of their choice, or throwing out a government they were done with, was not enough. If democracy was to take hold and survive, many other principles were needed, including the rule of law, freedom of speech, property rights, free trade unions, a strong civil society, an independent judiciary and much more. Or, to quote Mohamed, the young man in Benghazi, Libya would have to establish 'democracy as a way of life'.

Meanwhile, Gaddafi had not yet been found. At this point a long-term stalemate leading to chaos seemed unlikely, but some of us were nervous. It was increasingly hard to get decisions from the NTC, now formally recognised by the UN as Libya's legitimate political representatives. They were being overwhelmed by EU foreign ministers flying in and offering support in person and called to ask if I could stop them turning up one after another. Struggling to cope, the NTC were trapped in a loop of photo opportunities and meetings that went over the same ground. Too grateful to refuse to meet anyone, they were left with little time to work out what to do.

My focus was on a coherent, coordinated set of plans to help the country through the difficult times ahead. I spoke with the UN, Arab League, African Union and Organisation of Islamic Cooperation (OIC) to propose we work together, calling ourselves the Cairo Group. Within our group there were differing and sometimes opposing views about the military action, but we were united in wanting to support Libya.

In Brussels our EU teams met regularly, identifying four areas where we could usefully provide assistance. First, the delivery of food and medicine through Médecins Sans Frontières, the Red Crescent and Red Cross, and getting in fuel, especially for the vital water pumps. Second, training and advice for a new police force and border controls. Third, the removal of sanctions, help for the external workforce to return and transparent processes by which to introduce cash into circulation. In London, suitcases full of Libyan banknotes were ready to be sent over once the banks were working. Fourth, support for the civil structures that underpin a democratic society.

Jim Moran, a highly experienced British diplomat in the EU, arrived in Tripoli in September to set up our delegation. It was dangerous, with the opposition militias and Gaddafi loyalists trying to regain control, and Jim had very few resources. Banks didn't work and the only flights were provided by the UN. Everything, including bundles of cash, had to be flown in. Miozzo and Moran did a stunning job of getting everything organised in the most challenging of circumstances.

As Gaddafi evaded capture and we waited for a new government, we made our plans to get help into the country from day one. An assessment team of experts in development, security and humanitarian aid would be deployed immediately, joining up with their UN counterparts there. They would establish what was needed where and how quickly. While this was happening, the Political and Security Committee of EU ambassadors would approve the lifting of sanctions. Other teams would plan the arrival and distribution of resources to follow the assessment on the ground.

But all our plans were predicated on the existence of functioning leadership from Libya itself. We could arrange for food and medicine to be sent and distributed immediately, then turn our attention to security: individual EU countries were ready to send in experts to train local police officers and customs officers to set up the border management. But they needed an invitation to go in from someone in a position of authority, not least because they in turn would need protection as well as logistical support. If the NTC did not step up, there was no one to facilitate this process.

Gaddafi evaded capture until 20 October, when he was cornered in the city of Sirte and killed. On 23 October 2011 the NTC officially declared an end to the war, and the liberation of Libya. If only it had been that simple. Mahmoud Jibril, who had effectively become interim prime minister and had made it clear he would leave when Sirte was 'liberated', resigned. His time in office had been difficult, with accusations that the NTC had been slow to act, and that he spent too much time out of the country. I saw him only once more in 2019, when he told me he feared that the quest for democracy had been a mistake. When I said it surely was, in the end, the answer, he shook his head. He could see no path to democracy for Libya. He died in Cairo in 2020, hospitalised with heart problems and diagnosed with Covid-19.

In November 2011 I flew to Tripoli to meet the president of the NTC, Mustafa Abdul Jalil, and the new prime minister, Abdurrahim el-Keib, to formally open our first EU delegation and to speak at the Libyan Women's Rights Forum. The willingness of women to participate in demonstrations and action had been warmly welcomed, but their desire to field candidates to be part of the new government was less well received. I had seen this before, most recently in Cairo. I told them about a young woman I had met in Tahrir Square. 'The men were keen for me to be here when we were demanding that Mubarak should go, but now that he is gone they want me to go home,' she said to me. She was determined to stay. 'Do not go home!' I urged the women in the meeting.

A few weeks before, we had taken women from twelve different Libyan cities to observe the elections in Tunisia. On their return they set up the Association for Election Observation in Tripoli. Their energy was incredible, and I promised to urge Jalil to come to their conference and see the 200 women determined to support Libya's future. The women presented me with a large gold-coloured metal plate. On it they had carefully scratched the date, the event and my name. I was deeply moved by their gesture, and have kept it ever since.

Opening our delegation felt especially poignant to me. The circumstances were not easy: there was always the possibility of a militia attack. During the women's forum I was vaguely aware of perturbed looks and hurried phone calls from my team. When I asked what was happening, they assured me everything was OK. I later discovered that the plane that had brought me to Tripoli was being held by the Zintan militiamen who controlled the area, and who were arguing with the civil aviation authority about our permission to leave. Thankfully, by the time we were due to depart, the incident had been resolved and the plane was back in our custody. But it demonstrated how precarious things were: nobody was really in control. Those who had formed the interim government were unable to decide what they needed and couldn't agree a mandate for the UN or the EU to allow us to deploy people there. They even seemed to question their own legitimacy as an interim government when it came to asking for outside support and expertise. The head of the UN, Ian Martin, together with Jim Moran made it clear that they were the only people who could give us the mandate, but they seemed paralysed by indecision. The EU aid was still getting in —worth €155 million by this point – but there was so much more to do, not least in working out how to integrate the thousands of armed men who had fought Gaddafi and obtained weapons from his unsecured stocks, and who now needed jobs and a future. Meanwhile they roamed the streets fully armed, controlling highway checkpoints.

El-Keib told me the NTC had a plan, of sorts, to integrate them one by one into the security forces, or to find them other work. It sounded, and turned out to be, too slow, too ineffective. El-Keib was cautious, I thought in part because he had been elected by only twenty-six of the fifty-one members of the NTC. The expanded NTC reflected the diversity of, but also the division between, those who had come together to overthrow Gaddafi. It was clear that the type of bold action necessary to get the country back on its feet was not going to happen. Instead, the NTC would focus on the elections to be held the following July.

As the power vacuum grew, so did the differing views on Libya's future, the gap widening between those who saw democracy as the future goal and those who did not. The removal of a brutal and ruthless leader created opportunities for others to try to take control, of their own area of the country if not all of it. As the militias grew in strength, the situation became increasingly precarious. Libya, a country with so much potential, was falling into anarchy. During the build-up to military action Sir Robert Cooper, a senior British diplomat who had led foreign policy work in Brussels for some years, had reminded me of the old truism: 'No battle plan survives contact with the enemy.' It fitted all too well with my constant refrain of 'And then what?' The international community's determination to save lives in Benghazi and support the opposition was not matched by a sufficient focus on what could happen next.

The UNSC resolution did not seek Gaddafi's removal – Russia and China would not have supported it on that basis – but in Paris this had been the clear aspiration of most around the table. In the UK, the Foreign Affairs Committee in Parliament had concluded that by the summer of 2011, British government policy in Libya had become regime change. Despite everything we had learnt from the errors made in Iraq, there seemed to be an unquestioning assumption that the liberation of Libya would lead to a different outcome.

Tragically, the political chaos that followed in Libya was the loudest echo from Iraq. The momentum towards military action was intense, and anyone suggesting a pause or change of tactic was suspect. I witnessed it – was part of it – in the days leading up to the bombings in Benghazi, especially at the European Council, where several countries raised their fears of the consequences of military action. Their agreement under the three conditions – UN resolution, Arab League request and a clear threat – was real enough and their support during the operation was evident. But there was an uneasiness that we were not thinking beyond the immediate action to what could happen next. They looked over their shoulders at Iraq and shuddered that we might end up with another country in a similarly chaotic mess.

It was a very difficult choice and there were no perfect solutions. Had the international community not taken military action against him, Gaddafi could have massacred the people of Benghazi and waged war against those who opposed him. Thousands of Libyans might have been killed, imprisoned or tortured under an increasingly brutal dictator. But our focus on the display of hard power was not matched by long-term planning for the use of soft power that should have followed. Against the backdrop of a wider region in crisis, we struggled to understand what we were looking at and how best to respond, while a howling media demanded slogans that sounded decisive and strong, unlike the messy reality of trying to work out what to do. Those with years of experience

LEFT: Prime Minister Gordon Brown greets Catherine Ashton (CA) after the announcement of her appointment as the first High Representative for Foreign Affairs/Vice President of the Commission in 2009.

LEFT: The press conference line up after the announcements. Left to right: Herman Van Rompuy, President of the European Council; Prime Minister Fredrik Reinfeldt of Sweden, Jose Manuel Barroso, President of the Commission; CA.

LEFT: Somali President Hassan Sheikh Mohamud with CA at 'A New Deal for Somalia' conference, Brussels, September 2013.

TOP: Inside one of the tents erected by NGOs to help children and families after the Haiti earthquake in 2010.

MIDDLE: Agostino Miozzo [left] and CA discussing the reconstruction plans in Haiti, with the military and NGOs from Europe working together.

BOTTOM: The remains of a village near Sendai, Japan after the earthquake and tsunami in 2011.

ABOVE: The Task Force meeting in Egypt 2012, in support of democracy and economic growth. The then president, Mohamed Morsi, held the meeting to reassure European business leaders.

ABOVE: After Morsi was removed, CA visited then Defence Minister Abdel Fattah el-Sisi to discuss events in summer 2013.

ABOVE: President Barack Obama and CA at the summit between the EU and USA in Brussels 2014.

ABOVE: CA and the EU team with activists in the Freedom Square, Benghazi 2011.

ABOVE: Prime Minister Ivica Dačić of Serbia (second from right) and Prime Minister Hashim Thaçi of Kosovo (second from left) meet for the first time in October 2012. Italian diplomat Fernando Gentilini and CA sit between the two delegations at CA's office in the EEAS building, Brussels.

ABOVE: US Secretary of State Hillary Clinton with CA at the Community of Democracies event in Vilnius, Lithuania, June 2011.

ABOVE: Handshake between the prime ministers of Kosovo and Serbia in Brussels, 2013, as they arrive for a round of discussions that eventually led to the Brussels Agreement.

ABOVE: 5am press conference with representatives from the six nations and Iran to announce the interim agreement on Iran's nuclear programme, 24 November 2013.

ABOVE: Foreign Minister Mohammed Javad Zarif of Iran and CA walking to a press conference during the Iran negotiations.

ABOVE: US Secretary of State John Kerry hugs CA after the announcement on the Iran nuclear negotiations.

ABOVE: Foreign Minister Sergei Lavrov of Russia and CA meeting in 2014 against the backdrop of the beginning of the Ukraine crisis, 28 January 2014.

ABOVE: CA in Maidan, the square in Kyiv, 2013, accompanied by Arseniy Yatsenyuk, later to become Prime Minister of Ukraine.

ABOVE: President Vladimir Putin and CA wait for the meeting in Minsk in summer 2014 to begin.

ABOVE: First meeting convened to discuss the Ukraine crisis in Minsk, 2014. Left to right: President Nursultan Nazarbayev of Kazakhstan; President Vladimir Putin of Russia; President Alexander Lukashenko of Belarus (host of the talks); President Petro Poroshenko of Ukraine; CA; Günther Oettinger, EU Commissioner for Energy; Karel De Gucht, EU Commissioner for Trade.

of working in Libya were not consulted in the rush to action, or if they were their views were lost or drowned out. Requests for support to stem the flow of looted weapons went unanswered, initially because military action was imminent and people could not be deployed, and later because the resulting anarchy was too dangerous.

The violence in Libya escalated, and before long I had to give the order for EU staff to leave, for their own safety. The November day when I had opened the EU delegation seemed a painfully long time ago.

As we failed to make headway, inevitably attention turned elsewhere, to other problems and other demands. Crises and disasters did not arrive one by one in an orderly fashion; rather they crashed into view jumbled up together, with no respite in between. I heard the cries for justice, democracy and freedom echoed in different towns, cities and countries by those who saw similar chances of a better life. Over the same years I watched their dreams be buffeted or wrecked by other forces with very different ideas for the society they wanted to create. A common theme would thread its way through much of what we had to do: how to build deep democracies that could survive being battered, and how to invest time and resources for the long haul necessary to achieve that.

6

THE WESTERN BALKANS: SERBIA AND KOSOVO DIALOGUE

Srebrenica is a place of overwhelming sorrow. A small mountain town in Bosnia-Herzegovina, it saw genocide in post Second World War Europe when, after the collapse of Yugoslavia, conflict and terror consumed the region, leaving thousands dead and many more missing. Under the leadership of Ratko Mladić, Bosnian Serb fighters massacred nearly 8,000 Muslim boys and men. To hide their crime Serb forces dug up and scattered the bodies' remains over eighty different sites, some far from Srebrenica, making it impossible for any individual to be recovered intact. Mladić evaded capture until May 2011, when, as my plane entered Serbian airspace for my first formal visit to the capital, Belgrade, I was notified he'd been arrested and the Serbian president, Boris Tadić, eagerly shared photographs of his capture with me.* Coincidence or not, it was welcome news.

I visited the Srebrenica memorial site in the spring of 2013, travelling from Sarajevo, the capital of Bosnia-Herzegovina, where the effects of the war were still visible on buildings splattered by artillery fire. At Srebrenica I met the group known simply as the Mothers: women who

---

* Mladić was later convicted in The Hague for genocide and crimes against humanity.

had lost sons, husbands and brothers in the massacre. They led me round their place of remembrance. Each grave is marked by a white headstone shaped like an arrow, inscribed with the victim's name. Row on row, the fields of stones stretch far into the distance. Over the years, DNA testing, US satellite technology and analysis of soil, fragments of clothing and remains have helped many families bury something of their loved ones. One woman who walked beside me told me softly that she was burying the one bone of her twelve-year-old son that had just been found. After eighteen years it was all she had of him. Maybe, she said, one day there would be more. Some families had nothing at all.

The Mothers led me to the memorial hall, inside the former battery factory where families were separated before the executions, to rows of glass cases where the stories of the dead were told through photographs and personal items. Some wept as they touched the glass that held fragments of a loved one's life.

They beckoned me to sit on one of the long, narrow benches arranged in front of a screen. For the next thirty minutes we watched those terrible days unfold before us. Peter Sorenson our head of delegation, who'd visited Srebrenica many times, was quietly crying, his arms wrapped round one of the Mothers. The story was devastating; the only reason I did not completely fall apart was the dignity of the women. They had suffered rape and torture, been terrorised and traumatised, forced to watch their boys and men taken away and killed. To survive was its own kind of hell. It was excruciating to be there; a day I will never forget – and it came less than twenty-four hours after I feared the talks I was leading between Serbia and Kosovo had collapsed.

Europe's answer to the horrific wars and genocide that followed the collapse of Yugoslavia was a commitment to all seven former Yugoslav nations to become part of the EU. Beyond the political stability, the region hoped to find greater economic security. Many people still lived in poverty, and the marks of war were everywhere. It was impossible to travel far without seeing buildings pockmarked with bullet holes or blown apart completely. Hotels still had plastic sheeting in place of windows twenty years after the war had ended. By the time I took office Slovenia had already joined the EU, while Croatia would do so in 2013. But before the remaining countries could join, the many problems that had been parked at the end of the wars had to be dealt with.

One of the most challenging was the relationship between Serbia and Kosovo, where tensions stretched back hundreds of years. Serbia controlled Kosovo from the twelfth century, building beautiful monasteries and churches that are still accessible today, until both came under Turkish Ottoman rule from the fifteenth to the twentieth century. At the end of the First World War, the ethnically and linguistically Albanian Kosovars became part of Serbia, where they were regarded as second-class citizens. During the Second World War, most of Kosovo was taken into Italian-controlled greater Albania. As the war ended, they were absorbed into President Tito's Yugoslavia, gaining de facto self-government in 1974. When Tito died, turbulence took over, and in 1989 President Milošević of Serbia revoked the autonomy, closed Albanian-language schools and fired Kosovar doctors and public servants. Some left; others went into internal exile.

In 1995, as the war in other parts of the Western Balkans ended, the Albanian state collapsed, creating a power vacuum that helped the emergence of a Kosovo Liberation Army (KLA), calling for an independent Kosovo. Serbia's response to KLA attacks was brutal as an escalating pattern of provocation and retaliation took hold. Attempts by the West, working with Russia, to negotiate a settlement failed. Forces from what remained of the government of Yugoslavia (Serbia and Montenegro), sometimes helped by local Serbs, drove 1.2 million Kosovars – more than half the population – out of their homes. The pictures of streams of women and children crossing the mountains looking for shelter were shown around the world.

In March 1999, NATO began air strikes to persuade Milošević to withdraw. After seventy-eight days of bombing, the distinguished UN mediator Martti Ahtisaari, supported by a Russian envoy, presented NATO's terms. Milošević agreed and withdrew his forces. NATO deployed 50,000 troops as a Kosovo peacekeeping force known as KFOR. Though now much smaller, it remains in place. The UN Security Council ratified the arrangements through its Resolution 1244, which said nothing about the status of Kosovo.

In February 2007, Ahtisaari produced a proposal for Kosovo's 'status settlement', outlining the 'supervised independence' under which Kosovo declared independence in 2008. It included a period of supervision by the international community to safeguard minorities, especially Serbs unable to leave or attached to the medieval monasteries of the Serbian Orthodox Church. Serbia formally rejected Ahtisaari's proposals and refused to recognise Kosovo's independence, asserting that it remained part of Serbia. Kosovo claimed the right to determine its own future; Serbia demanded that its territorial integrity be respected.

Over the next few months, around a hundred countries supported Kosovo as an independent state. Five EU member states did not (and still do not) for a variety of reasons, including a fear of breakaway territory in their own countries. A UN Security Council resolution to recognise Kosovo was blocked by Russia with support from China. At the end of 2009, President Tadić applied for Serbian membership of the EU in line with his election promises. Some member states rejected his application, citing Serbia's stance on Kosovo. Tadić requested an opinion from the International Court of Justice (ICJ) on the legality of Kosovo's declaration of independence, buying time and allowing him to resist domestic pressures for a more destructive response.

Two years later, as the ICJ prepared to deliver its opinion, the EU put forward a resolution to the UN General Assembly, proposing that it welcome an offer from the EU to facilitate dialogue 'between the parties'. Serbia put forward its own resolution, and as both were being considered I had dinner with Boris Tadić in Brussels to see if we might merge the two, but we failed to reach agreement that night. Overnight, and under pressure, Tadić sent a message offering to drop his draft and co-sponsor ours. Thus we found ourselves responsible for the first negotiations between Serbia and the breakaway province it did not recognise. Meanwhile, the ICJ found that 'the declaration of independence of Kosovo, adopted on 17 February 2008 did not violate international law'.

Given the history, it's not surprising that when I brought together the prime minister of Serbia, Ivica Dačić, and the prime minister of Kosovo, Hashim Thaçi, at the 2014 Munich Security Conference it left many in the audience open-mouthed. After all, Dačić had been Milošević's spokesman, and Thaçi the leader of the KLA. As we sat there, discussing the Brussels Agreement that began the normalisation of relations between their countries, I was struck by how commonplace being together had become. It is easy to overlook or downplay such moments, but it was an extraordinary achievement, given what had gone before. When I think about what it took for both men to reach this point, it never ceases to amaze me how quickly life can feel normal.

We'd started small, bringing together advisors from both sides to deal with the most innocuous issues: the civil registry books recording births, marriages and deaths that Serb officials had taken away, and the customs stamp to be used when goods crossed between the two territories. UN Resolution 1244 had recognised Kosovo as a separate customs area, though not a state. We proposed 'Kosovo Customs', but after Serbia refused to discuss it the meeting was cancelled. Kosovo closed the border with Serbia and sent paramilitary police units into the Serb areas in the north of Kosovo. One policeman was shot and the customs post burnt down by the local Serbs.

This was the outcome of long-standing tensions in the north of Kosovo, a mainly Serb-populated area of around 1,000 square kilometres and about 65,000 people. Law and order collapsed: makeshift barriers littered the bridges and streets and smuggling across the border was rife. The main town, Mitrovica, was effectively divided in two parts. KFOR and the EU's civilian team of police and legal experts monitored the situation and attempted to contain the violence.

The Serb population there looked to Belgrade, aggrieved that their country and culture were being torn apart. When the conflict ended in June 1999, 200,000 Serbs, Romani and others had fled from Kosovo as Serbia became home to the highest number of refugees and displaced people in Europe. Their voices added to the calls for Kosovo to remain part of Serbia. Some argued that the solution was to give back the territory to the north of the Ibar River, effectively moving Serbs living in the north back into Serbia. There was no appetite for this in Pristina, the capital of Kosovo, and little in the international community. The long-term goal was to ensure that the governments were willing to provide for all their citizens, and that people were willing to live side by side.

Our process ran out of steam. Whatever problems we dealt with, the question of the north of Kosovo would always come up. Without political engagement neither side could address it. On their return to Pristina, the Kosovar team had been pelted with tomatoes for even talking to the Serb enemy. In 2012 Serbia elected a new government, replacing Tadić as president, which felt little obligation to be bound by what had gone before (though nothing had been implemented up to that point), rendering the whole exercise ineffective. Both sides seemed to have different interpretations of what they had agreed, which made progress even harder.

Formerly the head of the KLA, Hashim Thaçi emerged from the negotiations that ended the war as Kosovo's de facto leader. The dark hair of his youth had been transformed by age and war into a shock of grey, just as he had transformed himself from soldier to statesman, determined to make Kosovo a UN nation and ultimately a member of the EU. He understood that, in order to join, he needed to put relations with Serbia on a more normal footing and was prepared to talk despite knowing many at home considered any discussion, let alone compromise, unacceptable. His detractors included Vetëvendosje, the political party headed by Albin Kurti, who opposed any dialogue without prior conditions, while other parties were at best sceptical. But any discussion of the status of Kosovo was off the table: it was and would remain an independent country, he said. I readily agreed to that.

Serbia had recently elected Tomislav Nikolić as its new president. His victory was unexpected as all the polling suggested Tadić would win. Nikolić described himself to me as an old war horse when I met with him in New York. I asked whether he would be interested in sending someone if I convened a meeting in Brussels. He declared that in 100 years no president of Serbia would recognise Kosovo as an independent country – and then said yes to a meeting between Serbia and Kosovo. I was so surprised I asked him again. He laughed and said, 'Why don't you believe me?' His reputation had tempered in recent years, and 'only a fool never changes their mind', he observed. Serbia was €300 million in debt; by the next year that would be €700 million. To get economic investment, he needed to be closer to Europe. But he reiterated there was no question of recognising Kosovo. I understood. The red line was clear. Nikolić nominated his prime minister, Ivica Dačić, to lead the talks for Serbia. Dačić appeared to be from the most pro-European political party in the new government coalition, had been in the previous government and was the same age as Thaçi. I wondered how he would react to being asked, but was pleased we had two prime ministers ready to start discussions. Whatever their histories in the past horrors of war, I was ready to work with them for a better future.

I flew back to Brussels and went to meet Fernando Gentilini, an Italian diplomat with a wealth of international experience, who knew the region and had spent years working with both Serbia and Kosovo. Fernando brought humour and exasperation, sometimes at the same time, to dealing with them. He exuded calm and good sense and both sides respected him. Without him the process would have failed from the start. With him I had the best chance of success.

We didn't have to worry about the recognition of Kosovo. Recognition of a country lay with the individual member states and not the EU as a whole. Some of them were very interested in the Western Balkans, especially if they bordered the region, but nobody was hopeful that this process would get anywhere. The relationship between Serbia and Kosovo was considered an intractable problem. With expectations so low,

I had plenty of breathing space to get the talks moving. Nobody was putting conditions on what Fernando and I wanted to do – they were not anticipating success.

It was agreed that the two prime ministers would come to Brussels and meet for the first time in my office in the External Action Service building, as the European Council ended its meeting on Friday after-noon, 19 October 2012. I sat through the day's agenda with a growing sense of excitement and worry. Would either of them turn up? If they did, would they stay? As news of the meeting spread a few government leaders wished me luck and I smiled and grimaced at the same time. As soon as I could, I raced across the road to see what was happening.

Fernando told me that both prime ministers had arrived with small delegations, including their foreign ministers, and were safely ensconced in separate rooms down the corridor. We'd worked out a plan to first see them separately, so I invited Thaçi into the office. Tall and well dressed, he had presence, but I could tell he was nervous: this was uncharted territory that would not win him friends at home. His concern was justified. The same was true for Dačić, who used his time to explain the position Serbia was in. He was from a different political party to President Nikolić, and he knew his room for manoeuvre was limited. But he was smart, and I genuinely wanted to help him get his country into a better position.

I explained to each the rules of their first encounter. They need not shake hands. There would be one photo and, after it was taken, the memory stick would be removed from the camera and handed to me in front of them. I guaranteed it would not be released without them both giving their approval. I showed them where they would sit on the purple sofas in my office, facing each other, with their interpreters next to them. Fernando and I would make up the third side of a square, sitting on the middle sofa. It would last one hour, and I would begin the conversation. I explained what I would cover. A time-limited encounter gave less scope for moving into territory that would lead to argument – something I was very keen to avoid at this first stage.

Fernando and I had worked out a list of what we wanted to cover – as far as possible, this was the easier stuff. Before Christmas, each should open a liaison office in the other's capital to aid communication between the two. I explained to Dačić that Serbia needed to be transparent about the money it was sending into the north of Kosovo, so Pristina would know what they were funding. I told Thaçi that Kosovo needed to protect the religious and cultural sites important to Serbia, such as the monasteries. In addition, Kosovo needed to consider decentralising activities from Pristina, and Serbia to implement the border management plan, agreed in earlier discussions in Brussels. Finally, I made it clear that we would respect the position of each on the status of Kosovo. Recognition was not on the agenda for these talks.

It went down well. Each was comfortable, knowing how it was all going to work. I was less confident, as I had no idea what would happen when they got into the same room. Fernando and I closed all the blinds so the meeting would not be seen from any surrounding building, then I took a deep breath and asked them both into my office. They appeared, flanked by their translators, and I said, 'Prime Minister Thaçi meet Prime Minister Dačić'. To my surprise they shook hands, both leaning forward with little hint of a smile, before the photographer captured us all sitting together.

I started by telling them how brave they both were, and that our purpose in meeting was to make the lives of the people living in the north of Kosovo easier. I explained that I was not asking Serbia to recognise Kosovo, nor asking Kosovo to see itself as less than a country, but I was asking them to find a way through some of the practical problems the people in the north faced. I went through the list of issues I hoped they would tackle together.

Dačić spoke first, for about fifteen minutes, and was direct. He was pleased we were meeting, but reiterated that Serbia was not going to recognise Kosovo. However, he was ready to discuss 'all topics, including property, war crimes on both sides and so on'. He wanted the economy and infrastructure, particularly the possibility of a highway, to be part of their discussions.

Thaçi followed and said to Dačić: 'Our joint future is in the EU; we belong to the same generation. Let's talk of the future.' He talked about the need to find answers for the north and his concern about security. Most importantly, he said he was ready to start the process of normalising relations with Serbia.

I closed the meeting while the mood was positive. I told them that I recognised their willingness to move forward and that I had enjoyed the meeting, which I hadn't been sure beforehand would be the case. I invited them to continue their dialogue over dinner in early November. I also asked them to be realistic if we were not to get stuck. My job would be to convince twenty-seven member states to proceed alongside them. They slapped each other on the back and shook hands again. The relief on their faces was clear.

Thaçi was happy to release the photo immediately, but Dačić, fearing a backlash in Belgrade, was more cautious. By the next morning, however, he said I could release it to the press. It was a sensation. Messages came in from all over the world saying how astonishing it was to see them together and wishing the talks well. I put out a brief press statement emphasising my firm belief that dialogue was in the interests of both sides. Our objective, I said, was 'to improve the lives of people and help solve problems and, in so doing, bring Serbia and Kosovo closer to the European Union'. I meant it.

US Secretary of State Hillary Clinton supported the talks with an enthusiasm not everyone in her team felt. The USA and the Clintons remained important in the Western Balkans: President Bill Clinton and the USA had led the NATO bombing of Serbia to stop Milošević's campaign against Kosovo. In Pristina a 3-metre-high statue of President Clinton stands on Bill Clinton Boulevard. But her team were unsure the talks would go anywhere, fearing it would only harden positions on both sides. I understood their wariness but thought it was worth trying. Using NATO's secure communications in Brussels – we had none of our own – I explained what I wanted to do. Hillary listened carefully then overruled her team, saying she thought it was the right time and I should do it – and suggested we travel together to the region.

A few days after that first meeting of the prime ministers I boarded her Boeing 737, a converted cargo plane, to Belgrade. There was a definite thrill in walking up the steps and seeing the blue and white plaques fastened in front of the main cabin, establishing that this aircraft was for the secretary of state of the United States of America. On board, a small cabin was set aside for the secretary of state, with a table and chair for her to work at and two banquette-style sofas. Outside the cabin the seats were café-style, two facing two with a table in between, for her closest team. In the next section there were four rows of two seats on each side like a traditional business-class area, where my team and I sat. The rest of the plane contained a standard economy section for the press. Clearly designed for maximum practicality, the aircraft had printers but no hot food galley; lunch appeared in brown bags.

We landed in Belgrade for a three-hour visit to see President Nikolić and Prime Minister Dačić. I was nervous they might consider it a waste of time, but Dačić made much of how well the first meeting had gone, describing me as his partner in looking for solutions. Nikolić was more downbeat, gazing at his hands as he ruminated on the impossibility of trying to do anything and reiterating that Kosovo was still part of his country. One of the US team joked afterwards that it was just as well. Things had been going so smoothly that the USA might have thought this was going to be a breeze.

We flew on to Pristina, where Hillary and I had dinner together. We'd spent a long time in conversation on the plane, at one point joking that we might need to fly around in circles to give us time to cover everything. Thaçi greeted us warmly and spoke with great enthusiasm about the talks. In both capitals, Hillary made it clear she backed the initiative – and me personally – and would continue to do so. It was typical of her support for others, especially women. When we parted she wished me luck and asked Phil Reeker, a leading State Department official with responsibility for the region, to assist us. Phil came to Brussels for each round of talks to offer US support as needed. From the US embassy he focused his attention on Thaçi and his team, reassuring the Kosovars, and kept in touch with Fernando and me, helping me to push hard when asking them to think creatively.

On our trip I had confirmed my dinner invitation with both leaders. Thaçi suggested bringing members of Kosovo's opposition parties to the preliminary meeting beforehand, which was a great idea. His power base was limited and talking to the Serbs was far from popular. A few days later, I welcomed him and the opposition to my office to go through what we were asking of Kosovo and take their questions. Fernando and I explained what would be on the list of topics over dinner, hoping to make some progress so we'd have specific points to discuss with the two prime ministers. We started with what we called Integrated Border Management – the customs and border crossings between Kosovo and the four countries it bordered. Our focus was on the two gates between Serbia and the north of Kosovo known as Gate 1 and Gate 31. Someone driving through one gate would be in a kind of no man's land before reaching the gate run by the other side. The plan was for a future border run by both sides, getting rid of the no man's land in between. The previous year the gates had been in flames, so this was not going to be easy to resolve. Teams from each side had been meeting daily in our offices to work out what to do. Serbia's team said they should control the gates as the people living in the north of Kosovo were primarily Serb. The Kosovo team were clear – this was Kosovo's territory and they needed control of their own gates. They argued their points carefully, without rancour, but it was depressing.

I saw both prime ministers on their own before dinner. Thaçi had some ideas to discuss and a more conciliatory approach than Dačić, who just reiterated Serbia's overall position. We met together in a small area outside the dining room, where an EU flag stood ready to backdrop a photo of the three of us. Just as we got there, the building's lights fused; the subsequent jokes about omens of disaster broke the ice at least. After canapés and drinks we sat down – Dačić on my left, Thaçi on my right.

The table was oblong, and Fernando and I sat opposite each other on the short sides, with the prime ministers and their translators on the long sides. Initially we reversed their seating position each time – so nobody could argue who was more important – but after a while things were going sufficiently smoothly that we simply forgot about it. The table gave us enough space while enabling intimate conversation. Other than staff bringing in food – velouté of mushrooms, lamb, and a pear and chocolate dessert – we were alone. Both men ate well but drank little. Translation into English meant that Fernando and I could follow their conversation. After a while, I raised the five issues we'd identified and suggested we start with the liaison offices, which were intended to sort out problems before they got serious, and help build a relationship for the future. I reminded them that these were not embassies – impossible, as Serbia did not recognise Kosovo. After some debate they agreed, if the office could be in the EU delegation in each country. Fine by us, if they paid the costs.

While I led the first discussion, I left the next one on the gates largely to them, keeping a close eye on who was giving on what. To my surprise, they quite quickly agreed that four gates would open: three initially, including one in the north, leaving the second in the north to open three weeks later if the first had not gone up in flames. I asked them to get the first three open and operational before the next EU meeting, when I would report on progress: it would be a good demonstration that the talks were effective.

We moved on to Serbia's funding of groups in the north of Kosovo. There were two types of funding coming from Belgrade. The first was for health and education in poor areas needing support. Kosovo was mainly concerned that Serbia be transparent about how much money was going to which communities. Dačić asked Thaçi directly, 'What do you want? We can give you the information on funding.' It was an interesting moment: they had moved into a conversational style that allowed them to discuss problems rather than simply swap statements. Thaçi replied that he wanted Serbia to set up a fund that Kosovo would administer openly. This was clearly difficult for Dačić, but rather than rule it out immediately he offered to discuss it further. Meanwhile he would provide the information on what was already being funded. It was a small step, but definitely progress. The second type of funding was more challenging. Serbia was giving resources to what were called 'parallel structures', such as a police force and justice system, that were run separately from the Kosovo ones. Some officials received two salaries, and others were employed directly from Belgrade. This had to be replaced by one system, funded in Kosovo, but the system needed to serve and gain the confidence of the population in the north. I knew this would be very difficult to resolve: it was an issue we had to save for later if the talks were successful. I moved on to the next topic.

The government in Pristina needed to do more to reach out to the many thousands of Serbs living in both the north and the rest of the country. Dačić raised a practical issue: Serbs had removed Serb number plates from their cars but had not been issued with new ones. It clearly rankled with him. Thaçi agreed to investigate. Next I raised religious and cultural sites. The most important monasteries and churches of the Serbian Orthodox Church were being protected by NATO troops. One such was Visoki Dečani, a medieval Serb monastery built in the fourteenth century. Beautifully preserved, it became a shelter during the war. I'd visited it the year before and discussed the fears of attack, with both the brotherhood living there and the Italian NATO troops who protected it. I'd already told Thaçi that any desecration of the monasteries would have a devastating effect on Kosovo's relationship with the EU, and whatever solution he suggested he needed to be confident that they would be fully protected. Thaçi proposed a special unit of police that would be 50 per cent Kosovo Serb and 50 per cent Kosovo Albanian. The commander would be a Serb. Dačić listened carefully, and I suggested that together we work out the detail of how this would be implemented.

By this point it was late, and enough for a first session. Thaçi and Dačić looked tired and Fernando and I were exhausted. I brought out a little brandy to mark our progress and we all relaxed. They asked me to tell the press about the conversation, which I did via a short statement – every word agreed with both sides – with an accompanying photo that would not feature a handshake. Neither was ready for that image to be made public yet.

After they left the building, Fernando and I reflected on the evening. We were encouraged by how willing they were to talk. There was a long way to go, of course: easy-won agreements would not necessarily convert smoothly to facts on the ground. But the more they got to know each other, the greater the chance of avoiding conflict. As we made plans to meet again, with their officials meeting in between, I saw the beginning of a relationship that could bring change.

By January 2013, after real progress on the first set of issues, we needed to move on to more complex ones. For Serbia this meant dismantling the parallel structures of police, courts and security; Kosovo in turn had to make the Serb communities feel valued and supported. A fully integrated justice system meant that the Kosovo vision of a unified country came a little closer, but Kosovo had to ensure that the Serb population in the north felt ownership of their lives and identity. At our next meeting I explained to both sides separately that we had reached these more difficult issues, and over dinner we had to talk openly about what needed to be done.

I reminded them that on 1 April I had to submit my report to the EU with recommendations on their progress towards EU membership. Both Thaçi and Dačić were serious and thoughtful. Thaçi had been confronted by demonstrators in Brussels, protesting against the talks with Serbia. Many at home were opposed to what he was doing too. Dačić said it was hard for him to be out in public as well. I was conscious that they were at significant risk politically, and possibly personally too, but recognised their determination to keep going.

I kept the food arriving at regular intervals to create natural pauses in our conversation. It gave a sort of rhythm to the evening, and, given enough space in between each course, provided time to reflect and mull over the issues. By the time we got to the main course, Thaçi had offered amnesty to the people in the north of Kosovo who were working for the parallel structures and paying no tax. He was careful to rule out any thought of amnesty for war crimes.

Dačić explained he wanted to see the end of parallel structures, but the local Serb population needed a justice system they could have confidence in. Thaçi made it clear that while he could not support a separate layer of government for the north, which could bring all the problems Bosnia faced with Republika Srpska,* he was not opposed to some form of local devolution.

They were soon locked in deep conversation on how to solve these problems. Fernando and I exchanged glances of disbelief alongside our delight that this was happening. After a while Thaçi told Dačić they were close to agreement. They would try to bring the Kosovo Serb municipalities into a group and work out how to give them identity and purpose without threatening the Kosovo government's role and without their needing to recognise Kosovo as a separate nation.

To remove the parallel police force Fernando and I suggested we look at creating special Serb units within the Kosovo police force. Both Thaçi and Dačić agreed it was worth exploring. With that, I decided to recap the many hours of talks, reminding them that they had discussed amnesty for those in the parallel structures and considered how to give the Serb communities in the north a clearer sense of identity without moving towards a new layer of government. I suggested that meant looking carefully at what the communities had the power to do – the competencies they held – and whether there was more that could be devolved. For this we would need legal and local government advice which Fernando and I undertook to look at.

Thaçi suggested we reconvene for two days in February, to see if we could make real progress and have plans for the police, judiciary and

---

* RS, as it is known, was created as part of the Dayton Agreement that ended the war in Bosnia-Herzegovina. Although subject to Bosnian overall control, its Serb leader, Dodik, took as much authority as possible, a constant challenge to attempts to move the country away from ethnic divisions towards a united nation.

local municipalities ready for my April meeting with the EU ministers. It was a lot to do, but worth a try. For now, we had exhausted our conversations and ourselves. These meetings always came on the back of punishing schedules for all of us, and usually just before a long overseas trip for me.

During our dinner, experts from both sides had been finalising a plan to collect customs revenue at the newly opened gates. Gate 1, in the north, was not yet operational, but the others were working well, though without collecting customs at this stage. We had decided this would help to reduce friction in the short term, but we needed a plan to start collection, and I invited their two key negotiators to join us and explain where they had got to. At this point, nobody outside the room had seen Thaçi and Dačić together: the two negotiators stared wide-eyed at the relaxed conversation, the debris of dinner surrounding them. How quickly we had created a new normal, I murmured to Fernando.

By 2 a.m. we had hammered out a plan. All customs revenue would go into a development fund to be spent in the north of Kosovo, via a commercial bank account which the EU would open in Pristina, with three signatories. Serbia would represent the interest of the Kosovo Serbs; Kosovo would represent the government; and the EU would make sure it was all done correctly, with the account frozen until the agreement had been negotiated. What was left was how to get the money from the gates into the bank account. Thaçi's team suggested they collect it, put it into the treasury and transfer it, but Dačić worried that this implied Serbian acceptance of Kosovan statehood and refused. We were stuck, but by then I was too tired to care. I proposed we stop worrying about it. The important point was that the money got to the bank – how it got there should not concern us for now. Dačić accepted the 'for now' solution as something he could live with. Good, I said, because if we get stuck on small points it will be impossible.

We said goodnight and, after a brief chat to my weary but pleased team, I gave a short press statement that the two prime ministers had reached a provisional understanding on the collection of customs duties, levies and VAT. That showed some progress from our five-hour conversation without saying anything about the more complex discussions that had taken up most our time. I went home to grab a few hours' sleep.

Before the two prime ministers came back to Brussels in mid-February, I got a message from Serbia's President Nikolić that he would like to meet President Atifete Jahjaga of Kosovo in my office, just as Dačić and Thaçi had met at the start of the talks. I was surprised that he would risk elevating her importance in Serbia, but I was keen to get them together. Jahjaga was a former police officer, smart and clear-thinking with an air of poise and calm, a strong symbol of the future. She was tough, but I guessed she would be nervous at this encounter – I never underestimated the toll of years of oppression and war seared into the minds of everyone in Kosovo.

We arranged for them to come on 6 February, a couple of weeks before the prime ministers' meeting, and just as before we saw them separately first. Nikolić was quick to tell me Serbia would never recognise Kosovo, and I was quick to point out this was not the purpose of our talks. I reminded him that this meeting was his idea and hoped he would be respectful. With a huge grin, he told me he knew how to behave. Which of course he did. He was a much more interesting politician than the gruff character he chose to show. Next, I greeted Jahjaga and asked if she wanted to speak first or second. She requested that Nikolić begin.

Our bilateral meetings over, we arranged for the two of them to arrive at my office together, where they shook hands and we took our seats – Fernando and I swapping places from the last time so there could be no accusation of favouritism towards one side. Dačić told me that after the first meeting, the media in Belgrade had speculated why I sat closer to him. The simple answer was I had to sit somewhere, but it was a valuable lesson. Everything matters – so this time I sat closer to Kosovo.

I asked Nikolić to begin, and he courteously offered Jahjaga the floor. I told him she would like him to start and he did, in fluent English. She replied in Albanian, he reverted to Serbian. They referred to each other as Mr Nikolić and Mrs Jahjaga – not a presidential title in sight. So far, so predictable.

He said Serbia would never recognise Kosovo, but if she could accept that, he could offer a great deal. She politely told him Kosovo was a country, and she was its president. He said he was disappointed. It was very cordial. Both expressed firm support for the dialogue and agreed to meet again if that felt necessary. After about forty-five minutes it was over, and I thanked them both. Outside were thirty or so TV cameras, and I spoke briefly using an agreed script to say it had been a constructive meeting and released a photo. It made headlines globally – the US State Department sent me a copy from a Pakistan newspaper. Apart from the UK, where interest was selective, the dialogue was becoming big news.

Inevitably, President Jahjaga told the press this was proof Serbia recognised Kosovo – otherwise why would a Serbian president bother to meet her? Serbia professed great offence, though I was sure the Serbian side would have anticipated this. They lost nothing by the meeting, in any event, and Nikolić's reputation as a statesman was enhanced. They knew too that he had been clear – there was no recognition. He was under no real pressure from home as Serbian support for joining the EU was at 42 per cent, its lowest to date. But I thought he understood that some things had to change, and doing so might as well start now.

Our fifth round of meetings with the prime ministers took place a couple of weeks later, drilling down into the questions we had posed over our last dinner. Thaçi had a meeting with President Barroso at the European Commission to discuss the future of Kosovo with the EU. It went well – Barroso put out a press statement: 'The results of the dialogue are critically important for EU relations with both Kosovo and Serbia. I wish the prime minister courage and wisdom for the days ahead. He has an opportunity on his hands to make a big step to the next stage on Kosovo's European path.'

By the end of February, discussions had taken us into the detail of how Serb communities in Kosovo might work together. Kosovo had already incorporated the EU charter on local self-government, devolving powers to local councils – apart from police, judicial system and security, which were sensitive issues and subjects of our talks on parallel structures. Much of what we were discussing was already legally possible under the charter. The question was whether we could, or should, add more.

We met again on 4 March, beginning with our usual bilateral discussion. I explained to Thaçi that preventing the Serb municipalities from working together was 'a ship that has sailed'. They could under the EU charter, and already did. But in Pristina Thaçi was under fire from opposition parties in parliament and groups outside opposed to any discussions with Serbia – many of them suspicious that he was giving away too much.

For this round of talks Thaçi brought with him Blerim Shala, a former journalist and now a deputy leader in the opposition. Shala would look intently at whoever was speaking, arms folded, exasperated by what he saw as unreasonable Serb behaviour. Dačić meanwhile brought Marko Đurić, a key advisor to President Nikolić, who knew his boss's position and was determined to stick with it. The dynamic in the room changed immediately: the rhythm and style of the two prime ministers was replaced by a more abrupt, confrontational atmosphere. But if the two newcomers could be brought on board, the chances of success were greater.

I started by reminding them of the EU's timetable, and the need to make progress for my reports. The key date now was the General Affairs Council meeting on 28 June. Instead of concentrating their minds, the date sparked a long discussion about the Battle of Kosovo in 1389, commemorated in Serbia on the same day. A bloody conflict between Ottoman forces and Serbia, with huge losses on both sides and Serbia coming off worst, it was associated with conflict and revenge. Oddly, on the same date in 1914 Archduke Ferdinand was assassinated in Sarajevo, a crucial moment in the start of the First World War. I dropped my pen, sat back and waited. It was great that they could have these conversations, but I wished we had chosen a different date for such a vital discussion at the Council.

Eventually talk turned to the municipalities: Serbia asked that they be called a Community of Serb Municipalities; Kosovo countered that it had to be an Association. Though I never understood why, each rigidly stuck to their choices. But by the end of the day each agreed the other could use their own term. It was also accepted that its creation would be based on Kosovo law, via indirect elections – but we still had the difficult question of whether to devolve further powers.

Serbia was concerned that if they dismantled the parallel police force, making all police officers members of the Kosovar force, commanders who hated the Serbs might be put in charge. They wanted the Community/Association to have some influence on who was appointed as regional police commanders. At present, the mayor of each area produced a shortlist of candidates for the local station commander from which the Kosovar authorities made appointments. Dačić asked why this could not be the basis for more senior appointments. Thaçi was reluctant, stressing the importance of qualifications and suitability for senior positions. However, Fernando and I thought there was a conversation to be had on the possibilities to 'influence' the choice without removing decision-making from the government. I suggested to both sides that they view any overall agreement they were able to make as working within EU rules, rather than linking it to Kosovo. That way each could rightly claim they were doing what was necessary to get into the EU. It was important that we used the pull of the EU to help them look to the future, rather than fall back into the hatred and bitterness of the past.

Throughout our meeting I could see how the relationship between the prime ministers was developing. Dačić quipped that he wanted the relations with Kosovo sorted out because 'as Serbian PM I can't go anywhere in the world without hearing about Kosovo and I am fed up with it'. Thaçi smiled. They joked they'd put forward a joint application for political asylum in Brussels if they got this wrong, though behind the laughter the strain was clear.

At times the pressure was obvious. When Dačić made clear he was at the end of the mandate he had from President Nikolić, and any decisions would have to be ratified in Belgrade, Thaçi's smile turned to anger. The Kosovars were furious that Dačić had no power of decision when so much was at stake. Within a few minutes discussions became deeply acrimonious. I calmed everyone down. Dačić was being honest, and it was better not to make a deal than to say yes to something that fell apart instantly. Dačić explained that next to President Nikolić, the most powerful person in Serbia was Deputy Prime Minister Vučić.* He was the one who had to be convinced. Both Nikolić and Vučić offered to come to Brussels, and I said I would be pleased to see them. However, I pointed out it was not my intention to sell the plan to them. It belonged to the prime ministers, and they had to get agreement to it.

We had some good news. Customs officials on Gates 1 and 31 in the north of Kosovo had always been flown in to work by helicopter due to safety concerns. Today, for the first time, they'd arrived by car; a photo showed them inspecting vehicles lined up to cross the border. All six gates were now open and functioning normally. It was a sign that change was possible. Fernando and I stared at the photo for a long time.

As promised, Nikolić brought his political ally, Deputy Prime Minister Vučić, to Brussels. Vučić's focus was on the economy and the benefits a closer relationship with the EU offered. Over a relaxed dinner it became obvious that Vučić was at the heart of political thinking in Belgrade and a future leader. He needed to be brought into the decision-making as Dačić had said. Always determined to treat each side equally, I took a short trip to Pristina, mainly to see some of the opposition leaders in the parliament. They offered their support, even when I told them that the way forward would include some uncomfortable decisions. Both discussions augured well for the next. It was nearly spring, and time to find solutions.

Our next meeting was set for 20 March, and I hoped we'd finish by early evening. It was my birthday, and I was looking forward to dinner afterwards with James and his wife Helen, the closest to family I had in

---

* Vučić was later prime minister then president of Serbia.

Brussels. Fernando and I'd spent a long time considering the format we should use and had decided to start with just the two prime ministers and their translators.

On their arrival I went over the results from our previous discussions and moved on to the challenge of appointing the regional police commander and the judiciary, which revolved around the Court of Appeal in Mitrovica North. Serbia had to have confidence in the court for an area where the population was 90 per cent Serb. If we could get this right, then the parallel structures could be dismantled. I reminded them both that it was up to them to find a solution and opened the discussion. After a while we took a break, and they stopped to chat in the corridor. Officials from the EU, some of them old Balkans hands, watched in amazement. I took a photo: I never knew when it might be the last one of them together.

Thaçi told me he was prepared to make offers on both police and courts. He suggested shortlisting candidates for police commander based on competence and skills, followed by a process in which the municipalities could influence the final choice. That way Kosovo would get a commander with the competence to do the job that both sides would be happy with. He also proposed that the Appeal Court judges would sit as a panel of at least three: two Kosovo Serbs and one Kosovo Albanian. Other population groups would have to be represented, and that could be worked out in what was a significant move from Kosovo's original position of requiring Serbs in Mitrovica North to go to Pristina for the Court of Appeal – a non-starter for Serbia.

While Thaçi worked on the detail, Dačić – increasingly worried about the politics at home – was unable to concentrate on any kind of agreement. Vučić was about to take leadership of the Progressive Party, which made him an extremely powerful figure back in Belgrade, and Dačić felt Vučić needed to be making decisions with us. Otherwise it would be easy to make Dačić the scapegoat for failure.

We reconvened in a larger format with a mixture of advisors and ministers. The dynamic was harder to manage, but I hoped it would motivate them to find solutions. It did – for thirteen hours. But they got stuck on the Community/Association's powers, with Nikolić's advisor pushing for a new layer of government, which was never going to work. I advised Thaçi to hold back his formal proposals until we were deeper into the detail, making clear to Dačić that new ideas would not be put forward until we resolved the issue of powers. I knew that Thaçi was worried that without a deal at this late stage, his credibility would be shot back home. The whole Kosovo team were scared of failure, and I didn't blame them. So I piled the pressure on Dačić to find a way through.

The arguments grew more heated, tempers frayed, and I was completely fed up. We had spent the whole day going nowhere. I'd arranged sandwiches for lunch but no dinner, in the hope hunger might concentrate their minds. It didn't; they were shouting at each other. I closed my file, put my papers in my bag, folded my arms and looked at the floor. Dačić began speaking loudly, but as time went on and I wouldn't look up he started to speak more softly and to say over and over he really wanted an agreement. When he stopped, nobody spoke for about six minutes. I let the time tick by and then looked up: 'What are you doing here? If you don't want to do this, don't do it. Go home.'

It seemed to work; everyone calmed down and we carried on talking. Dačić asked for several breaks, ostensibly to smoke cigars; our building was smoke-free so he would disappear into the garage below. I knew that he was on the phone to Belgrade frequently and felt sorry for him, because he really wanted to find a way through but could only do it if he had the confidence that Belgrade would follow him.

Around 10 p.m., after fourteen exhausting hours, I called a halt and asked them to join me for a glass of champagne on what remained of my birthday. We sat in a mixed group on the sofas, and I took another photo to remind myself of this extraordinary day. I raised my glass to them, saying I believed in them, but if they left now with no agreement their countries would be in worse shape and their political lives finished. The words tumbled out; my language was tough in my frustration. Dačić drew me into a corner, telling me again that Vučić was the key and he needed a few more days. I told him to work it out with Thaçi. I said I would reconvene one more meeting in ten days' time. After that I was through.

To demonstrate they were serious, I asked them to join me in talking to the press. I gave a short statement: 'We have been together since early this morning determined to make progress . . . it is my personal view that we are very close to a solution on some of the most difficult issues concerning northern Kosovo . . . it is now time for consultations to take place before we come back together on 2 April for what will be the conclusive meeting of this set of issues . . . my birthday present is that they should keep working tomorrow and we will, I hope, reach conclusions.' Dačić looked tired and strained and I reminded him to take care of himself. Thaçi was worried, but holding up better now that he could see another opportunity to hammer out the details. We agreed Vučić should join our next meeting: it was our best chance of getting an agreement.

James and I raced off to his house, where Helen had cake and delicious white wine to celebrate the final few minutes of my birthday. It was good to have a little fun; it helped shift my mood. I was pretty sure things were about to fall apart: I didn't think at this stage that President Nikolić could agree. Russia was starting to comment publicly, saying I had played the talks unfairly. It was a good sign that they were taking an interest, clearly worried we might be getting somewhere. From time to time I had talked to the Russian foreign minister, Sergei Lavrov, explaining what we were trying to do. This was not about Serbia's relations with Russia, but failure could push Serbia closer to them.

I was sure that Vučić would only come if he had ideas to try out, so I set aside a full day for our 2 April meeting. I put out a statement the night before: 'Tomorrow I will host and support the eighth round of dialogue between Belgrade and Pristina. In the six months since the prime ministers first met in my office, I have seen the commitment and determination on both sides to reach an agreement . . . I believe an agreement is within reach – though it will not be easy. But when we began, we all knew this would be difficult and would require strong political leadership. I believe those coming tomorrow do so in the spirit of finding a solution in the best interests of the people they represent and to help offer a better future for them all. We must not let this opportunity pass.'

To my delight I heard Vučić was coming. I got to the office early for what would be a difficult but important day. I told my staff to deal with anything else that came in; member states' requests and the impending Iran negotiations I was to chair would all have to wait. Tomorrow I would begin a heavy ten-day trip, but for the next twelve hours my only priority was to get the two sides over the final hurdles. Fernando appeared, and he joined me in gazing out of the window at the Brussels traffic. Words were unnecessary.

Thaçi arrived first with his deputy prime minister, Edita Tahiri. Harvard-educated, she was a powerful force in Kosovo and had been responsible for the early technical talks. Dačić was accompanied by the tall and imposing figure of Aleksandar Vučić, destined to be the most significant Serb leader of his generation. Neither deputy was used to the format and both were more combative than their prime ministers; neither was prepared to give ground they didn't want to. I thought it would be fun to watch them spar for a while.

I began by making it clear I'd reached the end of the negotiations. We were running out of time to get the EU agreement on moving forward with either of them. I needed full consensus from the member states, which was not going to be easy, and upcoming German elections made it harder for Germany to take big decisions in the meantime. I then invited them to start their conversations.

We talked for twelve hours, and although it became clear much earlier on that we weren't going to reach agreement, I stuck to my word that this was the eighth and final round. Speaking to the press afterwards I described the gap between both sides as 'very narrow, but deep'. The next step, I said, was for each to return home to consult with colleagues and let me know in the next few days of their decision. I wished them a good journey home and every possible success in reaching a conclusion.

I was deeply disappointed when the proposals were formally rejected in Belgrade. My statement in response was conciliatory, but clear that it was Serbia that had rejected the proposals, so the EU would know what had happened. I had said from the beginning that if one side rejected and the other did not, I would make that distinction in my report; it was only fair.

I pointed out that all the elements for an agreement on northern Kosovo were on the table, but it was for the two sides to agree and not for the EU to impose. I added: 'I regret the decision of the Serbian government to reject the proposals and call on them to make a last effort to reach an agreement, for the benefit of their people,' ending more optimistically: 'I hope that Kosovo and Serbia will not miss the opportunity to put the past behind them and move forward into the future. I hope I will be leading the discussion in the EU over the next few days in support of a real step forward by both Serbia and Kosovo towards their European future.'

The Kosovo team were restrained in public but desperate in private. They responded to the Serb rejection with a press release saying the dialogue was the way forward and they remained committed to it. Thaçi's advisor suggested that Serbia's 'no' was only a temporary one. Thaçi had bet on the success of this process and knew his political future was in question without it. If we couldn't resolve this now, there was little chance for the future of his country during his premiership or even his lifetime. This could so easily become a frozen conflict that went on for years. We had enough of those, in my view. I waited. Belgrade was silent.

Fernando and I held our breath. We were determined not to do anything that either side could use as an excuse to blame Brussels. Fernando kept in touch with both capitals as I headed off on a ten-day trip that encompassed the Iran negotiations in Kazakhstan, a visit to Egypt and a G8 foreign ministers' meeting in London. Fernando called to say he could sense Serbia's position was thawing, and I started to get messages from other countries who'd been talking with them that they wanted a deal. At the same time Kosovo was working up ideas it thought might help.

I was due to visit their region on 17 April, but decided instead to invite them both to Brussels. Publicly I declared optimism once again, saying that I had asked them to come in a constructive spirit, ready to explore different options and agree to a mutual compromise. Good words, but I wasn't too hopeful. When they arrived, I saw each of them separately as usual. Body language is an important factor in negotiation, and I knew if either side showed too much eagerness for a point, the other would be suspicious they had missed or conceded something important. I told Thaçi he was far too polite when I put forward ideas he didn't like. Ultimately it would help if each side thought the other had been dragged screaming to a compromise.

We had three outstanding issues, all of them now led by Vučić on the Serb side. If he agreed, we had a deal. The first two were ongoing questions: how the regional police commander would be chosen and how to construct the Court of Appeal in Mitrovica North. The third was new. Vučić raised concerns that the Kosovars might take military action against the Serbs in the north – specifically including tank manoeuvres. It was ludicrous – Kosovo didn't have any tanks – but I had learnt long ago not to underestimate the paranoia conflict can inspire. The Serbs were anticipating a future scenario with a more hostile Kosovo leadership. I asked NATO if they could help, and their deputy secretary general, Sandy Vershbow, immediately offered to come in person to the talks.

It felt clear by this point that Serbia was moving rapidly in the right direction. Vučić was keen to use some wording from the document they'd produced for their domestic audience. Overall, it was an unhelpful paper, focusing on Serbia's position on the status of Kosovo, but it was important to them, and we found a couple of points we could use without causing any problems for Kosovo.

Throughout our discussions I had strongly resisted writing down what they were saying or suggesting wording. They had to be the authors of their agreement. I didn't want them to blame us because they did not like a phrase or word, and to use that as an excuse to walk away. They had to own this plan or it would never work. I also had an aversion to people putting their names to plans, and when the question came up of what to call this agreement I told them firmly that there would never be an Ashton plan. Rarely, if ever, does the credit belong to one person – especially true in this case. It became the Brussels Agreement.

But by now Fernando and I began to believe they might just make it to a deal. Given how much had been agreed, I decided to try and capture, in a series of short sentences, what they were going to do. We regretted it almost immediately afterwards. Just as the Serbs had been extremely difficult in the last meeting, so the Kosovars became impossible in this one. Part of the reason for that was our fault.

In drafting the short document, the Kosovo side persuaded us to add a sentence saying neither side should block the other's path to membership of any international organisation. We thought it looked harmless enough, which only shows we were too eager to get it done and too focused on the EU. Vučić and Dačić immediately rejected it, claiming it implied recognition of Kosovo as a state and it was a new issue which had been added without discussion. We had made a mistake. Fernando didn't sleep that night, agonising about how we had been so stupid and how we were going to fix it. I kicked a lot of furniture, furious with myself for even trying to write it down. The process of doing so had been as treacherous as I had expected it to be, so what possessed me I didn't know.

Vučić tried to help, suggesting a compromise using the EU Council wording 'neither should block the other on its path to the EU'. It was potentially much more manageable and gave Kosovo something, so I showed it to Thaçi's team. They went nuts. I suspected they had sold their wording heavily back in Pristina, and having it changed would cost them dearly. Our discussions were brutal.

It got worse. To sort out the regional police commander's appointments we'd worked out a formula whereby the four local Serb mayors would put forward a list of suitably qualified candidates to the Ministry of Internal Affairs on behalf of the Community/Association of Serb Municipalities. The ministry would decide who was appropriate. After talking about and fine-tuning this for an hour and a half, the Kosovo team suddenly said that giving executive power to the municipalities was a huge problem. I pointed out that they were providing a list, but the ministry would take the decision. It made no difference. I was frustrated but was not going to be drawn into defending a particular proposal. The suggestions were coming from them, not me. They had to take ownership and agree a solution: I was not going to take sides.

So much for my fears that the Kosovo team were too polite: they were blunt and to the point. The words they did not like were 'on behalf of', as in 'the mayors would submit a list of suitably qualified candidates *on behalf of* the Community/Association'. It didn't seem at all controversial to me and I could not understand what the problem was, but by that point I was so exasperated and drowning in detail that I wondered if I had lost the plot, though none of our legal team or officials could fathom it either. But in any event, Thaçi and his team were not going to move so it didn't matter what I thought.

I moved on to the remaining two issues. If we could narrow the divide on those, we would be left with just one point, which could make compromise easier. The Ministry of Justice in Kosovo had accepted the Appeal Court in Mitrovica North, so we had an agreement nailed down. As proposed, there would be three judges in total with two being selected from the Serb community. With a bit more time spent discussing the selection process and how it would work, this was sorted.

I moved on to what I called the 'tank issue'. The Serbs wanted assurances that Kosovar security forces would not go into the north without NATO's knowledge and that NATO would consult locally before any such deployment. As he had promised, the deputy secretary general of NATO sent a senior official over to spend time with the Serb team. He assured them that if NATO was there, it would be involved in any decisions the Kosovars took. That in turn reassured Kosovo that NATO would stay engaged in the future.

We were back to the last outstanding problem – that of the regional police commander. There were seven districts under their responsibility, four populated by local Serbs and three by Kosovars. The Serbs proposed one regional commander for all seven areas, serving a maximum of two terms – eight years – by which point we hoped ethnicity would be much less of an issue. The Kosovo team thought that was too long. Serbia wanted a guarantee that the post would go to a local Serb, which Kosovo found very challenging. I could see both sides' point. After much debate I suggested we go for two commanders – a local Serb for the four Serb areas, and a Kosovar for the other three. It wasn't what I'd set out to achieve, but it would do for now – just. But we were getting nowhere on the language points – the 'on behalf of' problem, or the line about 'blocking of international organisation' membership.

Moods shifted wildly throughout the day. Initially we had seen some fairly dramatic behaviour from the Serbs, while the Kosovars remained calm and conciliatory, but as the evening arrived Thaçi and his team were becoming extremely bad-tempered. In response Vučić said he had twenty-plus amendments to proposals so far, and the atmosphere became deeply acrimonious. I suggested a break for everyone to cool off and to give me a chance to talk to them separately.

I went to the Serb room first. Dačić's team always made themselves at home, bringing supplies from Serbia with them: today it was oysters. A chessboard was laid out and Vučić and Dačić shook hands, joking easily in front of me, despite their uneasy coalition at home. When I asked where they thought we had got to, Vučić said that with one slight change he could live with the regional organisations point, drop the twenty-plus amendments and back the deal. I knew in that moment they were ready to sign. It would be a hard sell back in Belgrade, but they were ready for the challenge.

I went to see Thaçi. I had an agreed text from the Serbs that I knew I could not ask them to change. But I also knew it was going to be difficult for Thaçi, probably even harder than it had been for Dačić and Vučić. He was stuck on the wording 'on behalf of', and I gently pointed out that we had talked through this wording with his team before we wrote it down and were surprised at his reaction. He complained bitterly that we'd reneged on the text we'd agreed on regional organisation membership. I said it should never had gone in, but even so, this was an agreement between Serbia and Kosovo, so ultimately it didn't matter what I thought. If Serbia could not accept it, that was that. What I could not gauge was the political problem it created back in Kosovo.

I tried to convince Thaçi to move on – this problem didn't affect the fundamental agreement which was about the north. The Serbs were dropping all the other amendments and were ready to sign. Surely this was what he wanted? I made no impact. I understood that any concession would be considered a betrayal by some back home, especially in parliament. Kosovo would not see any immediate benefit from the EU – just the early prospect of trade discussions, or visa liberalisation to make travel to Europe easier. Thaçi was effectively taking the first steps to normalising relations with Serbia, with no guarantee of state recognition at the end of it. But without these first steps they would not get there at all.

To give him time to think I suggested a break for dinner, with both parties returning at 10 p.m. I cancelled my evening flight to Sarajevo, planning to fly instead at 6 the next morning. I ordered pizza to the office and we waited until they came back. I was worried they'd start to reconsider what they had already agreed. Everyone was nervous. We were so close.

At 10 p.m. I spoke to both prime ministers without their teams, relying on the strength of the relationship between Dačić and Thaçi. I asked them to think about 'on behalf of' and whether they could find a solution. I said I preferred to say nothing, leaving them to explain the wording as they needed to back home, but in the end it was only about creating a list. If asked I would say that requesting the municipalities put together a list was not giving them executive power. Dačić went to join Vučić, Thaçi to meet with his team. I couldn't believe everything might now fall apart because of one phrase. But the phrase represented a wider set of issues, and Thaçi had the more challenging job to sell this to his people.

Fernando appeared in my doorway – Thaçi had decided to leave. We had arranged for both sides to receive calls from supportive countries, and Thaçi had spoken with Phil Reeker back in Washington, as well as officials from Germany and elsewhere who said they'd help in as many ways as they could if he signed, so I was really perturbed. I rushed to see him.

It was a very difficult conversation. I asked why he would leave when he had what he wanted. I said again that 'on behalf of' had been in the original proposal so I didn't understand why this problem had arisen. I had some sympathy for him, but I was angry too. I told him that I'd have to say he had been the one to go, whereas the Serbs were ready to sign. I was prepared to fail, but failing over such tiny issues was unexpected and depressing.

Vučić and Dačić came out of their room as Thaçi and his colleagues swept by. I explained that the Kosovo team were refusing to sign and were leaving. They were astonished and confused. What should they do now, what should they say? At that point I couldn't hide my anger. Tell the truth, I said. You were ready to sign, they were not. I felt utterly defeated. Thaçi went to the press and accused Vučić of behaving like Milošević – a comment that would inevitably draw a response. An escalating war of words could make any future talks impossible. It felt like the end.

After very little sleep I woke with a raging headache and headed to Sarajevo and Srebrenica. Fernando called around lunchtime. Thaçi and his team had taken a flight to Ljubljana, but not their connecting plane to Pristina. They were waiting. The Serbian press meanwhile were running stories that a deal was close and it was a good one for Serbia, which was partly why Thaçi had been so upset. Win-win was a concept lost on a region that had suffered so much. Thaçi was right to worry that he would be accused of failing his country. But they hadn't gone home yet, so there was a chance they might come back. Thaçi called Fernando and asked his advice. Turn round, said Fernando, come back and finish what you started.

The question then was, had we lost the Serbs? By this point I was in Croatia, where my trip had ended. As I headed back to Brussels the

Serbs would not confirm their return. Fernando had the brilliant idea of asking the Belgian Protocol Service at the airport if they were scheduled to greet the Serbian prime minister; they would know before anyone else. They confirmed a request for their service. We were back in business.

We decided to keep the teams apart. They had come to sign the deal, and after some acrimonious exchanges in the press I didn't want them yelling at each other. I typed the document myself and we photocopied it. It was short – just over one side of A4 with fifteen separate points. It described how the Association/Community (we didn't care which name they used) of Serb-majority municipalities in Kosovo would be created by statute, and that other municipalities could join it. It would have an overview on economic development, education, health, urban and rural planning.

It said there would be one police force called the Kosovo Police. All police would be integrated into it and their salaries would come only from it. It covered the regional commander post and the nominations for this post from the list. 'On behalf of' remained in the text. It described the Court of Appeal and its panel, the majority of whom would be Kosovo-Serb judges. Finally, it set out the implementation process for the agreement. However difficult it had been to get this far, there was still a very long way to go.

I saw Dačić and Vučić first. They said they would initial the agreement, then take it to Belgrade for their government processes. They told me this could be done over the weekend, including meeting with the northern Kosovo Serb leaders, and they would send me a letter confirming their agreement. Then on Wednesday it would be discussed in their parliament, where Vučić assured me he would get a majority vote. 'It will be worse than hell, but I will do it,' he said.

We had the Serbs. Now for the Kosovars. They were still unsure about 'on behalf of' and I offered various ways in which we could ensure it was not seen to be giving away a new power, including mentioning it my EU Council report, which would be a public document. I could see Thaçi was still worried. I called Phil Reeker in Washington for his advice.

He asked me to give him a few minutes, then he called Thaçi. He told me later he was blunt, explaining how not taking this opportunity would be seen in the USA, and the importance of showing leadership. Thaçi asked for more time to think and talk to his team. We left him alone.

I'd suggested we sign at 2.40 p.m. and arranged for us all to go to NATO afterwards, which would be seen positively in both capitals. I showed Thaçi the final document. We had given it the title 'First agreement of principles governing the normalisation of relations between Belgrade and Pristina'. It was, I thought, the least controversial part of the document. It used familiar language and we avoided further details, allowing both sides to stay on their side of the red line of recognition. But Thaçi suddenly shouted, 'I am not the mayor of Pristina' and took off down the corridor. I ran after him – there was no way I was letting him leave a second time. Others watched astounded as we hurtled down the corridor. Fernando, calm as ever, caught up with us and suggested we delete 'between Belgrade and Pristina' from the title. The document itself referred to Kosovo, not Pristina, so I hoped Thaçi could agree. He did.

I walked into the first empty room I found: I didn't care which room it was and had no idea what it was normally used for. It had a table and chairs, and somebody produced a desktop EU flag together with a photographer. I sat with Thaçi and waited until the new copies appeared with the offending words changed. He initialled his copy and I initialled alongside him. The photographer snapped the moment, and I saw Thaçi's smile reappear.

I went to see the Serbs, who were much more relaxed. Vučić told Dačić that the document was for him to initial as prime minister. We found the flag, got the photographer, and Dačić initialled his copy alongside me. He also added a line after his signature: 'I hereby confirm that this is the text proposal on whose acceptance or refusal both sides shall submit their respective decisions.' He was making sure it was understood that Serbia had yet to formally agree. By doing that, though, I knew he and Vučić were serious about delivering the deal.

It had been incredibly hard for both sides, knowing many people they led and respected would never forgive them. This was leadership – and in those last hours I saw its price written on their faces, watched their agony as they made their decisions, and saw the weight lift when it was done.

We headed for NATO, and they met for the first time that day. The road ahead was going to be difficult – it is far from finished even today – but in a region that had known such turmoil, the message the whole process sent of the possibilities for a better future was important.

Kosovo's minister for Europe, Vlora Çitaku, was the first to break the news, tweeting 'Habemus Pactum' (we have an agreement). Word spread quickly and the messages flooded in. Across Europe it was front-page news, except in Britain, where initially it didn't make the news until Misha Glenny, an expert on the region, wrote a piece in the *Financial Times*. The *Economist* described it as a 'huge breakthrough for the two countries, for the Western Balkans as a whole, and a triumph for Lady Ashton and her team'. Jon Snow of Channel 4 tweeted: 'Cathy Ashton has pulled off a massive peace deal between Kosovo and Serbia. First full-blown deal in 100 years.' Roger Boyes in *The Times* wrote: 'if it holds, Belgrade Kosovo pact big win for EU foreign policy . . . USA impressed'.

The US administration was delighted, sending messages of support to both leaders and to my team. Both parties in the US Congress nominated the two leaders and me for the 2014 Nobel Peace Prize, which Malala Yousafzai rightly won that year for her bravery and courage. I was honoured even to have been on the same list.

The arrangement represented a historic milestone, both in potentially ending the long-standing enmity between both sides and in overcoming widespread public distrust of such an agreement. It was a genuinely collaborative effort, requiring persistence and patience from all involved. But there was no time to bask in the – for once – positive press. Fernando and I knew the harder job was to implement the agreement. I was under no illusions – it would not be easy. But almost no one had believed we would ever get this far, and we were not giving up now.

Fernando took on the responsibility of getting the implementation started, with up to fifty officials each week from Pristina and Belgrade heading to Brussels to work out the detail. I turned my attention to getting member states to support it by offering closer links to Brussels – opening accession talks with Serbia and trade links to Kosovo. Sessions almost as complex and long as the negotiations themselves finally reached agreement on my recommendations.

At the beginning, most EU member states had assumed failure was inevitable and paid little attention to the talks. It helped to be out of the spotlight while we slowly built up trust in the process between the two sides. Now there was much more interest in the outcomes and curiosity about how it had been done – especially from those who knew the region well. I explained what I thought had worked. In Fernando I had someone both sides knew and trusted and his team had acres of experience. Together we were a good team, trusting instinctively in each other and testing out ideas carefully. We were prepared for failure – at times expected it – and were ready for the anticipated sneering from those who thought us mad to even try. There were no egos at work on our side; we just wanted to help. We gave the process time, spending long hours and where necessary several days to get it done. Afterwards both teams said how much it meant to them that we were always there, didn't give up or leave for something 'more important'. We understood what we were trying to do – and what we were not – crossing no red lines on either side. Most of all we stuck to our job of facilitating their agreement, not ours. It may have Brussels in the title, but it belongs to Serbia and Kosovo.

7

THE IRAN NUCLEAR
NEGOTIATIONS

A few days after I took office, in the autumn of 2009, as I was still getting to grips with the scale of the job, a colleague mentioned that I was now responsible for chairing and leading the international negotiations on Iran's nuclear programme. I looked at him in disbelief as he explained that in my new role I was mandated by the UN Security Council to convene and manage the meetings. I already had plenty to worry about, but this was in a different league. I knew little about Iran, and was immediately daunted. Yet, by the time I left the job five years later, I had devoted more time to this than to any other issue and spent many more hours with the Iranians than with my family.

The international community's main concern was that Iran was enriching uranium beyond the 3–4 per cent necessary for a civil nuclear programme and had been putting together the infrastructure necessary to develop nuclear weapons. At their nuclear plant in Natanz they had enriched to 20 per cent with no obvious civil use. Getting from 4 per cent to 20 per cent was the most challenging step – if they continued, they would reach the 90 per cent enrichment level necessary for nuclear weapon production within two years. As a signatory to the Non-Proliferation Treaty, Iran had obligations not to acquire nuclear weapons and to allow International Atomic Energy Agency (IAEA) inspectors to monitor its activities. Its failure to comply led to sanctions being imposed by the UN Security Council, banning the supply of nuclear-related materials, freezing the assets of those connected to the programme and introducing an arms embargo.

France, Germany and the UK began negotiations with Iran in 2003, inviting the EU to take on a coordinating function. Russia, China and the USA joined in 2006, creating the team of six countries, plus the EU.* Proposals were put forward, including that Iran would ship out its low-enriched uranium to be held in a sort of fuel bank where it could be further processed to make fuel before being returned under supervision. Later, when I raised this proposal with Dr Saeed Jalili, the secretary of Iran's Supreme National Security Council and at that time their chief negotiator, he explained that having a nuclear programme was like having an expensive car. If they agreed to send the fuel out of the country, and we decided not to send it back, they would have the car but no petrol. 'What would be the point in that?' he asked, rejecting the idea with a shrug.

During my first couple of years we held seven meetings in Switzerland, Turkey, Iraq, Russia and Kazakhstan but made little progress. Dr Jalili, a candidate for the presidency of Iran in 2013, and I talked for many hours, exchanging letters and phone calls in between but got nowhere. It was small consolation for the six countries that we had a process in place if a new president was serious about talks.

The small EU team had led the work to ensure we had a strong, agreed position on the outcomes we were looking for. The most challenging question was Iran's right to enrich uranium, which sorely tested the unity of the six countries.

The collective view was officially that the Non-Proliferation Treaty conveyed rights and responsibilities on its members, and one right could

---

* In Europe, to recognise the European origins of the talks, the group of six was known as the E3 plus 3 (E being European), but was described elsewhere as the P5 plus 1 to promote the key role of the Security Council. Either way it was six countries, and either way the role of the EU was given little prominence, or added in rather clumsily as EU/E3 whenever the European description of six was used.

not be read in isolation. If Iran followed all the rules it was entitled to a civil nuclear programme. But there was no real consensus on how best to achieve that. Some countries thought it was dangerous for Iran to have the capacity to enrich in any circumstances. Others, including Russia and China, thought the Non-Proliferation Treaty did convey the right and we should all acknowledge it. It was a disagreement that we had to resolve at some point. But despite the frustrations, nobody considered for a moment giving up. Instead, we waited for the outcome of the presidential elections in the hope that the next leader might be more willing to engage.

I was surprised that Hassan Rouhani won on the first round with an absolute majority. A former nuclear negotiator, he had positioned himself as a unifying candidate for the more reformist groups, promising new respect for civil rights and freedom of the press, equality for women and minorities and, most pressingly, a vision to fix the economy – a task that required the lifting of sanctions imposed by the UN Security Council, the USA and the EU. The EU oil embargo alone cost Iran $50 billion a year in revenue; banking sanctions and the almost total restrictions on trade from the USA had dealt significant blows to the economy. A deal which removed most, if not all, economic sanctions would give a dramatic boost to industry and business. During one of the presidential debates before the election, Rouhani said: 'Our centrifuges are good to spin when the people's economy is also spinning in the right direction.' His clear focus on the economy might be the incentive to come to the negotiating table. We surmised he would build as much consensus as possible, which could make it harder to find a deal, but if successful it would be more likely to stick, at least in Iran.

I wrote to Rouhani congratulating him, saying we were keen to continue the talks. While waiting for the new team to be assembled we worked on our strategy, which I often described as like creating a jigsaw puzzle. When complete the puzzle had to form a clear picture – in this case of a peaceful nuclear programme in Iran, with monitoring and verification in place. The individual pieces could vary if the finished picture was unambiguous. So if Iran was willing to do more in one area, we could afford to ask for less in another, giving us some flexibility. One of the challenges was that, for some, a particular piece was more important than the bigger picture. If it looked different to their expectations, they would declare the agreement a failure.

The EU team spent hours talking to their counterparts. Helga Schmid, a talented German diplomat, led much of the discussion with the teams across the six, and with the Iranians. Working closely with her was Stephan Klement, an Austrian nuclear expert, who chaired and led the technical discussions. They were supported by the rest of their team, which, with James and I, made up the EU side.

Brussels, 16–17 July 2013

The delegations from the six countries were led day to day by either a deputy minister or a senior civil servant reporting directly to their foreign minister. Each team consisted of nuclear experts, policy analysts, political advisors and sanctions experts as needed. Some were large – the USA had over fifty people on a regular basis, and more as the talks became more serious. Together they had the ability to analyse and agree proposals put forward from within the six, the EU, or from Iran. Technical experts met as necessary during or between the negotiations.

Helga Schmid, as the EU political director, led many of the internal discussions and met regularly with Iran's deputy foreign minister. The formal set-piece talks were led by me and the chief Iranian negotiator, bringing in other ministers if we needed them to take political decisions or to be consulted as a group. Only the USA would play a much larger part, with Secretary of State John Kerry taking a lead role in the negotiations, not least as US sanctions relief was a key part of the discussions.

To prepare for Iran's response, the six joined me in Brussels. Each had their own ideas, but prior consultation, especially between the three European countries and the USA, meant some of the wrinkles were already ironed out. Still there were differences. The UK political director,

Simon Gass, a former ambassador to Iran who exuded calm and good sense even in the most challenging debates, proposed we produce a short document explaining our vision for the talks. In the jargon it was called a political chapeau, from the French for hat. Shared with the Iranian team, it would sit on top of the negotiations as a description of what the endgame could look like. Jacques Audibert of France thought it was too early to put a comprehensive plan forward. He was a veteran of the talks, with an impish grin that belied his steely-eyed watchfulness, ready to pounce on any sign that France's position was being undermined or ignored. Wendy Sherman agreed with him. As the head of the US negotiating team she came with experience from negotiations with North Korea as well as a wealth of knowledge in foreign affairs. She reminded everyone that the USA remained open for bilateral talks with Iran – something we encouraged all six countries to continue to do, within the framework of the overall negotiations. Iran had expressed no interest in talking with the USA, shunning even short exchanges during our meetings. We hoped this would change with a new government in place. Hans-Dieter Lucas, Germany's political director, known for his pragmatic approach, thought we needed to be bolder and focus on setting out a comprehensive plan in which small steps or 'confidence-building measures' would sit. The four divided neatly into two positions. All accepted that small steps were the best method; the question was, did we lay out our endgame now, or later?

Ma Zhaoxu, a senior official from China, joined the discussion. China's perspective was that we would see a change of tactics by a new Iranian team but not a fundamental shift of position. He wanted new talks quickly, in the hope of 'an early harvest'. I turned to Sergei Ryabkov,* Russia's deputy foreign minister and a veteran of the talks. He was generally good-natured but tough when he saw it was needed, either with Iran or with others in the six. Russia wanted a deal but he thought

---

* Relations with Russia went downhill over these years, but in the Iran talks we kept our focus.

there should be more 'give and take', and that I should consider going to Iran to talk to the new government there. I was not against visiting Tehran at the right time, and I was cautiously optimistic that we might begin a real dialogue. But from our discussions I saw that getting into real dialogue would test our abilities as collaborators as well as negotiators.

I spoke to Iran's new foreign minister, Mohammad Javad Zarif, in mid-August to congratulate him on his appointment. He knew the USA well, having studied at San Francisco University and the University of Denver. He'd worked for Iran at the UN, rising to become Iranian ambassador to the UN from 2002 to 2007. I told him we were ready to meet as soon as the new negotiating team was appointed. Shortly afterwards we learnt he was to lead the team himself.

Zarif said that although he was comfortable working directly with me, in 2002 all his meetings had been at ministerial level and he regretted the change from foreign ministers leading the talks to deputies taking this responsibility. I pointed out that ministers would engage at critical moments and to endorse the results. I knew that ministers had less time and weren't familiar with the detail, and we risked other disputes spilling over into the negotiations. Political directors and deputies were more able to keep focus. I didn't convince him, though, and as it made sense to bring all six ministers together in late September at the UN in New York to meet with him, I parked the problem. In reality, the talks in the media spotlight were always going to be staged to show the outcome of what was done behind the scenes. The most important of the private conversations would be between the USA and Iran – vital if we were to make progress – but all the detailed work needed to be done quietly. I think of it as the difference between front of house and back of house – like staging a play.

We reconvened during ministerial week at the UN General Assembly. The week is best described as 'speed-dating for diplomats'. Hundreds of bilateral meetings take place, each in a small booth with portable room dividers and containing two armchairs, one small table, a jug of water with two glasses, and four or five chairs down each side for the entourages. Every thirty minutes or so, everyone shuffles round to meet someone else, creating bottlenecks each time a minister stops to talk en route to the next meeting and leaving anxious officials looking at their watches and trying to shepherd their minister onward.

When Zarif and I met at the beginning of the week, I remembered not to offer my hand. For many Muslim men physical contact with a woman to whom they are not related is prohibited and for the Iranian team of men this was an absolute. Instead, they placed their right hand across their heart in greeting. I found it hard to remember, especially when the men were shaking hands freely; James, knowing my instincts, would whisper in my ear, 'Don't touch.' Some of the press wrote up the lack of a handshake as a snub. I was keen to correct them – we had enough problems without such basic misinterpretations.

Zarif's first suggestion was that we meet at one UN location rather than wandering around the planet. But for the strict observance on physical contact, I could have hugged him. Getting agreement on where and when to meet, let alone the logistics of arranging it all, had been nothing short of a nightmare. He wanted it to be a UN location and we landed on Geneva, to which the six readily agreed. I formally invited him to meet with the ministers on Thursday in the reopened conference room, refurbished by Russia and named the Russian room.

I planned the seating arrangements carefully, putting Zarif next to me, as chair, with his deputy next to Helga, and the six countries spread around the horseshoe-shaped table. The US team went nuts: they wanted John Kerry sitting next to Zarif. Sherman pointedly said this would be the only photo anyone would be interested in. We changed it – and she was right of course. The photo of a US secretary of state and an Iranian foreign minister sitting together was sensational. I noted with irony that the *New York Times* chose a photo that included me, on the other side of Zarif, while the *Financial Times* in London cut me out. Kerry and Zarif were the story.

Zarif made clear Iran's interest in getting a deal, but restated Iran's conviction that it had the right to enrich uranium under the terms of the

Non-Proliferation Treaty. When he finished, I invited ministers to contribute; each reinforced their commitment to the process, their hopes for a positive outcome and the need to get on with it. We agreed that talks would start soon in Geneva.* Afterwards Zarif and Kerry met together in a side room – the first formal bilateral meeting at this level since before the 1979 revolution. It was big news across the world.

Geneva, 15–16 October 2013

All of us bar Russia and China (who stayed elsewhere) used the Intercontinental Hotel in Geneva. I had a room on the seventeenth floor; the USA took half a floor directly below. The Iranians were on the seventh floor. The four meeting rooms, away from the main hotel areas, formed the basis of our negotiating space and were named Moscow, Brussels, Berlin and Amsterdam. Late one night a young woman in the bar made a bet with friends that she could break into our discussions. Racing down the corridor, she got close to flinging the door open before security stopped her. Combined with the hundreds of journalists doing their best to get information, it added to the sense of drama.

I arrived a day early for meetings with the European and US teams, followed by dinner with Zarif, a tradition I'd begun with Jalili. It gave me the chance to check the mood music for the days ahead. The rhythm of the Jalili years was well known to us but Zarif was new, and I knew little of his views.

As soon as her team arrived, Sherman took me aside to explain that the USA had begun private discussions with Iran. I'd always expected the breakthrough to come via back-of-house discussions between the USA and Iran, so I was relieved they had begun. But a bilateral agreement between the USA and Iran, though necessary, was insufficient to get a deal and everyone had to be on board. We had to hold the talks together.

---

*   In the meeting, Russian Foreign Minister Lavrov drew one of his spectacular doodles; this one was in black ink with a moon, flower, heart and words decorated with different fonts. I suggested he publish a book of them with a description of where he drew them. He laughed and gave it to me. I still have it.

Later that evening I headed for dinner with Zarif. It was a small affair. Helga and James and I on our side; Zarif with his two deputies, Majid Takht Ravanchi and Seyed Abbas Araghchi on theirs. We knew Araghchi already from previous talks but Ravanchi was new to us. During these relaxed dinners we had the chance to learn more of each other – they both spoke perfect English. Araghchi had got his first degree from the University of Kent in the UK and Ravanchi at the University of Kansas in the USA, which gave us a couple of *Wizard of Oz* jokes; we were certainly not in Kansas any more. Together the two played a vital role in getting the negotiations done. On this occasion, we checked Zarif and his team were happy with the format, timings and discussion areas, without getting into any detail. Zarif was clear that over the years there had been missed chances to come to an agreement. It was obvious he did not want to miss this one, if there was a way to get it done.

The next morning we met to open our first plenary session in front of the press. Photographers were so numerous that we had to bring them to the room in waves. They jostled for the best position, despite the careful shepherding of security staff. Zarif proposed a new seating plan to show we were working as one team. He sat next to me, his team fanning out in one direction and mine the other. All our discussions would now be conducted in English, which speeded up proceedings, and we asked Zarif to open the discussions. He gave us an hour-long PowerPoint presentation entitled 'Closing an unnecessary crisis and opening new horizons'. I grinned to myself. We were used to obtuse, complicated slide shows; this was very different. Its first slide simply said, 'Iran does not need or want nuclear weapons.' Zarif said our common objective was to ensure that Iran's exercise of the right to nuclear energy, including enrichment activities, 'would remain peaceful'.

To achieve that, he proposed a year-long timetable from the endorsement of an initial agreement to the UN Security Council and the IAEA, treating them the same as any other signatory to the Non-Proliferation Treaty. The IAEA had responsibility, under the treaty, for monitoring and inspection. Their regular reports were sent to the UN Security Council, which assessed whether Iran was compliant and therefore no longer a 'threat to international peace and security'.

Zarif proposed a joint commission from the six countries, convened by the EU, to review and approve the changes undertaken by Iran, monitor compliance and resolve disputes. When I invited comments from the six, Sherman welcomed his proposals and it was clear to some on our side that she'd known roughly what he was going to say. After we broke up the meeting Zarif expressed his impatience: he'd expected more from the six. I reminded him that the day had been about Iran's ideas; tomorrow we would put forward ours.

By the next morning the air was distinctly tetchy. I wasn't surprised. The closer we got to finding a possible agreement, the more the differences between the six were exposed. The risk was these differences could pull apart the outline of our jigsaw puzzle. A procession of political directors put their views to Helga or me, suggesting we were ill prepared for the talks or did not have a common position. Capitals got in on the act, with London leading on Prime Minister Cameron's desire for a swift grand bargain – much in keeping with his personality. I sensed that his foreign minister William Hague, who was closer to the talks, was more cautious. Hans-Dieter Lucas and Jacques Audibert, troubled by what the USA might be doing, wondered how far the positions of Germany and France were being taken into account. Only the Chinese delegation were upbeat, pushing hard for talks to start. I never knew if they really felt that positive, but it helped.

I worried our collaboration would unravel and recognised there was no time to work out how to manage the impending revelation of the US talks. Helga gathered the teams together, working tirelessly to deal with their issues and get everyone to the same positions. We ploughed on, by late afternoon reaching the point of agreeing a joint statement with Iran to close the meeting and set up the next. These statements mattered. They demonstrated that the six held the same views, showed progress and indicated what would happen next. The only unresolved point on our side was the adjective used to describe the meeting. We had chosen 'important'. Back in Washington, Susan Rice, President Obama's national security advisor, worried that an inconclusive first meeting was far from that and wanted to delete it. I knew there would have been uproar in the room if the USA had downgraded its significance. Susan understood and withdrew her objection. 'Important' stayed in.

Zarif and I led a final plenary to say goodbye, at which Sherman read out a prepared statement.

She was putting on record the US position in light of their bilateral talks, and it was obvious to everyone in the room that a closer working relationship had been established between the two countries. Ultimately, however, any agreement had to be between the six and Iran and it was time to merge what they were doing into the main body of the talks. The challenge would be keeping everyone on board while we did it.

Geneva, 7–9 November 2013

US Deputy Secretary of State Bill Burns was a career diplomat. In my years of working with him I never found any country or individual who had other than the highest praise for him. Now, it transpired, he was leading the US secret discussions with Iran. If anyone could pull off the challenge of getting everyone to accept these talks, it was him. He was working closely with Senior Advisor Jake Sullivan* – the perfect foil to Burns. His sharp mind and forensic questioning style contrasted well with Burns' more gently persuasive approach.

Wendy Sherman led the official talks for the USA, folding the work Burns and Sullivan were doing into the substantive negotiations. As we got together in Geneva, she told Helga and me of her plans to reveal the substance of the US talks to the other five, beginning with the Europeans that evening. I was relieved – bringing their work into the open would help us to get on with constructing a deal that everyone could support. But I didn't underestimate the challenge of winning everyone over,

---

* Under President Biden, Jake Sullivan was appointed national security advisor.

despite her undoubted abilities. She could lead the conversation with
her strong, no-nonsense approach, but her natural warmth and humour
would be required in bucketloads if she was to get them on side.

Over dinner with me, Audibert, Gass and Lucas, Sherman went
through in outline what the US team had been doing. As she did so, she
glanced frequently at a short document. I could sense irritation in the
room that she was not sharing its contents, or giving out copies when
it was obviously a key paper of some description. Irritation grew
when it became clear that she was not able to share anything more. It
turned out that an important meeting to be held in Washington was
going to determine if the US talks had given a good enough basis to push
forward with negotiations. She was not at liberty to share what had been
done until authorised to do so after that meeting. Pieces of the jigsaw
puzzle were hidden in plain view. She went on to brief Russia and China
as well and I wondered, with some trepidation, what the next morning's
coordination meeting would bring.

My first meeting of the morning was with Zarif to discuss a text that
the six, under Helga's leadership, had put together. It was intended to
form the basis of an interim or initial agreement. The USA had helped
prepare it, so we were relatively confident it was in line with the bilateral
discussions between the USA and Iran. I explained to Zarif that I wanted
to share this text with him. What I didn't know at that point was that
the US–Iran talks had already produced a separate document – the one
in fact that Sherman had been unable to share – and Zarif assumed I
was referring to this.

I was puzzled by some of his comments about a text I believed he had
not seen, but before I could ask him about them he made the proposal
that he and I should write a new text together. In that way there could
be no suggestion of anything being imposed from any side: it would be
seen as a joint plan. He suggested an opening session at the UN for the
cameras, and a variety of meetings on proposals after that in which he
and I could work up the document.

When I put forward Zarif's suggestion to the six at our next meeting, there was a distinctly perturbed response from the US team. They were working on the basis of their jointly negotiated text being the starting document, not a newly created third text. But the rest of us knew nothing about their text and assumed they had left the negotiation of a document to the Geneva talks. Tempers frayed as everyone struggled to understand what was happening. The process was in trouble. To make it worse, the Americans assured us that the Iranians were ready to negotiate immediately: something flatly contradicted by the Iranian team in their discussions with the Europeans.

I spoke to Sherman, who suggested I call Burns and get his advice. I called him a few times, and as we talked it dawned on me he was not in the USA – the timing was all wrong and the distinctive long-distance ringing tone wasn't there. I had noticed, too, when I was talking to Zarif and Araghchi that some of their team were elsewhere. It turned out that Burns and Sullivan had been in Geneva for five days, holed up in a hotel, meeting with some of the Iranians. I was confident that so far only James and I had worked out there was a parallel process going on elsewhere in Geneva. At one level that was great news, but I knew the others would feel unhappy – if these were the serious negotiations what on earth were the rest of us doing back at the Intercontinental Hotel? It was vital to our overall success that the USA and Iran could hammer out some of the issues between them. Sanctions relief would be largely driven by the American team, with the EU working closely beside them. Making sure the USA got what it needed to demonstrate the peaceful nature of Iran's programme was vital to getting that relief in place. The broader formal negotiations couldn't do this detailed work which is why every country had bilateral meetings with Iran both during the talks and outside. The USA and Iran could not, in the political climate that surrounded their hostile relations, consider that. So this was the best and only way forward. Once they had laid down the overall parameters, I could lead the discussions to try to close the deal.

While I tried to work out what to do, John Kerry called to discuss coming to Geneva. A major part of the agreement concerned US sanctions, which fell to him and the US team to deal with. He had stayed in the Middle East at the end of a series of meetings, rather than flying back to the USA, hoping he would be able to help finalise a deal. It made sense to get him to Geneva, both to deal with the complex US elements of the negotiations and also to help pull the bilateral talks back into the main discussions.

In Washington the key high-level meeting had been convened to decide the status of the text negotiated between the USA and Iran. If it was agreed as a basis for negotiation, Sherman could give it to me to circulate to the others. It had not been easy for her, caught between the White House and angry colleagues. She had handled it well, but I knew she would be relieved to move forward. The evening wore on and I waited.

Meanwhile, the news that John Kerry might be coming to Geneva filtered back to the other five capitals. Laurent Fabius, the French foreign minister, called me. He was charming but direct: if Kerry came, so would he. I emphasised that the talks belonged to France as much as to any other country, but urged him to be clear about what he wanted to achieve. Kerry was coming to deal with US sanctions; Fabius should decide what he wanted to discuss. I knew that if Fabius came, then so would Guido Westerwelle from Germany and William Hague from the UK, even though there was little for them to do at this stage. It would be impossible not to be at the most important talks in the world if their counterparts were there. Moscow and Beijing would also be watching closely to ascertain whether they needed to have a ministerial presence. I parked the problem until the morning and returned to thinking about the text.

Towards midnight Sherman and Richard Nephew, the Americans' leading expert on sanctions, came to my room with their document. Washington had given them the go-ahead to pursue the proposals and try for an interim agreement with Iran.

James, Helga and I pored over the three-page text and were relieved to find that, although short on detail, it was a good outline of what an interim deal might look like. It described the goal of the negotiations, Iran's responsibilities, and what we would do in return. There were lots of brackets and blank spaces, which meant there was still a lot of work to be done, but it was an impressive start and, reassuringly, not hugely different to the approach we'd taken as a team. The challenge now was to get this accepted by everyone else. Clearly this was going to be my job. I chaired the talks; I had not been party to the US discussions and my relationship with each country was in a reasonable state. I might as well have had a huge arrow pointing over my head.

We thought it best for each political director to get the document separately, with an explanation from me. We needed agreement from capitals overnight if we were going to be able to use it the next day in our discussions. The Americans were adamant: small amendments would be OK, but not substantive alterations. It would be harder to get everyone on board if elements of the deal were set in stone, so I steeled myself for some difficult conversations.

I began with Sergei Ryabkov; he was coldly polite as I explained that I hadn't seen this document before and, that although the process was terrible the product was good. I needed to know by tomorrow morning if Russia could live with the document pretty much as it was. Unimpressed, he agreed to send it to Moscow.

I gradually worked my way round each political director. Jacques Audibert was particularly angry and made no promises. I thought he took it personally that the US team, whom he had worked with for a long time, had not taken him into their confidence earlier. But nobody was happy. While delivering unpalatable messages, I decided to deal with Kerry's arrival too. I said I wanted him to negotiate US sanctions relief and the release of Iranian assets, which had to be done at a political level. Nobody argued against it, partly because they understood the point of him coming, but also because they were too busy being angry about the text. Eventually it was done. Each political director had the document to send to their minister. Each knew they couldn't make major amendments. Each had made clear how affronted they felt by the process – at length in some cases. It was now early in the morning and I was exhausted and fed up.

Sitting down with James, I was ready to call it a night when the door flew open and Sherman and Nephew rushed back in. 'We gave you the wrong text!' she said. It was an earlier draft. I had to track down the political directors and stop them sending the document to their capitals. I ran to find those I could and sent messages to those who had left. Eventually I collected all the papers and shredded them, handing out the right version instead. Insult to injury was written all over their faces. I used a few expletives myself to explain what I thought of what had just happened, and Richard told me later it was the only time he ever saw me angry.

I got a couple of hours' sleep and hoped things would improve the next day. Overnight Kerry's press team had announced he was joining the talks at my invitation. Secretaries of state always travelled with journalists, and about fifty of them were currently on his plane. They all had to know what was going on. At 9 a.m. Laurent Fabius announced that he was heading for Geneva; immediately Simon Gass told me that William Hague was on his way. Hans-Dieter Lucas said Guido Westerwelle would come too. The decisions were partly press-driven: ministers had to have their photo snapped on the tarmac somewhere or else they faced criticism for not doing their job properly, despite their presence often being a waste of time and money or sometimes a hindrance to making progress. China and Russia meanwhile made it clear that at this stage their ministers were not coming. Good, I thought. Easier. Responses to the overnight document started to arrive. The British wanted to strengthen the language and France had three major amendments. I sent a message to Bill Burns to arrange for us to get together. While I waited for ministers to arrive the six and I had a coordination meeting. I began by apologising for the process, sensing the political directors felt quite sorry for me and for the charade of the night before. I was fine but it did no harm to get a bit of sympathy. Wendy Sherman was conciliatory and, with Helga working her magic to hold everyone together, we ended in reasonable shape.

I briefed Fabius, Hague and Westerwelle at the hotel. They were content to use the opportunity to talk together, and I gratefully left them to it. Kerry arrived in the afternoon and we held our meetings at the EU delegation – a smart suggestion from Helga as it moved us away from the UN and the Intercontinental, differentiating our conversation from the formal talks. Fabius came over to see Kerry and had a candid discussion about the document and the process. Kerry was open and direct and did a lot to assuage Fabius's concerns, but Audibert had detailed a few changes that France wanted to see – some were just clarifications, but others were more substantive changes to what was expected from Iran. Afterwards, Fabius went back to the hotel to brief Hague and Westerwelle.

Suddenly we seemed to be moving forward together. The last bit of the puzzle was to talk with Burns and Sullivan, who had surfaced at the US embassy. Sherman joined us and Burns explained that they had been talking to Iran for some time, first with Jalili's team and now with Zarif's. I thought back over the long negotiations pre-Geneva, feeling a little foolish that I had not known then: my talk of front of house being the public view, and the breakthrough coming behind closed doors, had turned out to be more accurate than even I expected.

I needed to understand more about the document, and what the brackets and blank spaces represented. Burns said they were mainly outstanding American proposals to which Iran had not agreed. He agreed the proposed British and French amendments made sense and said the USA had some further changes after consultations back in Washington. The push to keep the text from being altered had probably focused attention on only major issues of contention, and I thought us fortunate that we had so few to deal with. He emphasised that both the USA and Iran knew there had to be only one process from here on. He assured me that the USA had made no commitment to the Iranian team that the rest of us would accept the text as it stood.

It had been a long and difficult day and there was still a long meeting to come, but everything was now running better: we had one document to work with, on behalf of everyone involved. With our core teams, Zarif, Kerry and I sat down at the EU delegation and went through the USA/Iran text, word by word, for five and a half hours. In the main it was a bilateral discussion as Kerry and Zarif knocked words back and forth; only the USA and Iranians knew what had been discussed and abandoned in their hidden talks. It was a chance for me to see their talks in action and pick up on any difficulties. At some point Kerry mentioned Oman, and I wrote a note to James to say that this was presumably the location for their secret talks. Until that moment I had had no idea where they'd met. As each word was assessed, each sentence agreed or disputed, the shape of a document that could capture an interim agreement began to emerge. Until it was all agreed by the six and by Iran, it was simply words. Once agreed it would provide the basis for final negotiations, stop any moves towards building a nuclear weapon in Iran and provide some relief for their economy in return.

Often the solution involved finding the right formulation of words that would give each side what they needed. At the beginning of the document, the USA proposed: 'Iran confirms it will not seek nuclear weapons . . .'. Iran said it had already been confirmed by the Supreme Leader. Instead they proposed the phrase 'As the Supreme Leader has confirmed . . .'. That didn't work for the six because the emphasis was on a leader rather than a nation. Much later we settled on 'Iran reaffirms'. Other issues were less straightforward to conclude. France wanted Iran's right to enrich linked to the outcome of a successful negotiation. Iran wanted it recognised as a right, regardless. We ended up with six important issues still unresolved – progress, but nowhere close to a final document.

It was late, and ministers and political directors had spent all evening back at the hotel waiting for news. I explained the six points, asking them to outline their red lines and where they could be flexible. At 1 a.m. the meeting ended and Ryabkov told me that Lavrov was on his way to join us. The Chinese had no option but to bring their vice minister, Li Baodong, and wanted to be sure that no decisions would be made before he arrived on Saturday. I grimaced and joked that I hoped we would be home by then. They smiled wearily: we all knew we were there for the weekend. Sleep eluded me as I pondered Lavrov's arrival. I wished we had more time to get everyone on board.

I joined Zarif's meetings with European ministers the following morning at his insistence. He wanted to avoid any further bilateral negotiations. It was a positive conversation; everyone expressed commitment to get an agreement. After that it was time to meet with the US team, this time bolstered by Bill Burns and Jake Sullivan joining in, after the cameras had gone. Over the next two hours it became clear that the mood had changed from the previous day's long meeting, as Zarif seemed more reluctant to engage. Lavrov arrived in the late morning, clearly unimpressed that the USA had been talking to Iran secretly, but content to sit tight with a tennis match on TV until he and I met Zarif together. That turned out to be a blunt conversation, with them agreeing that the original text Lavrov had been shown was good enough. That didn't help: it was unfinished and contained none of the European or US amendments. I told them it wouldn't work, conscious that this meant the six were no longer united.

Helga and Wendy Sherman produced an updated document after our meeting at the EU delegation; we named it the 9 November text, to differentiate it from the earlier draft that had gone to the capitals. Kerry got each minister to agree to use it as the basis for the next, and hopefully final, negotiations. His relentless energy and focus on the end goal was impressive. It was now Saturday – we'd been at this since Wednesday and we were all exhausted. At 6 p.m. Kerry called Zarif in to meet us both and raised the stakes. He said the USA would be willing to consider a special offer on sanctions relief, but for twenty-four hours only. He told me privately that this would either expose Iran's unwillingness to make a deal, or perhaps get us over the line to an agreement. We waited to see.

Chinese Vice Minister Li Baodong arrived, met Zarif and me, and pleasantly asked Zarif how it was going. Zarif launched unexpectedly into an outright attack on the 9 November text, describing it as demeaning. Li Baodong was taken aback. We both knew that the outburst was partly aimed at me; that both of us would take on board the strength of feeling expressed. Despite his undoubted tiredness after the long journey, Li Baodong pushed back hard, saying there was more negotiation to be done. At the end of the meeting Zarif asked me to stay and talk. In Oman, he said, the USA had told him that we would back the text as it was. He was furious to find himself trapped in a negotiation on the same points. I had no doubt the American team had assured him that their points reflected the views of all six, but I was also confident they would have been clear that each would want to scrutinise the detail. I pointed out to Zarif that he knew each of the six well enough to know that they would consider each word carefully, making sure the text reflected their priorities. Nonetheless, Zarif saw the 9 November text as being imposed by us, far from his proposal of a newly written, joint document. We were a long way off agreement.

I found Kerry sitting in his room, eating spaghetti while on the phone to Hague. As he ate, I talked him through my conversation with Zarif. Some upset was inevitable once we started firming up the specifics, but Zarif was angry about the new amendments. Kerry listened carefully. He understood that the US talks had caused some anguish but getting a deal was the priority. I nodded; everyone understood that. No matter how bruised they might feel, nobody was going to let a bad process get in the way of a good result. Not for the last time, I acknowledged that the document was a great piece of work. We just had to finish it.

By now it was late evening and I convened a meeting of the six for 11 p.m. Everyone was tired and fed up with hanging around for hours. Lavrov unhelpfully wanted to know why the language in the text used American English. I told him to blame Apple and Microsoft. He waved the paper in the air, saying it was American-sized foolscap – a not-so-subtle way of saying this was an American operation. Kerry then produced another 9 November text, in which the US had clarified some of their sanctions relief, which meant the Iranians had the wrong text – and probably so did I. Helga looked as if she could throttle someone, mirroring my thoughts clearly. Westerwelle was furious for a moment, saying this was no way to run things. I was tired enough to retort that this was how negotiations were: hours of detailed work and even more hours of hanging around being bored and not sleeping. He smiled at me, and I smiled back as our mutual frustration disappeared. He suggested asking the Iranians to join us and I agreed. If Zarif was prepared to come and explain his position, we had a chance of getting the negotiations back on track. Zarif was waiting for me when I got to his room and readily accepted the invitation. I told him I hoped he'd be as candid with them as he had been with me.

I need not have worried – he was polite, calm and very direct. He explained that he had put his cards on the table with the USA, believing that in addressing their concerns he was addressing the concerns of everyone. He had not expected to be confronted with a series of further changes, or to see a text that he felt did not properly represent the talks. Kerry watched intently for a way forward. Lavrov jumped in, expressing support for the document the USA had first shown us. The trouble was that set of proposals was incomplete; it had neither the technical details of what was to happen to Iran's existing nuclear programme, nor the political process to get us to a final negotiation. And since then the technical experts had reviewed it, and there were more detailed points to be gone through. Sherman, sitting next to Kerry, whispered in his ear. I guessed she was saying there was nothing more to be done for now.

I pointed out to Lavrov that without everyone's agreement we had no deal. Westerwelle asked what next, and Zarif said it was up to me. 'She is the boss,' he quipped.

There was nothing more to be done. Zarif needed to go back home and discuss where we had got to, and the political directors needed time to work through the issues. I suggested that we reconvene in our usual format without ministers. Kerry agreed, offering to come back if needed. Lavrov laughed, reached under the table and retrieved a bottle of champagne. This is for you, he told me, opening the bottle. The Iranians left immediately to avoid the alcohol and I half complained to Lavrov about bringing out a bottle in front of them. But he was mischievous by nature and dangerous by profession, and it broke the bad mood between us all. I followed Zarif to sort out dates for the next meeting. It was easy – we would come back less than two weeks later. I read out a bland statement to the press in English which Zarif repeated in Farsi. Somehow, we had another chance at a deal.

I spent the next two weeks mainly on a plane, with engagements in India, Thailand and Myanmar before returning to Brussels for two days of chairing foreign and defence ministers' meetings in Brussels ahead of my return to Geneva. Each meeting was important, but it gave no recovery time from the gruelling nature of our negotiations.

The US team spent the interim fortnight working with Congress. There was a lot of pressure on them from the White House, which wanted a good deal as soon as possible, as well as from large parts of Congress, deeply sceptical about a deal and favouring further sanctions against Iran. The process was pretty brutal, but Kerry and his team were relentless. We got enough breathing space to give us a few more days. Additional sanctions would make it impossible to work with Iran, who would see the move as bad faith and a loss of control by the White House. None of the other five thought new sanctions a good idea at this delicate moment. If the talks collapsed because of them, it would be in a cloud of recriminations.

Geneva, 20–24 November 2013

The plan was to start with lunch on Wednesday, 20 November, then move on to formal discussions. The Intercontinental Hotel meeting rooms were busy, so we opted to use the UN and EU offices. The Iranians told us they had amendments to the 9 November text – a sign that they were prepared to take it as a starting point. Zarif said he had to be back in Tehran by Saturday. Good luck with that, I thought, but still, it was something to aim for.

On 19 November I arrived in Geneva on a late-afternoon flight and went straight into a meeting with Wendy Sherman, who was ready to close the deal if at all possible. The pressure from Washington was now palpable. She proposed we went through the 9 November text, now formally to become the 20 November text, line by line, 'looking for sticking points'. Everything had to work in six languages – English, French, German, Russian, Chinese and Farsi – which inevitably caused its own problems.

Many hours later we met up with the rest of the six to update each other on what had happened since we last met. President Putin had met with President Rouhani and discussed the 9 November text; Russia was comfortable to move on if Iran was willing to accept the 20 November text as the starting point. 'Russia is hopeful they are not in the mood to give up,' said Ryabkov. Simon Gass said that Prime Minister Cameron wanted both success and transparency, which I took to mean no more secret discussions. Chinese President Xi Jinping had spoken with President Rouhani the night before, both disappointed at the failure to reach agreement. Zarif had made clear to all six that he wanted negotiations going forward to be with everyone. There was a murmur of agreement with that. We went through the document once again, line by line, and I could feel an air of expectation. It was now or probably never.

Around 2.30 p.m. I met Zarif at his consulate for a late lunch: kebabs, salad and rice followed by knickerbocker glories adorned with tinsel on cocktail sticks. The food there was always delicious and the desserts always a surprise. Eating together before the negotiations was an informal occasion – Helga and James sat on either side of Zarif and Araghchi, and Ravanchi was next to me – to show it was a team effort, as Zarif put it. The atmosphere was light, but we had a lot of work ahead. At the end Zarif suggested I do a quick statement to the cameras with him beside me, and I joked I'd announce we had a deal. Everyone smiled. Zarif said it was the last chance saloon and he was right. After three years of talking with no results we had reached the point of haggling over individual words. He had come to make an agreement but was prepared to leave empty-handed. So were we.

Zarif and I began negotiating the next morning at 9 a.m. For the first time James, Helga, Stephan and I represented all six countries without them being present. My mandate was to get as close as possible to the 20 November text, which would then form the basis for final discussions.

We began with the preamble, which described what a full agreement would cover. Zarif wanted to avoid a scenario where we simply rolled over the interim deal again and again, freezing Iran's programme without helping its economy further. 'If we address these issues what incentives are there for the six to come back to the negotiating table?' he said. I reassured him that any first agreement would not be enough for any of us but it would show progress and give time to get to a final deal.

We examined every word carefully. 'What we have put in the document we cannot take out. What we need now is to build a 21 November text,' I said. We came back again and again to Iran's right to enrich uranium. I reiterated that the right only existed alongside the obligations of the Non-Proliferation Treaty, which they had signed up to. If the Iranians fulfilled those requirements, including inspections and monitoring, then our proposed wording accepted that they could have a properly limited and monitored civil nuclear programme once we agreed a final deal. Iran wanted this to be an inviolable right, not a gift from the six as they saw it.

It came down to five words in the first paragraph of the draft document. Iran wanted 'if agreed' removed, rejecting the conditionality of their enrichment programme. But this was a red line for us: the enrichment programme could not exist regardless of what they were doing. A long debate centred on whether a civil nuclear programme was a 'basic' right. The Iranians said yes; we said no. They said it was bestowed within the treaty; we said it was bestowed only if they followed the obligations in the treaty. And so on.

The mood stayed broadly positive and professional as we continued, only occasionally heating up in frustration. Zarif was willing to defend a 'good deal', but there was little point in him agreeing to something that would be rejected in Tehran. I agreed, but pointed out that we had six countries to please, and a US president and Congress with high expectations.

Within twenty-four hours we'd nailed 95 per cent of the text, but the final 5 per cent was very difficult. Each session lasted over three hours, and during the breaks I'd report back to the six, gather ideas and arrange conversations that might be useful. In a later session Zarif made a few suggestions, some of which I thought might help – sometimes just using a different word, even with the same meaning, made a difference – but the USA rejected them all. Some objections were substantive but others seemed purely linguistic. Everyone in Washington was focused on getting the wording they wanted, conscious of the antipathy to an agreement in Congress. I tried to be creative with wording. In one sentence the phrase 'in practice' was used to indicate that if a solution was agreed, it would 'in practice' involve an enrichment programme. Iran thought it might render conditional the point that they were entitled (in their view) to such a programme. I discussed with the Americans and Europeans whether we could use 'in reality', 'in exercise', 'in operation', 'effectively' and so on. 'Take your pick' I said, as they mulled them over.

We kept going. At one point I suggested introducing a particular word, only to have an exasperated Zarif produce an earlier draft I hadn't seen before from 29 October that showed it had already been discussed and rejected. I had no idea what words had been tried in Oman or the reason why some were accepted, others rejected. It was hard to overstate how difficult it was, not knowing what might trigger a massive reaction that would put our conversation back hours. In our short breaks I would storm around the room with frustration. As James said, it was like walking through a minefield. But over time, with Bill Burns and Jake Sullivan working diligently in the background and all six countries collaborating closely, we gradually reduced the distance between us.

We were tantalisingly close to success and I judged it was time to bring the ministers to Geneva. Lavrov had in fact already arrived, but had been discreetly keeping out of the negotiations. He was supportive, but thought the USA was asking too much. The Chinese minister had the longest journey, but I knew he would keep a low profile to avoid alerting the media prematurely, so I suggested to the Chinese team that they should decide when the right time to bring him over would be.

The main press interest was in Kerry's appearance. He was eight hours away in the USA, and I suggested he take off, knowing that he could turn round if it became clear this was premature. I was seeing Zarif at 10.30 p.m. and would get a better idea of where things stood. After that I planned to tell the Europeans to ready their ministers so their arrival would roughly coincide with Kerry's the next morning. Unfortunately, the State Department leapt into action once more with a statement that Kerry was coming to help get the talks moving 'after consultation with Cathy Ashton'.

Wendy Sherman couldn't believe it. The statement was supposed to say he was coming to Europe to be on standby for the talks, due to the long distance he had to travel. The European delegations in Geneva were furious. I hadn't had the chance to ask them to ready their ministers; now, within minutes, they were tweeting or calling to say they were coming too. A small problem in some ways, but such were the sensitivities involved that it took hours to get the lid back on. Sherman reassured everyone that this was purely a cock-up and was readily believed: her feelings were written all over her face. I went to bed.

The next morning I got up early and went to see Zarif. 'The circus has come to town,' I said as the ministers' planes cluttered the skies above Geneva. Despite how close we seemed to a deal he was not in good spirits, focused on the final obstacles between us. We went back and forth on the outstanding issues. One concerned Arak, the plutonium reactor where we wanted our concerns to be 'fully' resolved. He wanted clarity on what that word meant in practice, saying he suspected we would never be fully satisfied and would use that to keep sanctions in place.

After debating the point for a while I suggested Zarif had a conversation with Fabius. A change of interlocutor might help understanding on both sides. He agreed and I left to greet Kerry, who'd just landed. He was keen to get going so I sent a message to the Iranians that he'd like to see Zarif. Hungry, I went to my room for some food, curled up in a chair and chatted to James. The food arrived just as the phone rang: the Iranians wanted me to join the meeting with Kerry. Eating would have to wait. I sent the food away and headed down to the meeting room, where Kerry was setting out what the USA was prepared to do.

The day wore on with constant meetings. I spoke with Zarif, then the USA, then ministers and political directors. Stephan led the technical discussions, looking at how ideas translated into the moving parts of a nuclear programme. By evening I had new wording from Zarif on centrifuges and a better preamble. Of the six points we had begun with only one remained: the heavy water reactor at Arak. I gathered the ministers together and asked them what more they needed to close this deal. All except the USA confirmed that if we could get agreement on Arak, they would be content. The USA, however, identified several outstanding points they now wanted resolved.

The mood in the room went from calm to exasperation. Lavrov said it was ridiculous; Hague lifted one eyebrow – a trademark query that always made me smile. Westerwelle acknowledged he was not a native English speaker but thought the language worked. Fabius would have preferred stronger language on centrifuges but could live with the agreement if we got the last point on Arak. I was happy to try to get the last Arak point, but beyond that I didn't feel I had anything left to offer. I suggested the group mandate Kerry to get what the USA needed. It was the best move I could have made. Suddenly all the angst about the Americans negotiating independently disappeared. I suggested Kerry met with Zarif and we'd all reconvene at 9.30 p.m. It was then about 7.15 p.m.; they had a couple of hours.

I went upstairs and ordered food, again, and a gin and tonic. As my drink arrived I was told Kerry needed to speak to me urgently, while a message from the Iranians said they wouldn't meet him. I put down the drink, untouched, and cancelled my food order.

I arrived as Kerry was on the phone to the president. I'd discussed the negotiations with Obama on a few occasions, at his meetings with the EU and on the sidelines of a NATO summit, and knew he took a keen interest. He was content for an interim deal to buy some breathing space before a full agreement, but he was not going to be easy to satisfy and, in his forensic way, would test what we were doing to destruction. After they had finished, Kerry said he'd heard the Iranians wanted me to join the meeting. Clearly he hadn't been told they were no longer prepared to come. I headed off swiftly to the seventh floor with James. There Zarif told me he was content to agree the sixth Arak point and I breathed a sigh of relief; I had got everything I had said I could. Now it was over to the USA – so the meeting with Kerry had to take place. There could be no agreement if Zarif refused to talk to the secretary of state, who now held the mandate for the six. I sensed Zarif needed to let out his frustration, but even if all he would do was tell Kerry that Iran wouldn't do any more, he had to see him. To my relief, he agreed.

I returned to Kerry and told him we would meet in fifteen minutes in the Amsterdam room. I was present, but made it clear I was there only to observe and support. Bill Burns and Jake Sullivan joined for a surprisingly constructive conversation before we were interrupted by urgent messages for Zarif. After he left, Burns and Sullivan went off with Araghchi and Ravanchi to tweak and tighten the language to resolve the final US concerns.

James and I hadn't been outside for days; we were hungry, sleep-deprived and desperate for the end. We had started at 8.45 a.m. and it was now 1 a.m. the next morning. We waited. The time dragged by, interspersed with calls from Burns and Sherman updating us on their discussions. Amsterdam was a typical hotel conference room, so there was nothing of interest in it. James invented Geneva skittles using small Swiss chocolates, of which the hotel seemed to have an endless supply, to knock over plastic water bottles at the end of the room. Some kind person put their head round the door and asked if we'd like roast chicken. Convinced I would get a call just as I put the first mouthful in, I gulped it down.

Just before 2.30 a.m. I got a message to say that both sides were content. Richard Nephew, in charge once again of the texts, worked with my team to make sure we had the final version. Stephan went through it to ensure the technical language worked. There had been fifteen different versions in just over two days; to say we were keen to be certain we had the right one would be something of an understatement. Helga drafted, and got everyone to agree to, the press statement that would accompany our announcement of the deal.

I brought ministers and political directors together and we went through the final version – four pages of well-spaced-out paragraphs. The preamble set out our purpose to 'reach a mutually agreed long-term comprehensive solution that will ensure Iran's nuclear programme will be exclusively peaceful', then explained what that meant, and how it would be done. The next part, the 'first step', described what Iran would do, and what we would do in return. The final page was headed 'Elements of a final step of a comprehensive solution' and listed what would be included in a final agreement, without going into detail. The agreement would come into effect in January 2014, giving us time to work out the technical details. (I knew what I would be doing through Christmas.) It would last for six months. (In the end, it lasted eighteen.) With relief on all our faces, Lavrov popped another champagne cork and with many congratulations we realised we had an agreement.

Almost immediately I started to worry that the agreement would leak, or someone would have second thoughts. I suggested we went to the UN at 4.45 a.m. to announce the deal. As I left the lobby of the hotel, I asked my press officer to tweet that we had got a deal – I wanted us to be the first to say it.

'Is there a deal?' one of the waiting journalists asked. 'Yes,' I said, and Fabius gave them a thumbs up.

I got in the car and panicked. I turned to James – what if the Iranians didn't turn up or changed their minds? I went into a cold sweat. Until we

were all in front of the cameras and Zarif said it too, I wouldn't believe
it. When I arrived at the UN, the Iranians asked that we make clear the
agreement was conditional on the details of the US sanctions relief,
which they had not yet received in writing. I said no, but I guaranteed
they would get it. They accepted my word.

We sat at the conference table, tired but with a sense of real achievement. This was a moment in history, and it was worth savouring. We also
had time to waste because the UN security teams hadn't been told to let
the cameras in and kept them outside until somebody realised. Lavrov
made jokes while we waited. Westerwelle asked how he kept producing
bottles of champagne and Lavrov told him he was given it free, in his
room. Westerwelle complained he was only given two apples in his room,
but then remembered he got chocolate too. 'In this country, chocolate is
like dust,' said Lavrov. I laughed out loud.

Finally, we walked out to the cameras. I was the only woman in
the line-up. It dawned on me that at the end of the statement there'd
be handshakes and hugs and I'd be left out. I whispered to Kerry to
shake hands or hug me so I wouldn't be alone. Standing slightly to the
front, I announced we'd reached an agreement and thanked everyone.
Cameras flashed, some clapped, others murmured their delight. Our
teams turned to each other for congratulations. Kerry gave me a huge
hug and the photo went global.

The Iranians asked to have photos with me, and I was happy to do
so. We had done the impossible – and done it well. Six nations divided
by much and working together for years had reached an agreement with
a country nobody believed would do a deal. It was a moment to treasure,
whatever was to come. I would later be asked many times to compare
negotiations in one situation with another – Iran with Serbia–Kosovo,
for example. The truth is that every crisis or problem is unique and the
solutions are bespoke. There are no shortcuts. Being prepared to spend
months or years working quietly, often behind the scenes, building relationships, developing trust, is what gets a deal over the line; being willing
to keep going even when it seems hopeless.

Afterwards we gathered our things, said goodbye, and walked out of the building. Kerry offered me a lift back to the UK on his plane, and I gratefully accepted. We were too tired to talk much on the way to London. We had a jigsaw puzzle in place – not yet complete but with clear outlines and some pieces joined together. It all seemed possible, and I was glad to be home.

8

REVOLUTION
IN UKRAINE

Viktor Yanukovych strode into the Grand Hotel in Vilnius. The Ukrainian president's tall, large frame was imposing, and he towered over the crowded lobby. It was a cold November day in 2013, and the room was full of people ordering coffee, greeting old friends or arranging meetings. Lithuania's capital city was playing host to a summit of EU leaders, the European Commission and the Eastern Partnership countries – Armenia, Azerbaijan, Belarus, Georgia, Moldova and Ukraine. Most of the prime ministers or presidents of the twenty-eight EU countries, and their Eastern counterparts, were arriving that morning, so the main hotel was buzzing with staff teams, logistics crews and security. I grabbed a coffee, said hello to a few colleagues and watched Yanukovych.

The centrepiece of the Vilnius Summit was to be the signing of an Association Agreement between the EU and Ukraine. Negotiations had spanned seven years, led during the last four by Commissioner Štefan Füle and his officials in the Commission. The final details had been agreed in March, when the documents had been initialled, confirming that the text was ready for formal signatures. It would establish free trade between Ukraine and the EU, opening up new opportunities for Ukrainians in agriculture, technology and energy. It also paved the way for a closer relationship, with cooperation on border management, rule of law, legal and institutional reforms and more.

One week earlier, Yanukovych had announced that he was suspending preparations to sign the agreement in Vilnius, describing his decision as 'a pause', which caused puzzlement and alarm among EU leaders. I was interested that he had nonetheless arrived and watched as he moved through the room. He caught sight of me, stopped, and beckoned me over. Moving to a convenient corner to speak more quietly, we exchanged pleasantries about his journey, my health, his family, my work. We had first met when I attended his inauguration in February 2010, squeezing it into a day that involved travelling to four other countries in an attempt to fulfil the demands of my, then, new job. He had made Brussels his first stop on being made president – a clear indication, I had thought, that he planned to fulfil his election promise to sign an agreement with Europe as a priority.

He leant over and talked quietly, explaining that he was not able to sign the agreement right now. I shrugged. I said I was sorry to hear this; that EU leaders would be very disappointed after so much work had been done and that I was surprised at the timing of his decision. We had been negotiating since 2007 and had reached this point with his support. All that remained were the signatures to the document, which was why we were all there. He shook his head and said, nonetheless, he could not. I shrugged again. He was the president and it was his decision. I had a good idea what lay behind it. It all came down to the relationship with Russia.

Ukraine and Russia's connected history went back a thousand years. Of Ukraine's 46 million population, 7.5 million were ethnic Russians and roughly 10 million spoke Russian as their primary language. Many Russians saw Ukraine as one and the same country, and the birthplace of the region's Orthodox Christianity, claiming that only those in the western regions of Ukraine looked to Europe. Ukraine had been part of the Russian empire, then the Soviet Union, and regularly talked of as the most important Soviet republic after Russia. An agreement with the EU appeared to the Russian leadership to be a significant step away from this relationship.

There was pressure on Yanukovych to join Russia, Belarus and Kazakhstan in a customs union. His prime minister, Mykola Azarov suggested in December 2012 that Ukraine could cooperate with both the Customs Union and the EU. Yanukovych proposed that Russian and Ukrainian experts should look at how Ukraine could join without disturbing plans for 'other agreements'. He nonetheless avoided a trip to Moscow to sign the same month, saying Ukraine was not yet ready, but continued to propose links with both Moscow and Brussels. That came to an end when EU President Barroso made it clear in February 2013 that being part of a common free-trade area with the EU and simultaneously part of the Customs Union couldn't work. The initialling of the agreement with the EU in March seemed to confirm that Yanukovych had made the choice to forgo the Customs Union.

Instead Yanukovych offered Moscow a three-plus-one formula: Russia, Belarus and Kazakhstan with Ukraine – the plus one – having a sort of observer status, dangling the possibility of becoming a member over time. As Kyiv moved closer to a deal with Brussels, the Customs Union launched a new round of talks ending with a signed memorandum of Ukraine's observer status in May 2013. This went down badly in Brussels, though Yanukovych rang Barroso on the day he signed it to reassure him that this did not contradict his determination to sign the Association Agreement.

In August 2013 the Russian government stopped importing goods from Ukraine, causing big problems for the Ukrainian economy. Seventy-five per cent of Ukraine's machine-building production had been exported to Russia. Experts predicted that losses from Moscow's actions could cost up to $2.5 billion for just the second half of 2013. Yanukovych nonetheless continued to talk up his relations with Europe, saying to a meeting of his political group, known as The Party of the Regions, that Ukraine was going 'full-speed to Europe'. His declaration fed growing concern in Moscow and the pressure mounted. Russia made it clear that if Ukraine signed an agreement with the EU it would call in loans and raise energy costs. Ukraine was one of the biggest markets for Russian gas, and a crucial transit route to Europe. These threats were greeted in Kyiv with dismay.

President Putin met with President Yanukovych in October, in Sochi, the site of the Russian-hosted Olympic Games. It was clear that Russia was not going to ignore the signing ceremony scheduled for Vilnius in November, especially as some in Ukraine were enthusiastically describing the Association Agreement as the first step towards membership of the EU, or even membership of NATO. Although Putin was on record as saying that in principle he would not oppose Ukraine joining the EU, the move to a closer relationship between the two was raising a red flag.

Looking back, we should have looked harder for trouble and examined more closely the politics as well as the economics. A year before, in October 2012, Sergei Lavrov, the Russian foreign minister, had joined EU foreign ministers for dinner in Luxembourg. He was highly critical of the trade parts of the agreement. Europe was an important market for Russia, he said, and the EU should take account of Russian trade interests by adding Russia as a third party to the discussions. Commission trade officials were clear that the agreement was between two parties – Europe and Ukraine – not three. The issue wasn't raised in the twice-yearly Russia summits until we moved closer to the signing of the agreement, when Putin proposed a closer collaboration between his Customs Union and the EU, which meant reviewing Ukraine's relationship to both.

In easier times we would have been able to consider potential problems more effectively, but at this point we were swamped by live ones, not least the interim nuclear agreement with Iran and the aftermath of the dramatic events of the Arab Spring. There simply wasn't the bandwidth within the EEAS to stay on top of everything, and Füle and his team seemed to have the relationship firmly under control.

So why did Yanukovych choose to turn up at the summit, which must have been a deeply uncomfortable experience for him? He was creating maximum turbulence at home for himself in front of the press of thirty-four nations and drawing attention to his refusal to sign in the most public way. At any earlier stage he could have stalled, nit-picked around a small issue, or simply said 'I can't do it.' My view was that he didn't because he thought he wouldn't need to. He was relying on Europe to give him an excuse.

One of the enduring problems affecting the agreement from the EU side was the imprisonment of former Ukrainian Prime Minister Yulia Tymoshenko. First jailed in August 2011, she was sentenced to seven years for abuse of office in her negotiation of a gas deal with Russia. Later, charges of embezzlement, tax evasion and eventually involvement in murder continued to be brought forward over many months and years. She was prosecuted and convicted in a trial that fell far short of international standards, which the European Court of Human Rights later described as 'a politically motivated violation of her rights'.

For many in the EU her imprisonment was a scandal. In 2011 I warned the Ukrainian government that, though talks would continue, the ratification process 'will face problems if there is no reversal in the approach of the Ukrainian authorities'. Debate raged over whether the EU could or should sign an agreement with a president who would abuse his political opponent in this fashion. The outcome of the Court of Human Rights threw this into sharp relief. Any agreement would require unanimity among the twenty-eight member states and the consent of the European Parliament, where many had become vocal opponents of signing any deal without her release. The many attempts to persuade Yanukovych or his prime minister, Azarov, of the need to release Tymoshenko had been futile. Listening politely, they'd accuse us of not understanding her criminality or their judicial system; meanwhile her situation went from bad to worse. Denied medical attention and with lights on in her cell twenty-four hours a day, she became an uncomfortable reminder of the sort of government we were dealing with.

The European Parliament sent Pat Cox, its former president, together with Aleksander Kwaśniewski, former president of Poland, to Ukraine several times from June 2012. Both highly respected men, they and their team had a number of meetings with Yanukovych, Azarov and Tymoshenko herself over the period before Vilnius and beyond. By March 2013 they had made fourteen visits, held tens of dozens of meetings, but failed to get her released. The noises against signing grew louder.

The EU proposed that Tymoshenko be allowed to travel to Germany for medical treatment, conveniently shipping her out of the country and solving the problem. A week before the summit and the day before the proposal was debated in the Ukrainian parliament, the Rada, President Dalia Grybauskaitė of Lithuania, the host of the summit, warned explicitly that 'If the law that solves the Tymoshenko issue is not adopted, EU member states will not sign the Association Agreement.' The next day the Rada refused to adopt it. At the same time Ukraine's government suspended preparations for signing the agreement, proposing instead the creation of a three-way trade commission between the EU, Ukraine and Russia reminiscent of Lavrov's request a year before.

I wondered if Yanukovych knew that, despite the strong rhetoric calling for Tymoshenko's release as a condition, the European Parliament and member states had concluded they should sign the agreement. Tymoshenko asked the EU to sign, saying her country was more important than her plight and any request for her freedom to be a condition of signing should be dropped if it helped Yanukovych to sign. It was clear to me that any opposition would have disappeared by the time we all arrived in Vilnius. If Yanukovych had relied on our not signing so that he wouldn't have to – his 'get out of jail free' card – by keeping Tymoshenko locked up and telling Russia the EU would not sign, he was to be disappointed.

A week before the summit, as word spread that preparations for signing the agreement had stopped, demonstrations began in Kyiv and across Ukraine. In bitterly cold conditions people gathered to demand that their president fulfil his commitment to signing the agreement with Europe. Every night until and throughout the summit, people gathered together in Maidan Nezalezhnosti (Independence Square), commonly known as Maidan,* in what eventually became famous as the Maidan demonstrations.

Back in Vilnius, public irritation with Yanukovych was widely reported in the press. Individual leaders met with Yanukovych to try to get him to sign, or at least to understand what was going on – especially Chancellor Merkel, clearly frustrated at his intransigence.

Over and over again Commissioner Füle met with the Ukraine team that had travelled to the summit with Yanukovych to try to find a way through. At one point Yanukovych proposed signing a different document. I was completely against the idea. I did not want him waving bits of paper around and confusing the issue at home. If he was not signing, he would have to explain why and deal with it. Füle brought the idea to a meeting held in the office of President Grybauskaitė. She had been a commissioner in the previous European Commission and left the Commission early to become president of her home country. President Van Rompuy, President Barroso and I joined her in rejecting the idea of a separate document. We agreed not to support any signed papers other than the agreement itself. There was genuine anger that the centrepiece of the summit was being wrecked and no desire to give Yanukovych a way of avoiding his decision.

I stared out of the window on my flight back to Brussels, feeling much gloomier than when I had arrived. Only a few days before, we had concluded the interim agreement with Iran on its nuclear programme. Although it had been a gruelling period, we had something tangible to show for it. Now it felt like a lifetime ago. I knew that member states would expect me to engage with the Ukrainians. I had not expected to visit Ukraine again before my mandate ended the following October, but a visit, or more likely several, was now a priority.

The demonstrations became bigger and more agitated. On 30 November the police moved in using batons and stun grenades to disperse the protestors, detaining dozens of people and injuring dozens

---

* *Maidan* is the Ukrainian word for 'square'.

more. The demonstrations grew in number and spread further across the country. EU flags flew or were carried by protestors. Another crisis was brewing on our borders, and again I cleared the travel schedule, this time to head to Kyiv.

I arrived in Ukraine on 10 December and went straight to see Yanukovych. Assistant Secretary of State Victoria Nuland had arrived from the USA around the same time and had gone directly to Maidan. I decided to go and see the president first. The presidential palace was a large, seemingly empty building; but the main reception room, where Yanukovych greeted me warmly, was an ornate affair. After the obligatory photos were taken for the media, we sat down opposite each other flanked by ambassadors and officials, including Prime Minister Azarov. We talked for over three and a half hours – I say 'we' but, as always, he did the majority of the talking. I pointed out that I wasn't there to tell him what he could or should do – he was an elected president – but he had to understand that we needed to know what was going on, to know why he had changed his mind and to find out if we could help.

More importantly, he needed to talk to the people gathered in the square in Kyiv and in squares across the country who deserved an explanation. I urged him to do that. It was freezing outside – they wouldn't be there if it didn't matter. I was concerned about their safety and told him to condemn violence against the peaceful demonstrators.

Yanukovych tried to convince me that he would eventually sign the agreement and that this was only a pause. He explained that industry in the east was heavily reliant on Russia for exports and in urgent need of modernisation, that he was under pressure from Russia to join the Customs Union, and he feared that Moscow might start a trade war. Then he moved on to his concern about Ukraine's finances, his worry that the IMF would not help and that the EU would not come up with short-term funding. He asked the EU to encourage the IMF to continue loans, and I added it to my list of issues for my next meeting with Christine Lagarde, head of the IMF, in Washington.

The more he talked, the clearer it became to me that he would never sign the agreement. He simply could not resist the pressure exerted from Russia. No short-term loan or long-term industrial strategy was going to change that. But at that moment it was not my concern; I was much more worried about the escalating chance of violence against the protestors and the lack of a plan from him about how to address their concerns.

The conversation ended and I headed for Maidan. The demonstrations were about the future relationship between Ukraine and the EU; I was representing both member states and the Commission, and I needed to understand who was there and see for myself what was happening. I told Yanukovych I was going – he didn't ask me not to. I would have gone anyway.

The square was full of people, thousands of them, some carrying banners, others waving EU flags. I could hear lots of singing and chanting, which I guessed was partly to ward off the intense cold. It was freezing – minus 30 degrees, someone told me – and they had been there for hours. Many were prepared to stay all night. The cold air made me gasp as I got out of the car. I could see families with children, though was told they would go home before too long, leaving the core demonstrators who never vacated the square, but took it in turns to be there. I met up with Arseniy Yatsenyuk, the leader of the opposition party, Batkivshchyna (Fatherland), among others.

We set off across the square. I found it hard to stay upright; the snow and ice underfoot made me skid frequently. Setting out from Brussels, I had not had time to get back to London first to pick up my boots. Falling over was not the image I wanted to project on the news broadcasts. People were cheering and shouting in what was a peaceful, almost festive atmosphere. Well wrapped up in coats, scarves, hats and gloves, they were prepared for the weather. It was clearly reasonably well organised, good humoured and full of ordinary people who were very concerned about their leader's broken promise.

I walked from one end of the square to the other, clinging on to Arseniy to avoid sliding. It was very dark apart from torches and the light of buildings nearby, with occasional flashing neon lights of green, red and blue, like in a rock concert. Along one side of the square a makeshift stage had been set up for music and speeches. People called my name, shouted support for Europe and thanked me for coming. It was overwhelming. Back in the UK, the papers described it as a 'pop star' welcome. It was clear that the protestors would not easily be deterred, especially if Yanukovych failed to answer their questions or explain his position.

I had decided not to speak in the square but to talk to the press later. I did not want this to look like an EU-organised rally, which would be used to undermine the point that it arose out of frustration at the decisions being taken by the president. I told the press conference I wanted to make it clear that I had come here to be of assistance. And to show to the people I met that the EU really did care about the country. I was conscious that we needed to tread carefully if this difficult situation was not to get much worse.

It was very late at night when I got to the hotel and I was really tired and cold. I couldn't imagine how the people in the square were feeling; they were standing in freezing temperatures for hours. I fell asleep instantly but was woken around 3 a.m. by my phone ringing. It was the head of the EU delegation to Kyiv. An experienced Polish diplomat, he sounded extremely alarmed. I forced myself awake. He explained that the city was full of rumours that Yanukovych planned to send riot police to disperse the demonstrators. I asked to speak to the president's office. A short while later they called. I told them that any threat of that nature would mean I would feel compelled to go to Maidan and stay there for the rest of the night. It was one of the moments when I felt the strength of the twenty-eight countries – I belonged to all of them, and me being carted off by riot police, or worse, was not going to go down well. I was reassured that nothing would happen and after a while the rumours stopped. I grabbed a bit more sleep, conscious that I had probably only postponed the problem until after I left.

The next morning I went back to see Yanukovych and tried again to talk to him about how he was going to explain to people why he had changed his mind. Prime Minister Azarov, a seasoned politician who would later be subject to sanctions from Europe and USA for his role in the crisis, suggested trilateral talks. He wanted Brussels, Kyiv and Moscow to sit down and find a solution. I explained that a bilateral deal was precisely that – between two nations. Asking a third country to give its agreement was a precedent that was never going to be acceptable. If Ukraine wanted to talk to Russia about the details of its agreements, that was a matter for them, but there was no chance that Brussels would negotiate a bilateral agreement with a third country calling the shots.

Yanukovych was completely dismissive of the protestors and unable to see that his political future lay in sorting this out. He took the view that it would all just melt away and, failing that, he could intimidate his opponents, using force as necessary. As the weeks went by and the demonstrations across Ukraine grew in size, Yanukovych met the demonstrators with violence and abuse rather than dialogue, labelling them all as right-wing elements intent on destroying the country.

The situation worsened. Yanukovych met with opposition leaders through December and January several times and offered up the resignation of Prime Minister Azarov to the demonstrators as a sign of his willingness to find a solution, trying to get Arseniy Yatsenyuk to take on the job in a sort of government of unity, but he refused. I was not surprised. People wanted change. Tens of thousands were on the streets and Maidan had become a protest camp named Euromaidan surrounded by dozens of barricades. Many were calling for Yanukovych to resign and for elections to be held before they would end the protests. By the end of January 2014 Azarov had resigned and left Ukraine.

On 28 January, the regular six-monthly summit with Russia took place in Brussels, and I saw President Putin for the first time since the crisis had erupted. As usual the meeting was led by the two EU presidents on our side and President Putin on the other, with Sergei Lavrov and I there to discuss foreign policy issues. I was to leave the meeting and travel to Kyiv specifically to try to mediate and Putin warned me not to take part in opposition rallies. It was obvious he was unimpressed with our attempts to find a solution. He saw no role for the EU in Ukraine, and in his press conference at the end of our meeting he warned Europe to keep away. He said it was as if Lavrov, the Russian foreign minister, had turned up in Athens to mediate. 'I am sure the Ukrainian people will sort this out and Russia is not going to interfere.' I left for Kyiv, aware Russia was watching us closely and was increasingly openly hostile to what we were doing.

The days I spent in Kyiv over the next weeks went by in a whirl of endless meetings as we tried to find ways to help. I would arrive at the airport to be driven to my first meeting, then shuttle between oligarchs and activists by way of the presidential palace and press conferences. Each time I visited, the situation seemed more challenging and the atmosphere more tense. It was like a fog enveloping Kyiv, thick and heavy. People were wandering around heading for demonstrations or talking in groups on street corners. A statue of Lenin lay toppled near the city centre.

In Brussels there was growing interest in visiting and showing solidarity with the demonstrators. Some politicians were keen to be 'where the action was' and turned up to speak at the rallies in Maidan. They rarely let us know in advance or asked our advice about the situation. Those watching their occasionally provocative statements did not understand that they were free agents and not representative of anyone but themselves. Instead it was interpreted as a sign that we were formally working with the opposition to overthrow the elected president. This complicated matters, especially when members of the US Congress also turned up to speak in Maidan. While thoughtful elected politicians were trying to offer support, mindful of what they said and did when in Kyiv, others knew what to say to get the cheers they wanted. I was more cautious by nature, and I was worried how it would be seen. It was important, it seemed to me, that it did not come across – even fleetingly – as an EU- or Western-driven crisis. I knew that Moscow would be looking for any sign of our involvement, and could point to the evidence of Western politicians standing on platforms. Arguably Russia would claim this was the case regardless, but other countries asked me why so many Western politicians were in the square.

At the beginning of February, I went again to see Yanukovych. Waiting outside to be brought into the ornate room once again, I shuddered. Kyiv seemed on the brink. The atmosphere outside was heady and heavy; people were walking around in groups, talking with each other, as if waiting for something to happen. Yanukovych had been ill for a few days, and I hoped that time under the duvet might have given him chance to think more constructively about what to do. No such luck. We sat down to talk and it swiftly became obvious that he did not accept any responsibility for this mess. He preferred instead to drone on and on about how they were all anarchists trying to bring him down.

I had come to discuss a financial package the EU had put together with the USA to address some of the issues Yanukovych had raised with us. President Barroso at the European Commission made it clear that 'we are not in a bidding war with anyone for Ukraine'. He didn't want anyone to see this as us vying with Moscow for Ukraine's interests. Goodness knows where that would end – and not just with Ukraine. But he wanted to respond to what Yanukovych said he needed. I explained our thinking and he nodded, but seemed more interested in attacking the people on the streets.

I left more agitated than when I arrived, wondering what Yanukovych thought the outcome would be if he did not respond to the people who had elected him as I went to meet with the Maidan demonstrators. The representatives came mainly from NGOs, journalism and activism. They explained their shared desire to change how the country was run, to support minority groups and see an end to corruption. They didn't always agree with each other, but they were united in calling for change. Many supported a promise of EU membership. Some were looking for an opportunity for NATO membership. Whatever they wanted, they wanted it right now. Incremental change or participating in government was not on their agenda and my attempts to get a more pragmatic approach were only partly successful. I was concerned that their hurry would result in failure. I knew that member states of the EU would not be ready to offer the promise of membership in the middle of this crisis, even if all of them might be agreeable to that at another time.

Many of the activists believed their determination not to compromise was the anchor that kept people honest and held the promise of the future steady. Many of them bore the scars and bruises of being beaten; some had disappeared completely, others reappeared bearing the signs of imprisonment and rough treatment. One victim, Dmytro Bulatov, missing for eight days, was dumped badly injured from a car. In hospital police attempted to arrest him but he was kept safe by protestors, including members of the Rada, who formed a guard around him until he could be flown out to Lithuania for treatment.

One of those involved in protecting him was Petro Poroshenko, nicknamed the 'Chocolate King' because of his confectionery company interests. An oligarch with influence, he had served as foreign then trade minister during the last four years, and now positioned himself as the moderate who could try to bring Ukraine together, creating good relations with both Brussels and Moscow. He and I spoke at length on each visit, as I did with Vitali Klitschko, then a member of the Rada. Klitschko was famous as a highly successful professional boxer who combined his sport with a deep interest and involvement in politics. He founded his own political party, later linking up with Poroshenko after withdrawing from a presidential run. He became mayor of Kyiv a few months later.

I engaged with as many different people as possible, including former Presidents Kravchuk and Kuchma, who offered advice and help at each visit. Kuchma would later become a representative in talks to try to resolve the problems in eastern Ukraine. They used their experience as presidents to attempt to influence Yanukovych, but with little success.

As always, we coordinated where we could with the USA. Victoria Nuland was spending a lot of time in Kyiv, talking to Yanukovych and meeting with opposition leaders. Our relationship took an interesting turn the week after my February visit when a telephone conversation between Victoria and the US ambassador to Ukraine was uploaded to YouTube. It immortalised the phrase 'Fuck the EU', reflecting her frustration with what she thought was less effective action from our side. Victoria was mortified. She was a feisty official, always prepared to speak her mind, but she had never intended a privately shared thought to become a public pronouncement. Nobody at the EU minded very much. 'You should hear what we say about you when you are not listening,' said one senior official in response to Victoria's call to apologise. But it became a story, prompting the wearing of 'love the EU' badges by some state officials. I still have the gracious apology card that Victoria wrote – it was completely unnecessary, but typical of her. The only problem the whole episode created was a distraction from the tragedy unfolding in Ukraine. The press either began or ended with a question on it. Did this mean a rift? No. Was I concerned? No. Had I spoken to Victoria? Mind your own business. And so on.

In Maidan my worst fears were realised when on 20 February protestors were shot at, resulting in the deaths of over seventy-five people. Speculation aside, it seemed clear that the government was involved. It was my turn to be on YouTube, as a recording of a phone conversation between Urmas Paet, then foreign minister of Estonia, and I found its way on to the airwaves. He was commenting on reports that the snipers doing the shooting may not have been police. Those who leaked the call wanted to use it as proof that radical elements were deliberately making the situation more volatile. Of course, Urmas was only reporting to me what one person had mentioned to him. I replied that we should investigate it. We did. The evidence pointed directly to government.

My trips to Kyiv were interspersed with the negotiations with Iran that were now based in Vienna. It was an indication of how compartmentalised the talks were that Russia, the USA and the EU were able to continue working closely together despite the growing crisis. But I could only be in one place at a time and the demands for my attention showed no sign of abating. Frank-Walter Steinmeier, the German foreign minister (now president of Germany), suggested that he and Radek Sikorski, the Polish foreign minister (now a member of the European

Parliament), go together to Kyiv and that they invite France to join them. I was delighted. The three of them would be a strong team, balancing each other politically and able to represent the rest of the EU too. This was what I felt the EU should be about – a collaboration that lent weight and breadth to any problem. I gave my full support to them. I have sometimes wondered if I should have gone instead, but the Iran talks were at a crucial point and they had stacks more experience than I did.

They stayed closely in touch with me and worked hard to get a plan together to diffuse the situation. Participating in the long hours of nego-tiations were the key opposition leaders together with President Putin's special envoy, Vladimir Lukin. They reached an agreement which every-one signed up to on 21 February. Its measures included amending the constitution back to 2004, giving power to the parliament to appoint the prime minister; agreeing the formation of a national unity govern-ment; and making efforts towards unblocking squares and buildings. Radek told me later that Lukin helped persuade Yanukovych to sign the agreement but refused to sign it himself on behalf of Russia. Later that day Lukin said Russia does not 'quite understand what our role here is'. Distancing himself and his country, I thought.

The next day the parliament impeached Yanukovych as Yulia Tymoshenko was released from prison. Calls for Yanukovych to resign grew stronger, with accusations he had siphoned off billions in gold reserves and disappeared loans. Believing he could no longer trust the people around him, Yanukovych decided to leave the country. He resur-faced in Rostov-on-Don, a major Russian city that served as host to one of the many summits the EU had with Russia over the years. But it wasn't Moscow and I wondered why he had not appeared somewhere more obviously at the heart of the Russian political world. Nevertheless, he asserted he was still the president.

I flew to Ukraine again on 24 February and went straight to lay flowers at Maidan, to mourn those who had lost their lives. Hundreds of bunches of tulips and roses were piled together on a debris-strewn part of the square with thousands of people, some clearly shocked, standing by. I laid my bunch of yellow tulips on top, watched closely by a man in a black leather jacket and soldier's tin hat with slogans I didn't understand written in black felt pen. Sandbags were piled everywhere, with the occasional framed photo of one of the murdered. I lowered my head, conscious of the photos being taken on hundreds of cell phones and news photographers gathered around. I remembered the beginnings of Maidan, the rock bands and family groups. Now it was a grubby battleground of grim determination and the remains of long-term occupation.

Yulia Tymoshenko was a pale and drawn version of the woman I had met on my first visit to Ukraine nearly four years before. Confined to a wheelchair and awaiting medical treatment, she hugged me and sobbed with relief that she was free. The Rada was still functioning, and a new government was being put together. I was told billions of dollars were missing, transferred overseas, that needed to be found and returned. I appealed through the press for the Maidan activists to work with the Rada to deliver a lasting political solution to the crisis as well as a credible economic plan. I went on to stress: 'We are not in competition with Russia. There are strong links between Ukraine and Russia, and they should be maintained.' But I added, pointedly, that Ukraine should remain independent, with full territorial integrity and unity. This looked more and more difficult, especially in Crimea where events were making headlines.

Crimea had been part of Russia from 1783 to 1954 when Nikita Khrushchev, the leader of the Soviet Union, gave it to Ukraine. The official record explains this was to 'evince the boundless trust and love the Russian people feel towards the Ukrainian people' and to recognise the economic and cultural ties that existed between Crimea and Ukraine. More likely is that Khrushchev needed to shore up his support after Stalin's death, and getting the powerful leadership in Ukraine on side was an important part of that. Whatever the reason, after the Soviet Union was dissolved there were calls for Crimea to rejoin Russia, where some said it had always belonged.

Clashes in Ukraine grew intense from 26 February 2014, with the occupation of the Rada by a pro-Russian group. Poroshenko, a candidate in the presidential elections, went to Crimea a couple of days later and was attacked. Reconciliation looked unlikely. On 1 March the self-designated leader in Crimea, Sergei Aksyonov, appealed directly to President Putin in a signed statement calling for Russia to 'provide assistance in ensuring peace and tranquillity on the territory of Crimea'. Russia moved in.

I was driven to the Rada building, passing masked men carrying guns and standing round burning oil drums. We went through impromptu checkpoints where people peered in and smiled as they saw me, waving us on to the next group who would raise their arms to tell the car to slow down. I got out of the car at the Rada and walked into its imposing hall, listening to the sound of cheering from a free parliament taking the opportunities to pass all the laws it wanted. Some, like the temporary banning of the Russian language, were avoidable mistakes, usually quickly rectified, reflecting the headiness of the events rather than the calm rationality that was going to be needed. We tried to convey the message that the sooner they moved away from gestures the better.

I sat down and talked with the politicians now trying to work out what to do. Many, like Arseniy Yatsenyuk, the opposition leader, now prime minister, with whom I had walked around Maidan on my first visit to the demonstrations, had ideas for the future. Vitali Klitschko, soon to be mayor of Kyiv, was passionate about moving the country forward. We sat in high-backed leather chairs talking about the future to the sounds of cheers from the parliamentary chamber wafting towards us.

In Kyiv I was aware of a particular atmosphere that I had experienced before in Egypt, Tunisia and Libya. It was as if the wind had changed direction and you had to brace yourself against it as it whipped your breath away. A sense of excitement, mixed with fear and apprehension, and the knowledge that whatever was going to happen, the end was anywhere but here – that this moment could be savoured but would soon be gone forever. It would change, and the endless possibilities would be replaced by something else – with luck something positive, but there was no way of knowing. Revolution, freedom, chaos – I could almost taste it. I listened to the sounds and closed my eyes for a moment. Someone leant towards me and grasped my hand. His voice trembled as he asked, 'Do you think it felt like this in Russia in 1917?' I looked out at the men with guns walking past the windows, listened to the cheering from the Rada, saw people carrying parts of a statue they had removed, and the anxious faces of the men sitting with me, lost in thought. 'Maybe,' I said nodding; 'maybe.'

I called an emergency Foreign Affairs Council for Monday, 3 March and discussed the crisis with NATO. Membership of both the EU and NATO was high on the list of the new Ukrainian government and a key demand from the Maidan organisers. For some member states this crisis was on their doorstep and high on their agenda. But others had more complex relations with Russia based on energy dependence and economic links, and a few had other issues at the top of their list. Military advisors, from the member states and based in Brussels, told me that by their definition Russia had invaded Ukraine. I decided to use the word 'invasion' in the draft of the conclusions that I put forward to the foreign affairs ministers' meeting – the document that would define where all twenty-eight member states stood and to which they would be committed in their actions. I knew 'invasion' wouldn't stand; it would be too strong for some countries. But it would be a good place to start and keep on board those who feared that we had not understood what was going on.

All ministers except William Hague came to the meeting. He was in Kyiv, loathe to cut short his previously planned visit. Some foreign ministers grumbled that this was the UK wanting the headlines in Ukraine while they were all in Brussels. I had other things to worry about than where Hague might be and, knowing the challenges of setting up visits, was confident in his explanation. He was a highly respected colleague who worked closely with other ministers, but the signs of growing British disengagement made some nervous about anything that seemed to show the UK on a different path.

We spent six hours discussing the crisis, with lots of amendments to
the text from ministers. The word 'invasion' became 'act of aggression'
in the final text. I enjoyed negotiating the text directly with ministers,
rather than having it agreed by ambassadors first. We always managed
to reach a conclusion, though sometimes – and this day was one of them
– it was nothing short of miraculous. Germany was heavily invested
in setting up a contact group, involving Russia, Ukraine and the EU,
proposed by Chancellor Merkel in a conversation with President Putin
over the previous weekend. With a European Council coming later in the
week, our position was strong enough to give the heads of state a good
jumping-off point to decide what they wanted to say. I could, for once,
afford to dump this on them.

We took several small steps. We proposed to suspend discussions
on a new visa regime with Russia, and on the new comprehensive trade
agreement. We agreed with the G7 countries that they would not participate in any preparatory meetings with Russia while this situation was
under review, and I asked colleagues who were in Moscow for a variety
of regular meetings to return to Brussels. Small steps, unlikely to deter
Moscow from its attempt to regain Crimea, but we might prevent further
moves while we worked out how to get into reverse gear.

Afterwards I flew to Madrid to meet Sergei Lavrov in the private
setting of the Russian ambassador's residence. We sat by the fire
drinking tea. It was an interlude, a chance to talk calmly about how we
saw events in Ukraine; neither of us alerted the press to our meeting
nor spoke of it in public. It was a looking-glass moment for me. Lavrov
saw a mirror image of what I saw, a completely distorted view from
my perspective, but one that I could recognise from the events that had
happened.

He told me that Kyiv had been taken over by ultra-nationalists who
were refusing to put down their weapons and were holding the Rada
to ransom. He explained that he was worried they would seek out and
kill the Russian minority, whom he felt Russia had a duty to protect. He
pointed out that Russia's actions to date were consistent with the 1997

agreement between Russia and Ukraine, in which the port of Sevastopol in Crimea had been leased to Russia.

I replied that I knew there were a few elements around that we didn't like either – perhaps an inevitability in such a turbulent time – but they were not in control. President Yanukovych had left the country, and under the Ukrainian constitution it was the Rada that had to elect a new president and speaker and form a new government. The Rada was now doing its job. Lavrov was clearly unimpressed.

He stressed that everyone should stick to the agreement reached on 21 February. I guessed Moscow was aggrieved: it had helped to get the agreement and now the situation had got worse, not better. Now that the opposition parties had become the government, Russia's focus was on the commitments to stop occupations that were the responsibility of the new administration – in theory at least. I wasn't sure how far he realised that those in control in Maidan were by now an independent movement not likely to take orders from traditional political parties. I was clear in my own mind that the people in Maidan were going nowhere until they felt they had got at least some of what they wanted. There had been too much death and terror for them to give up now.

I asked him if Russia was interested in the contact group, the proposal that Germany was strongly backing to find a peace solution. I made clear that the EU wanted to find answers with Russia if we could. It was a difficult conversation. Sergei shrugged – he had no instructions to get involved in a group, but he would be in Paris the next day, which was when the group was due to meet.

I left Madrid and headed for Paris and the Quai d'Orsay, the French Foreign Ministry – a truly magnificent building embodying all the pomp and circumstance of a major power. Each of its beautifully decorated rooms, bathed in light from exquisite crystal chandeliers, gave way to another through ornately carved doors. The whole building exuded the perfume of the pride of France.

By contrast the meeting itself was chaotic. As well as the countries I expected to see there, namely France, Germany, the USA, Russia, Ukraine and the EU, there were lots of others claiming an invitation of sorts. Italy had asked France – socialist leader to socialist leader – to be invited, the British had been disinvited at the request of the Russians, which meant they *had* to be there and got themselves reinvited. The Canadians, with the largest Ukrainian diaspora, insisted on being there and the Polish foreign minister attended because of his role in brokering the 21 February agreement. The UN were there because they were the UN – a nameplate was hastily written for Jeff Feltman, their under-secretary for political affairs. Finally, the Swiss were represented as chair in office of the Organization for Security and Co-operation in Europe (OSCE), an organisation set up during the Cold War to work on dialogue between East and West, and which was to play an important mediating role.

Everybody gathered around a large table. It was shambolic. I was fed up with some European countries feeling they had to turn up at gatherings like this. It looked a mess. As a foreign policy actor, the EU was a twinkle in the eye of some countries and a plank in the eye to others who saw it as a threat to their role on the world stage. But none of that mattered. As the meeting began under the French chairmanship, it became obvious that the Ukrainians, Russians and Americans weren't there. They were somewhere else, making our own meeting pretty pointless. It was at some dark level actually funny. As people realised that the main act was missing, the speeches got shorter and the meeting disintegrated, and I abandoned the beauty of the Quai d'Orsay for a drink back at one of the hotels with Frank-Walter Steinmeier. A charming man whom I instantly warmed to, he was determined to play a significant role and for Germany to be at the centre. He told me that Chancellor Merkel's latest conversation with Putin had been difficult. The Russians were very unsure about a contact group. None of it sounded hopeful.

At around 6.45 p.m. I got a text message that Secretary of State John Kerry wanted to debrief from the alternate meeting, and I headed back. To my surprise it was US security who were on duty at the door of the French foreign minister's office, determining who could enter or not. I smiled to myself about the American capacity to be everywhere. In the room there was one available seat next to John Kerry and he tapped the sofa to tell me to sit down. Sergei Lavrov was sitting in an armchair with two of his team nearby. French Foreign Minister Laurent Fabius, an experienced politician, sat close by, together with William Hague. Drinks began to appear – large whiskeys for the Russians, white wine for John and me. The room was quiet and earnest.

John was trying to get some sort of process going, but it was clear there was a lot to nail down. The atmosphere was calm, with most of the talking done by him and Lavrov – the latter being occasionally provocative. We weren't discussing anything of substance, just how we were going to get the right people in a room. It was obvious that Lavrov wasn't going to commit to anything. President Putin had told Chancellor Merkel he didn't know why Lavrov was bothering to go to Paris.

Afterwards, William Hague, John Kerry and I went to meet with the representatives from Ukraine. Hague was worried that the Ukrainians' views would somehow get lost in the discussion, which was a problem linked to who would represent Ukraine in a contact group meeting. We wanted the government, but Russia wanted the leaders of the breakaway areas in Crimea and Eastern Ukraine, refusing to recognise the government that the Rada had appointed. John was prepared to consider a broader delegation to get the discussions moving at least. The Europeans were wary that this allowed Russia to decide who represented Ukraine, especially as the Rada had made appointments that were entirely constitutional. The Russians saw the Rada leadership as a Western-focused slice of Ukrainian political opinion and unrepresentative. We didn't get far.

I headed back to Brussels wondering if there was a way in which we could talk directly with President Putin. I wanted Russia to see the EU as a serious foreign policy force – or at least at this stage to see the potential. In any event this crisis had been sparked by a choice for Ukraine, as they saw it, between a relationship with Russia or Europe. The president of the European Council, Herman Van Rompuy, regularly met President Putin at our six-monthly summits with Russia. I asked if he would be willing to go to Moscow and talk to Putin before the European Council met. My plan was to join him direct from the next round of Iran negotiations. Herman wanted the meeting to be held in private and to avoid the circus of a media show put on by the Russians. I counselled that it was impossible to quietly slip into Moscow. Even if President Putin were to agree to keep it private, there were lots of people who would have to know, not least the protocol team who would greet the plane. Herman insisted that if the Russians said he was coming he would cancel the trip. Inevitably it leaked and Herman decided not to go. I was told Putin was offended, as he had given his agreement to the meeting very quickly. It was a blow for me. There was no way I would get the chance to hear directly from Putin what he was thinking, or at least what he was prepared to share with us.

I sought the wise advice of colleagues across the EEAS and friends I trusted. All agreed that, in the words of one, 'achieving some kind of standstill that allows more time for cooling off negotiation and de-escalation is vital'. The loss of Crimea was felt deeply in Ukraine. It was a core part of their territory, ripped from them. For the international community it was an issue that warranted strong pressure, but there was little to be done beyond sanctions. This was not lack of interest, rather a dose of reality. Military action was unthinkable. Russia consolidated its position, at least in its own eyes, with a referendum in Crimea on 16 March, when 96.8 per cent of people who voted were declared to have supported becoming part of the Russian Federation. In his speech a couple of days later, Putin cited the International Court of Justice's decision to allow Kosovo to declare independence as a justification for the absorption of Crimea. Merkel called the comparison 'shameful'. Many countries disputed the legitimacy of the vote in Crimea, but it nonetheless added to the sense in Moscow that this was a done deal.

Merkel persuaded Putin to agree to a meeting in Geneva in April between the USA, Russia, Ukraine and the EU foreign ministers. Helga Schmid, the EU political director, went to Moscow to meet with Putin's advisors. She came back with clear messages. Moscow was very angry with Kyiv and worried about who was in control there.

I arrived in Geneva on the Wednesday evening ready for the meeting on Thursday, 17 April at the Intercontinental Hotel, where just a few months before Kerry, Lavrov and I had completed the interim nuclear deal with Iran. It was odd to find ourselves in this new situation given how closely we had worked together.

I went to find the Ukrainian foreign minister, Andrii Deshchytsia, at around 10.30 p.m. He had only been in office for a few weeks and was understandably very nervous about the meeting. He was worried about being trapped into some statement in Geneva that would tie his hands back home. I reassured him Ukraine's interests had to be central to anything we agreed.

Next morning, I met Kerry in a room that had been called Moscow when we were last in the hotel, but which had hastily been renamed Madrid with a makeshift sign. The USA and EU meeting in Moscow would have been too much of a gift for journalists and cartoonists. John explained that his ambition was to come out of the meeting with specifics on who would do what, and when. He had Ukrainian Prime Minister Arseniy Yatsenyuk waiting by the phone in Kyiv to discuss whatever draft statement we might end up with.

At 11 a.m. we all met together. Four teams sat around a large square table – Ukraine opposite Russia, the USA opposite the EU. Kerry, Lavrov, Deshchytsia and I were joined by three officials each. Our first conversation was about which flags to have in the room. It always amazed me how much energy and time we could spend on this sort of stuff. I knew from experience that standing in front of the wrong flag could cause uproar – I had once been photographed at an angle that made a flag appear to be next to me when it was across the room and got a lot of grief as a result. The Russians did not want the Ukrainian team to be photographed in front of the Ukrainian flag, as they did not accept Deshchytsia represented all Ukraine. After a few minutes we just removed all the flags. There were much bigger issues at stake.

Kerry opened the discussion. His approach was lawyerly and pro-cedural, no doubt to keep the temperature in the room down, focusing on a draft text that Victoria Nuland and Helga Schmid had worked on together. It was a statement of who would do what, and when, to calm the situation. Lavrov presented a Russian version of a statement. He produced letters from 'people's councils' in the breakaway parts of Ukraine, outlining their demands and supporting Russia's efforts. Kerry kept everyone firmly focused on the text. I was fascinated by his choice to work this way – I would have started with substance then moved on to language – but John knew from experience what became obvious over the next hours: the moment we started talking substance the meet-ing would break down, with the Russian and Ukrainian teams shouting and arguing across the table.

Nonetheless it was difficult. Every word was fought over, moving from one draft to the other. Russia couldn't accept the word 'Ukraine' to describe what the people opposite them represented. Instead they wanted 'Ukrainian', implying they were people from the country but didn't speak for it. Lavrov spoke at great length, not once looking up from his papers at the Ukrainian team opposite, and was obviously very angry. He took the view that the situation in Kyiv was being driven by anti-Russian elements for whom he had no respect – as far as he was concerned, four of them were sitting opposite him. He wanted Maidan completely emptied of demonstrators before those opposing them would leave the nearby buildings. But the Maidan protestors would only dis-perse when they felt sure about the direction the country was taking. The Ukrainian government representatives were clear they did not control them, which strengthened Russia's view that they were radicals with an anti-Russia agenda.

We took a break and Kerry, Lavrov and I sat out in the sunshine of a hotel courtyard I did not know existed; leaving the building during the Iran talks with so many media and curious people around was impos-sible. Kerry continued to press Lavrov to commit to a plan to de-escalate the chaos. I told Lavrov he didn't need to like these Ukrainians, but we needed a deal to solve the problem. The atmosphere between us all seemed to improve, and we went back into the room.

Kerry moved on to specifics, suggesting we name places where the violence would stop, and proposed Donetsk in Eastern Ukraine as one of them. Lavrov agreed, though not to any specific timescales. Without some time frame nothing would happen, so I proposed the word 'immediately', which was accepted; I was well aware that translating this into reality on the ground was going to be extremely difficult. Tempers frayed again and again but slowly a document emerged – a de-escalation document promoting dialogue and specific immediate measures: 'All illegal armed groups must be disarmed; all illegally seized buildings must be returned to legitimate owners; all illegally occupied streets, squares and other public places in Ukrainian cities and towns must be vacated.'

From there, 'Amnesty will be granted to protesters and to those who have left buildings and other public places and surrendered weapons, with the exception of those found guilty of capital crimes.' 'It was agreed that the OSCE Special Monitoring Mission should play a leading role in assisting Ukrainian authorities and local communities in the immediate implementation of these de-escalation measures wherever they are needed most, beginning in the coming days. The US, EU and Russia commit to support this mission, including by providing monitors.' Using the OSCE had a number of advantages, not least that Russia and Ukraine were two of its fifty-seven members, along with all EU member states and the USA.

We kept talking as our original deadline of 3 p.m. for a press conference passed. One of the Russian team asked me what this day was called in English. It was Maundy Thursday, when traditionally the monarch distributed special coins, but I didn't know what the original meaning of the word was. The deputy foreign minister of Ukraine, probably wanting to do anything but the slog of the document for a few minutes, went off and looked it up, explaining on his return that it came from a command to love one another. We could have done with a bit of that in the room.

Kerry and I did the joint press conference a couple of hours later than planned. We were far from elated – one journalist described us as looking tense. We hoped the dynamics would change and that a three-way discussion between the EU, Russia and Ukraine on energy might restore some normality to the relationships. We had a document, but the level of anger and mistrust was very high so our expectations for its implementation were not.

Nonetheless the OSCE sent a monitoring mission to Ukraine and started dialogue there, often in the places that were most volatile. In those early months of the mission they were held at gunpoint and fired at, and in one terrible tragedy a US paramedic was killed by a landmine. Nonetheless, they worked for agreements on a ceasefire and supervision at the border with Russia. It was tough.

A couple of weeks later, in early May, I went to Washington to meet Susan Rice, national security advisor to President Obama, in her office at the White House. It felt very familiar to walk through the double doors flanked by the iconic white pillars into the West Wing reception. I sat with James and our EU head of delegation until Susan came out to greet us. In her office she was joined by a number of colleagues including Wendy Sherman, with whom I worked closely on the Iran negotiations. With more people in the meeting than usual, Susan suggested we sit around the table rather than the armchairs we often used. I thought nothing of it until the door opened and everyone quickly rose to their feet. President Obama had come to join the meeting. Giving me a warm, welcoming hug, he beckoned us all to sit down and relaxed into the chair at the end of the table, which I now realised had been left free for him.

For the next forty-five minutes he and I talked in detail about Ukraine. He always listened intently, giving very little away while I spoke. He wanted to get as much information as he could before making any comment. After I had finished, he told me America was interested in a diplomatic solution, recognising Russia had an interest in Ukraine, but we needed a resolution that allowed Ukrainians to make decisions without a foot on their neck. I said the election results might not be clear.

He was adamant that the election needed to go ahead, and that we should support the process. He was right. We thought Petro Poroshenko would be the most likely winner of the presidential election (he later won on the first round). We both hoped he would be strong enough to work out a way forward. We discussed sanctions and the challenges of the domestic selling job to be done in the EU as well as in the USA to get everyone on board. After what felt like a long time, another meeting demanded his attention, and with a hug he said goodbye. I sat down hard in a slight state of shock. The US team laughed – they thought I had guessed he would be coming but I had missed all the signals. The bigger meeting, sitting at the table, the empty chair were all clues. But it simply had never occurred to me. Shortly afterwards I got a text asking if I minded if they tweeted a photo of him joining my meeting – far from it. I had longer with the president that day than most heads of state ever had.

After his election in late May 2014, Poroshenko made clear his openness to get dialogue moving. Implementation of the Geneva statement had largely fizzled out – parts of it never got started. By June the best hope lay with the OSCE, which was brokering discussions for immediate de-escalation. But Poroshenko continued to work closely with the EU, coming to Brussels in June to sign the Association Agreement. 'This is what we have fought for over recent months and years,' he said.

Then the situation reached a terrible low with the tragic loss of Malaysia Airlines flight MH17. On 17 July a scheduled flight from Amsterdam to Kuala Lumpur carrying 283 passengers, including eighty children, together with fifty crew, was brought down by a Russian Buk missile fired from Eastern Ukraine. The surface-to-air missile had come across the Russian border that day and been fired from a field in a rebel-controlled area. The launcher returned across the border before investigations could begin.

Wreckage rained over 50 square kilometres, mainly near Hrabove, a village in Eastern Ukraine's Donetsk Oblast, scattering pieces of broken fuselage, bodies, passports, toys and other fragments of people's lives. Rescue and investigation were hampered by the chaos and fighting from pro-Russian rebels. Local militias prevented the Dutch investigators from removing the debris and returning the dead to their loved ones. Frans Timmermans, the Dutch foreign minister, went to Ukraine. A fluent Russian speaker, Frans was a skilled diplomat who knew how to deal with difficult situations. Nothing had prepared him for this. He called me during his trip, breaking down at the horror of the images he had been shown. Frans spoke of what he saw to the hushed room of a Foreign Affairs Council and to the UN Security Council, describing the looted possessions and the bodies left in the heat while foreign militias patrolled the area. In a voice cracked with emotion he said: 'To my dying day, I will not understand why it took so long for rescue workers to be allowed to do their difficult jobs; for remains to be used in a political game . . . I hope the world will not have to witness this again. Images of children's toys being tossed around, luggage being opened, and passports of children shown on television . . . we demand dignity for the victims and the multitudes who mourn their loss. They deserve to be home.'

I hoped the shockwave of horror might convince Moscow to start talking. How the missile ended up in the hands of people who brought down a plane of innocent men, women and children in such arbitrary circumstances was a question that I hoped would give pause for reflection. But, to my surprise, it seemed to make no difference. Phone calls and meetings continued at a frenetic rate but nothing much changed. I carried on shuttling between Kyiv and the Iran talks in Vienna.

In late July President Lukashenko of Belarus proposed that the Eurasian Customs Union, Russia, Belarus and Kazakhstan should meet with Ukraine (an observer to the Customs Union) and the EU in the capital, Minsk. The countries would be represented at presidential level. The head of the European Commission, President Barroso, who had devoted a lot of time to the Ukraine crisis, asked me to represent the EU and invited the commissioners for energy and for trade to join me. I was pleased they were coming. They were both experts in their fields and I was glad of their company and expertise. It was not going to be an easy meeting.

We flew to a warm reception of red carpet and military honour guard in Minsk. I was curious to see what the city was like. I knew it had suffered badly during the Second World War, when its entire infrastructure had been destroyed along with 85 per cent of its buildings. It had been rebuilt with some imposing structures, including the Independence Palace where the meeting was to take place. Looking beyond the city I could glimpse something of the lakes and forests for which Belarus is famous.

Our meetings began the next morning at the palace, a huge 50,000-square-metre building with hundreds of rooms, each one lavishly decorated in gilt and marble. I met President Poroshenko, who was concerned the discussion would focus purely on trade and energy and not on the raging conflict that was tearing parts of his country apart. Constant artillery and missile fire from across the border and helicopters firing on Ukrainian troops followed the capture of ten Russian soldiers the day before. Poroshenko was ready to work out a gas deal and wanted to meet Putin to try to de-escalate the armed conflict in Donbas, Eastern Ukraine. A few days before we arrived in Minsk, Russian artillery, personnel and a 'humanitarian convoy' had crossed the border into Ukraine. They did not ask for permission.

As so often in crises, the onset of winter focused everyone's mind. In Donetsk the winters were long and freezing. Poroshenko explained that separatists had bombed the infrastructure that supplied power to the population of several million people. Water levels were increasing in the mines; without electricity no pumps were working, and this water could contaminate the water table and drinking water. It would be a catastrophe. He looked and sounded under tremendous strain, but he was determined to put forward a plan. He wanted a ceasefire and control of Ukraine's borders. Whatever happened, he wanted to sign the Association Agreement with the EU but was prepared to discuss it with Russia.

I left Poroshenko and headed to meet President Lukashenko. I was unsure what to expect. Lukashenko was described as the last dictator left in Europe, a title he didn't try to escape. I was ushered into a large oval room where the president greeted me warmly. A large man with a comb-over hairstyle, he sported a moustache worthy of a caricature dictator. Impeccably dressed in a dark suit with blue tie and white shirt, he beckoned me to sit opposite him in a comfortable armchair. His translator sat beside me, quietly explaining what the president was saying. I looked around from time to time at the ornate room, where gold-painted flowers climbed from floor to ceiling in china-blue wall panels and a crystal chandelier blazed light above us. It was a room designed to make an impression – I couldn't keep my eyes from drifting around it.

Lukashenko said Belarus had been abandoned by Europe and was stuck close to Russia. He asked me what chance they had without support from the EU and elsewhere to develop as a truly independent nation. He had no choice but to be on the best of terms with Russia, and I sensed his relationship with President Putin was one of necessity. He started to talk about Chernobyl. If I had ever known it, I had forgotten that Belarus was badly affected by the nuclear reactor disaster in neighbouring Ukraine: 70 per cent of the fallout landed in Belarus, contaminating a quarter of the country and leaving 20 per cent of the agricultural land unusable. Millions of Belarusians were affected; thyroid cancers skyrocketed, especially among children. I was shocked. Later that day his deputy foreign minister talked about the day Chernobyl exploded. She remembered as a young girl the rain being full of some kind of dust and standing in her shorts and T-shirt while it covered her and those around her. It was the radioactive dust of Chernobyl – only nobody knew it then. Everyone she knew wondered what fate might ultimately befall them.

Lukashenko turned the conversation to the current crisis in Ukraine. He spoke of his personal links through family and military service and his good relations with lots of the politicians there, from 'nationalists to communists'. He hoped Ukraine would keep its territorial integrity and that the meeting would help. But he was clearly concerned that President Putin had different ideas.

Suddenly our conversation was interrupted. Putin had arrived, earlier than expected, and Lukashenko needed to greet him. He rushed away while I made my way down to the huge entrance hall. Every inch of the marble walls was covered in gold designs. People leant on the railings that ran the full length of the room, watching us gather together. We stood in a line. President Nazarbayev of Kazakhstan was next to Putin, Lukashenko in the middle, Poroshenko on his left. I stood next to him with my two colleagues beside me. I was, as so often, the only woman in the photo.

Everyone waited to see if Putin and Poroshenko would shake hands. They did; the photographers jostled for the best photo angle. This was their first serious meeting and I hoped they would meet bilaterally during the day. There was always a risk that painstaking work to get them into the same room would fall apart due to a misspoken word in the main session. We had a little time, as dinner would follow our meeting and I was determined to get it done. It was the best hope of moving forward.

We were ushered into another huge room to sit down around a table of ornately carved wood that easily seated the nineteen of us. Lukashenko sat slightly apart from his foreign minister with the Russian delegation on his right, then Kazakhstan, Ukraine and the EU completed the circle to his left.

The choreography of the meeting had changed at short notice, so the four presidents and I gave introductory statements in front of the press. Lukashenko had agreed and announced that the political situation in Ukraine was to be discussed first, but when the press left he gave the floor immediately to President Putin, who indulged in a long presentation – supported by Economy Minister Alexei Ulyukaev – on the disadvantages to their economy of the implementation of the Association Agreement between Ukraine and the EU. Ukraine was linked to Russia by centuries of economic cooperation, he said, with mutual trade in 2013 of $50 billion, equivalent to all of Ukraine's trade with the West. He said EU Presidents Van Rompuy and Barroso had admitted to him the agreement might be problematic. His team held up a photo: European vegetables, he said, in a container crossing the border into 'our region' that did not meet their hygiene standards. His argument was that the Association Agreement would allow 'substandard' European produce into Russia. We refuted his statements completely, while making it clear we were ready to be seriously engaged in discussions with Russia and Ukraine.

Lukashenko produced a draft communiqué setting up new structures with permanent meetings at the highest level among the five sides – Russia, Belarus, Kazakhstan, Ukraine and the EU. Nazarbayev offered to host the next meeting in the Kazakh capital city, Astana, and supported Russia's view that Ukraine should not ratify or implement the trade agreement. Putin went further, saying that if it did, Russia would immediately take defensive retaliatory action.

I tried to discourage a new process. The trilateral – Russia, Ukraine and EU – meetings were already set up, the next one being in September. No need, I said, for something new; we could keep Kazakhstan and Belarus in the loop. Creating new structures was often the reason to do very little except give the appearance of activity or give legitimacy to participants who were otherwise marginal to the main dispute.

After four hours, we agreed that Russia, Ukraine and the EU would meet on 12 September and Ukraine would not ratify the Association Agreement until then. In that case, Russia said, it would not retaliate with its own trade restrictions. I tried to turn the conversation to Eastern Ukraine. The conflict began, Putin said, with the agreement between the EU and Ukraine followed by a coup d'état against Yanukovych. He said part of Ukraine did not accept this, but instead of opening a political process with them Poroshenko had chosen a military way forward. In his view, the longer the conflict lasted, the harder it would be to find an agreement, and Poroshenko, in giving his 'ultimatum' calling for a ceasefire, was the same as issuing a threat. So far, he said, no talks had been set up to find a political solution; the 'so-called terrorists in the east of the country hadn't sent their troops to Kyiv – it was Kyiv who had sent their troops to them'.

I listened with fascination at his interpretation of events and wondered if we should refute his argument line by line. He did not accept that those in the so-called breakaway regions were responsible for the current violence; instead he blamed Kyiv. It was a reverse image of what I saw, and reminded me again that what you see is partly determined by what you choose to see and believe. Putin questioned whether Kyiv was in control of its supporters and told Poroshenko he needed to start negotiations. Why not, like the USA or Germany, have a federated country, he asked? He ended his long description of the political situation by saying that the chances of an end to hostilities would fall if the Ukrainian army continued its military operation in Eastern Ukraine.

The Russian position was clear. They were protecting their own interests and those of the people they said looked to them for help. In short, they had done nothing wrong. It was as if the EU agreement had come out of nowhere, rather than being the result of seven years of detailed negotiation. Russia's action had effectively inserted a 'wedge' into Ukraine so that pressure and violence could be ramped up if Kyiv took decisions it did not like. There was little likelihood of Ukraine being able to move closer to either the EU or NATO, since neither would import a country with unresolved problems into their midst. At this point, offering supplies, aid, monitoring missions, mediation and advisors was as far as they would go.

Meanwhile the problems in eastern Ukraine were turning into a semi-frozen conflict, locked in time and space without resolution. The cost to ordinary people from communities shattered by violence and destruction was immense. Thousands were killed and many more injured in the sporadic fighting, while towns and villages became uninhabitable. People who had fled the fighting returned to find a pile of rubble where their homes had stood. From this conversation it seemed Russia had little interest in solving the problems.

Putin moved on to energy; he was puzzled by Ukraine's behaviour. Ukraine owed Russia $3 billion, he claimed, which had not been repaid; it could not expect gas for free. He suggested the EU should give Ukraine the money to pay off all its debts, including to Russia. Somebody chortled at the idea. Putin did not smile. He finished his long contribution by pointing out that if the current government in Ukraine believed

Yanukovych had stolen money destined for the Ukrainian people, they should charge him – but they had no evidence, he said.

As he finished, I felt very apprehensive. Putin's version had been delivered with cold deliberation, and no suggestion of dialogue or compromise to resolve the issue – far from it. I wrote a note to Helga sitting next to me: 'This is quite like being on a roller coaster.'

After Putin finished, Nazarbayev followed with a short statement proposing multilateral trade links between Ukraine and its neighbours, both east and west. Even as he spoke, all eyes were on Poroshenko, whose turn was next. I knew he would be nervous – the future of his country was at stake. He explained that his plan was the way to peace, and hoped to talk to Putin in detail, signalling he wanted a bilateral conversation. He looked across at Putin, who did not meet his gaze. With that Lukashenko brought the meeting to an end. He had hoped everyone would join him to speak to the waiting press, but nobody was interested in doing that. I suggested some well-known phrases that were suitably vague – 'serious discussions on a range of issues', 'the talks were not easy, but the dialogue was very substantive and frank'. Lukashenko went to yet another huge room to give his press conference, promoting Minsk as a venue for mediation, a sort of Geneva in the east.

Upstairs, dinner awaited us and the chance to talk more informally. On the way, Putin asked me how the Iran talks were going. I gave him a quick summary of the latest meeting and my hopes for the next meeting in New York during the UN General Assembly. He made it clear that whatever was happening in Ukraine, Russia remained committed to the Iran talks. I nodded.

I was seated next to Putin. The conversation, led by Lukashenko, stayed well away from politics, focusing on football, music, holidays and so on. Everyone was relieved to just relax for a short while after such an intense set of discussions and it allowed the mood to lighten. In the end, discussion was our best hope of getting some resolution, so just being in each other's company was important. Lukashenko toasted the possibility that Russia would beat Germany in the 2018 World Cup – something that seemed like pure flattery at the time. (In the event Germany did badly, defeated by South Korea in the group stage. Russia did not win but made it to the quarter-finals.) I whispered to Putin that I thought it unlikely. He laughed, only too aware of how much everyone wanted to please him. Most importantly, Poroshenko and Putin exchanged reasonably friendly remarks, and agreed to the suggestion that they should meet later that evening.

At the end of dinner, I wished Poroshenko luck and promised to wait to hear from him. Just before midnight I got a call asking me to join him in his embassy in the centre of Minsk. The city was so quiet I felt we were the only people awake. At the embassy I met a visibly shaken and tired Poroshenko. He told me the conversation had been very difficult and Putin very tough, but his expectations had been so low the result was better than he had feared. Putin had promised to help in the release of hostages held by rebel forces in the east, and to start talks on border control between Ukraine and Russia. In theory that would prevent the movement of Russians wanting to help the breakaway areas. They'd agreed that the military commanders of both Ukraine and Russia should meet to try to stop the shelling between the Ukrainian army and Russian-led or -supported militia. Finally, they had agreed to talk more on energy and the agreements with the EU. He and I talked long into the night. His task was going to be extremely challenging in a country trying to determine its own future. When it was nearly morning, we said goodbye.

In early September we met again at the NATO summit in Wales. As an invited guest, Poroshenko spoke to the assembled leaders and met privately to talk in depth about the ever-growing problems in Ukraine. I heard that he had some new ideas to try to persuade Russia to de-escalate and find a way to stop the ongoing violence. As I walked down the long corridors at the venue in Newport, I saw President Obama and Chancellor Merkel heading in my direction. It was obvious from their fixed gaze that I was the person they were looking for. They took me aside and explained they had just had a long meeting with Poroshenko and wanted to see what parts of the Association Agreement might be delayed or possibly revisited.

They said this was important and, through a mixture of flattery and clear instructions, told me I was the one to get it done. I tried to explain that this was not my remit in the EU but it was clear Obama had no interest in the EU's inner workings. He put his hand on my shoulder and said he came to me because he knew I could get things done. If the lawyers try to stop you, he said, change the lawyers. I said I would do my best and headed to find President Barroso, who was less than impressed. For the last few months the Commission had been working hard to get the details of the deal through the EU and some parts of the trade agreement provisionally operational. Full ratification would not come until 2017. But, as always, Barroso moved swiftly to look again at the agreement.

On 16 September the European Parliament and the Rada of Ukraine both ratified the trade agreement. I saw Poroshenko only a couple of times more before I left office. I didn't know if he could achieve what he wanted, or indeed if he was the person to bring peace and prosperity to Ukraine. As I said my final goodbyes to him, I thought back to the extraordinary days of Maidan and wondered what Ukraine's future held. Recent history suggested it would not be easy to remove the 'wedge' that Russia had inserted to keep Ukraine from moving towards Europe or NATO, damaging or destroying what Putin saw as a key relationship. I had never believed Ukraine should choose all or nothing; rather it needed to be a strong independent state with relationships that worked to its advantage, economically and politically.

What I did not anticipate was that, eight years after these events, the conflict in Ukraine would transform into an invasion and a bloody war. Looking back, Putin's anger and determination to prevent Ukraine from moving to a fully independent future was all too evident. I had never heard such emotion and, at times, hatred from Russian leaders as I did during those months of discussions on Ukraine. It was brutal talk, since then translated into brutal action. While we weep for the loss of life and pointless destruction of towns and villages, offer what support we can, and help those fleeing the horror, we need to be willing to work with Ukraine to a sustainable future, however difficult.

AFTERWORD

A decade has passed since the period covered in this book and none of the challenges I have written about here are permanently resolved. Somalia and Haiti continue to struggle with poverty, political instability, armed violence and insecurity. Neither the historic agreement between Serbia and Kosovo nor the UN Security Council deal with Iran have progressed. Egypt may be stable, but it operates under an authoritarian leadership that has curtailed human rights. Despite ongoing attempts to broker a lasting peace, Libya still needs a government and an end to violent conflict. In Japan the echoes from the Fukushima nuclear disaster continue to reverberate, including in Europe, where choices for alternative energy sources to tackle climate change are affected by decisions made in the wake of what happened there. Worst of all, Ukraine is fighting for its very existence against Russian aggression as the shadow of war falls over the European continent once more.

Of course, these are complex and deep-rooted problems, and solutions were never going to be found in quick and easy remedies or grand designs that could be rolled out to fix all the interlocking difficulties in one go. Only the drip, drip of painstaking efforts to respond to immediate crises, negotiate long-term solutions and rebuild communities has any chance of success; and even then there is no guarantee. Without long-term investment and support we can only precariously manage what may begin as local problems but soon become global issues as their causes or consequences spread.

The roots of many of the challenges we face today can be traced back decades, sometimes even centuries. When a crisis erupts there is huge pressure to respond quickly. Acting fast may be necessary, but it's also essential to think beyond that. It is why I came back over and over again to the question 'And then what?' It is obvious that we need to plan for what comes after an event – beyond a war, an earthquake, a first negoti- ation or a revolution – to create a sustainable path to peace and security. Everyone may agree with the principle, but in practice the plans are often short-term and starved of resources. Dealing with domestic concerns or new problems takes priority for resources, even though many of these are caused precisely because of unresolved problems elsewhere.

In all the planning for the future, in all the thousands of pages I read, hundreds of meetings I attended and dozens of visits I made around the world, the same things came through loud and clear. Success is rarely the effect of one moment, but of thousands of interlocking actions over a sustained period; and tiny details, especially in difficult negotiations, can make the difference between success or failure even if they seem arbitrary or inconsequential.

If a crisis has taken decades to emerge, the sustained period we need to envisage afterwards is much the same. Resolving conflict for the long term means making sure more than one generation of girls goes to school, democratic institutions put down roots, economies flourish. We need to think differently about time.

During a visit to China, I travelled to Xi'an to see the terracotta army. As I walked around the site, the Chinese archaeologist accompanying me explained there was much more to find. She pointed to a small hill some way in the distance as the likely burial chamber of China's first emperor, Qin, where they hoped to find even more impressive treasures. I asked when excavation would start. Perhaps we will start some of it in fifty years, she said. Did she mind that she wouldn't see the results, I asked? No, she told me, doing this properly takes time to make sure it will survive for generations to come.

I like to think about international diplomacy as engagement on a spectrum, with the freezer at one end – no contact, all relationships suspended – and the warmth of an oven at the other, in which the ingredients of a good partnership can be baked together. The freezer is necessary (and as I write, Russia is rightly and firmly in it), but our long-term objective is to move towards the other end of the spectrum in all our relationships. In pursuit of preventing or ending chaos we engage with people we neither like nor respect, and whose views are wildly different to our own, posing for the official photo while hoping they will spend their days in a prison cell, not a government office or palace. Diplomatic effort requires constant decisions about where on the spectrum relations with another country or leader should be, and a recognition that in the end we may find ourselves confronting an enemy across a table as well as on a battlefield. To end a conflict, negotiate a peace, work out a way forward in a crisis we have to keep communications open, meet those we oppose and look for a way through.

I stand in awe of those who have made diplomacy their lives' work. Often operating behind the scenes, they understand that there is no room for individual ego, and that solutions are never neat outcomes to be admired by all sides from afar. At best they are workable compromises that can be lived with but rarely loved and which must be nurtured over time. In a crisis, politicians and diplomats may only get one shot at finding a solution; if they are wrong, they must live with the consequences of their choices. But always there is an obligation to ask and attempt to answer the question 'And then what?' and to recognise that engagement is not just for a few days or months, but for a lifetime and beyond. As Hillary Clinton once told me, 'Even when you do all you can, it's never enough.'

First and Last

I want to end this book with a reflection on being the first. In my generation many women have found themselves the first woman to hold a particular role. There is no roadmap then; nobody to give advice or warn of potential difficulties. I was the first woman in my family to go to university; I became the first female commissioner for trade and then the first HRVP. After leaving office I became the first female chancellor of Warwick University, and the first woman chancellor of the Order of

St Michael and St George. It is not always easy to be the first. But the main challenge that the first takes on is to make sure there is a second: the responsibility of ensuring that your appointment is not seen as an aberration, a case of having slipped through the net as a 'one off', not to be repeated easily, if ever. Women who get to be second prove themselves just as much. They show that the first is not an exception, but rather the norm. We should celebrate their achievements more.

To be the first is not so surprising, but what I had not expected to be was the last. With the departure of the UK from the EU, the opportunity for another British person to play a role in developing European foreign policy is lost. I will be the last woman UK commissioner, as well as the first; the last British HRVP as well as the first. For the first time in my life, I am the last. In its own way it is another first.

ACKNOWLEDGEMENTS

In getting this book to publication my biggest debt goes to Peter, my husband. His tireless support translated into his natural journalistic creativity, getting me to talk about the events and the people at the time. Gentle probing made me look more closely at what was happening and react to what I had seen as an ordinary person in extraordinary circumstances. Over the years that followed he encouraged me to listen to the tapes, transcribe them and turn them into stories for other people to read. Lorne Forsyth, the chairman of Elliott and Thompson, and Olivia Bays, my amazing editor, brought this project to fruition. Over many zooms and occasional cocktails, they transformed my rough stories and became dear friends. Without them there would be no book to read.

James, my chief of staff throughout those years, lived through many of the events alongside me, particularly the Iran negotiations. His depth of knowledge on how Brussels works was important in explaining how I came to be appointed. He read through the individual chapters as they took shape, and the final manuscript at the end. His advice was invaluable. James and I share a north of England heritage and with it the same sense of humour. Even now an exchanged look can reduce me to helpless laughter. It helped a lot during those years. His wife Helen and daughters Josie, Bea and Sophia were a constant support to him – and to me. They saw very little of him. Helen remarked at the end of a summer break as James left for the office, 'See you at Christmas!' She was being only slightly ironic. I owe them all a huge debt.

Some of my colleagues read parts of the manuscript and gave me their views and advice. Pierre Vimont helped particularly on Libya.

Fernando Gentilini read the Serbia-Kosovo Dialogue chapter twice. Sir Robert Cooper read it too, along with the Iran chapter. Christian Berger, as my companion in the visit to Morsi, read the Egypt chapter, having shared his recollections from the time. I am so grateful to them for their help.

Helga Schmid and David O'Sullivan offered advice and support as well as their knowledge and experience. Together with those who worked most closely with me in my 'cabinet', they allowed me to check facts and memories. The creation of a new foreign policy service was no easy task and took huge effort from EU foreign ministers, Commission officials, ambassadors, EEAS staff and European parliamentarians. Both Presidents of the EU Institutions played their part. Herman Van Rompuy brought wisdom and insight at a time of economic turbulence. José Manuel Barroso was an early cheerleader for the setting up of the EEAS and for my stewardship. Whether I lived up to his expectations at times, he remains a good friend. I remain forever in the debt of those who travelled on this journey with me. Emma Tunney ran my office and schedule with good humour, despite endless demands and extremely long hours. She was simply wonderful.

I am proud to be a Distinguished Fellow at the Woodrow Wilson Center in Washington DC. Senior Vice President Robert Litwak encouraged me to use my time with them to work on the book and offered the space and support to do so. Led by Ambassador Mark Green, the Center is a fantastic resource on foreign and security policy.

To do the job and write the book, my family had to put up with my seemingly endless travels. I am fortunate to have three amazing step-children who, together with their families, have enriched my life beyond measure. Tara, her husband Paul and children Alexander and Annabelle; Kate, her husband Jonty and son James; and Mike have, individually and together, been a source of great happiness throughout. My own two children Robert and Rebecca, who complete the Kellner five, mean more to me than life itself. Both have found great happiness in their partners, Robert with his wife Caitrin, and Rebecca with her husband

Jonny. Robert and Rebecca have both read the manuscript, eliminating the odd typo and expressing delight, and perhaps a little surprise, that I can put pen to paper, so to speak. Rebecca and Jonny produced our newest addition Luke, born as I completed this book. For him what I have written will feel like ancient history. I hope it will help him understand that history better.

The diplomats and politicians I served alongside or met during the extraordinary events of those years taught me a great deal. We are fortunate that dedicated, smart people are still drawn to public service. I am grateful to all of them. Above all I pay tribute to the thousands of people I met, many of whose names I do not know, who bore the brunt of chaos or disaster. I watched them mourn what they had lost and pick up the pieces to begin again. They want and deserve a better life.

INDEX

Notes:

1. CA is used as an abbreviation for Catherine Ashton
2. EU/ECOM is used in subheadings to refer to Catherine Ashton as representative of the European Union and European Commission and her team

A

Afghanistan 59, 93
African Union 22, 23, 29, 95, 102
Ahtisaari, Martti 111–12
Aksyonov, Sergei 196
Al Nahyan, Sheikh Abdullah bin Zayed 71
al-Qaeda 22
al-Shabaab 22, 30
al-Wasat Party, Egyptian 76
Albania 111
ALDE Party 12, 13–14
Ali, Ben 55, 89
Amr, Mohamed 61, 62, 66
Annabi, Hédi 35
Arab League 59, 66, 92, 95, 96, 97, 102
Arab Spring uprising (2011) xx, 55, 56–8, 88
Araghchi, Seyed Abbas 155, 159, 169, 174
Arak heavy water reactor, Iran 172, 173
Armenia 179
Audibert, Jacques 151, 156, 158, 161, 163
Australia 33
Azarov, Mykola 181, 183, 186, 189
Azerbaijan 179

B

Bahrain 66
Ban Ki-Moon 37–8, 96

Barnier, Michel 38
Barre, Siad 19
Barroso, José Manuel 4–5, 7, 12, 14, 16–17, 35–6, 90, 127, 181, 185, 191, 208, 211, 216
Batkivshchyna Party, Ukrainian 187
Battle of Kosovo (1389) 128
Belarus 179, 181, 208–9, 210, 212
Belgian Protocol Service 142
Belgium 12, 13
Bellerive, Jean-Max 41–2
Berger, Christian 60, 64, 65, 67, 68, 73, 77, 78, 81, 82, 84, 85
Berlusconi, Silvio 6, 16
Biden, Joe 157
Blair, Tony 14
Boal, Pilar Juárez 35
Bosnia-Herzegovina 109–10, 124
Bosnian Serb forces 109
Bouazizi, Mohamed 55
Boyes, Roger 144
Brazil 94
Brexit 220
Brown, Gordon 1, 3, 4, 14, 15–16
Brunei 66
Bulatov, Dmytro 192
Bulgaria 89

Burns, Bill 84, 94, 157, 159, 162, 163, 165, 171, 174
Buzek, Jerzy 12

C

Cameron, David 58–9, 88, 90, 101, 156, 169
Canada 6, 13, 92, 96, 200
Caribbean 33
Chernobyl nuclear disaster 210
China xviii, 24, 33, 94, 106, 112, 148, 218
Iran nuclear negotiations and deal 151, 156, 158, 160, 164–6, 169, 172
Çitaku, Vlora 144
Clinton, Bill 38, 118
Clinton, Hillary xviii, 38, 57, 70, 93, 96, 118–19, 219
COMESA (Common Market for Easter and Southern Africa) 23
contact group, Ukrainian crisis 199–200, 201, 203–5
Cooper, Sir Robert 105
Cox, Pat 183–4
Crimea and Crimean annexation (2014) 93, 195–6, 198, 199, 201, 202
Croatia 111

D

da Costa, Luiz Carlos 35
Dačić, Ivica 113, 115–18, 119, 120–6, 130, 131–44
Darroch, Lord 'Kim' 3
Darroch, Vanessa 3, 4
Daul, Joseph 39, 41
Dayton Agreement 124
democracy xx–xxi, 19, 57, 58–9, 68, 82, 85, 92, 99, 100, 101–2, 104, 105, 107
Denmark 48, 52, 96
Deshchytsia, Andrii 203
DG ECHO 36, 37
diplomacy, CA on international xiii, xiv– xv, xvi–xvii, xviii–xix, 218–19
Djibouti 23, 30

Dodik, Milorad 124
Dominican Republic 37
Đurić, Marko 128

E

E3 xviii
E3 plus 3 xviii, 148
see also China; France; Germany; Iran and Iranian nuclear negotiations and deal; Russia; United Kingdom; United States of America
earthquake (2010), Haiti xx, 33–47
earthquake and tsunami (2011), Japan 33–4, 47–54
Eastern Partnership 179
Economist 144
Egypt 98, 217
anti-US sentiment 67
Arab Spring uprising (2011) 55, 56–8, 88
CA's visits 55, 57–8, 60–2, 63–5, 68–9, 71–84, 85–6
coalition/interim government and unrest 66–77, 84–6
elections 58, 59–60, 85–6
EU delegation premises 86
EU economic task force 60–2
EU/ECOM socio-economic support 58–9, 63–77, 84–6
human rights 61–3, 77
Islamic coalition 76
meeting with Morsi in detention 77–84
Morsi government 58, 59–60, 61–6
Mubarak government 56–7, 59, 63, 67, 89
Muslim Brotherhood and FJP 56–7, 59, 63, 65, 67–8, 69, 72, 73–4, 75–6
National Salvation Front 63, 64, 66
Salafists 75
Tamarod movement 76
Egyptian Gazette 61
el-Haddad, Essam 65
el-Keib, Abdurrahim 104, 105

el-Shater, Khairat 59, 66
el-Sisi, General Abdel Fattah 66, 67–8,
    69, 71, 74–5, 77, 83, 85–6
Elaraby, Nabil 66
ElBaradei, Mohamed 63, 64, 66, 68,
    70–1, 72–3, 77, 85
EPP Party 12, 13–14
Estonia 193
Eurasian Customs Union 181, 182, 186,
    208–14
European Bank for Reconstruction and
    Development 60
European Commission 4, 5, 9–11, 12, 13,
    16, 36, 37, 127, 179, 187, 191, 216
    CA as Commissioner for Trade 4, 5–8
    see also Barroso, José Manuel
European Council 4, 9–11, 12–13, 14, 16,
    90–2, 197
    see also European Union (EU); Van
        Rompuy, Herman
European Court of Human Rights 183
European External Action Service (EEAS)
    xiii–xiv, xviii–xix, xx, 4, 18, 47, 202
European Investment Bank 60
European Parliament 9–10, 11, 12, 16, 36,
    39, 89, 183–4
European People's Party 38
European Union (EU) xiii–xiv, xvii–xviii,
    xix–xx, 220
    Association Agreement with Ukraine
        179, 180, 181, 182, 184–5, 187,
        189–90, 207, 211, 212–13, 215–16
    Foreign Affairs Council 11, 66, 85,
        197–8, 208
    Foreign Service 36, 100–1
    General Affairs Council 128
    hierarchy of countries 12
    Mercury network 24
    Military Staff 20, 88
    Situation Centre 34–5
    trade portfolio 4, 5
    and the Ukrainian international crisis
        contact group 199–205
    Vilnius Summit (2013) 179–80, 182–3

    see also Egypt; European Commission;
        European Council; Iran and
        Iranian nuclear negotiations and
        deal; Japan; Kosovo; Libya; Serbia;
        Somalia; Ukraine

F
Fabius, Laurent 160, 162, 163, 172–3,
    175, 201
Fahmy, Nabil 74
Feltman, Jeff 200
Financial Times 144, 153
fishing industry, Somali 19–20
France xviii, 12, 14, 37, 38–9, 90–1, 92–3,
    97, 148, 194, 199–200
    Iran nuclear negotiations and deal
        151, 156, 158, 160, 161, 162
    see also Sarkozy, Nicolas
Freedom and Justice Party, Egyptian 59, 69
Friends of Syria xix
Fukushima nuclear plant 48, 217
Füle, Stefan 179, 185

G
G8 meetings 92–3
Gaddafi, Colonel Muammar xix, 87, 88,
    89, 91, 95, 102, 103, 106
Gass, Simon 151, 158, 162, 169
Gates, Robert 89
Gentilini, Fernando 115–16, 117, 120,
    121, 123, 129, 130, 131, 134, 135,
    141, 142, 145
Georgia 179
Georgieva, Kristalina 37
Germany xviii, 12, 33, 91, 92, 93, 96, 134,
    141, 193–4, 197, 199
    Iran nuclear negotiations and deal
        148, 151, 156, 158, 160, 162, 167
Glenny, Misha 144
Grand Imam, Egyptian 66
Greece 13
Grybauskaite, Dalia 184, 185

H

Hague, William 156, 160, 162, 163, 173, 197, 201

Haiti earthquake and aftermath xx, 33–4, 47, 217

EU/ECOM aid and support 34–44, 45

CA's visit 34, 36–7, 39–46

earthquake fatalities 35, 38, 42, 46, 47

government 34, 41–2, 43–4, 46–7

hospital ships 44–5

support from the military 35, 36

Harper, Stephen 96

Hoon, Geoff 15

House of Lords 1–2, 4

HRVP role (High Representative for Foreign and Security Policy/First Vice President of the Commission) ix–x, 5, 9, 11–12, 13, 14–18, 23, 219, 220

see also Egypt; Haiti; Iran and Iranian nuclear negotiations and deal; Japan; Kosovo; Libya; Serbia; Somalia; Ukraine

Hudson, Rear Admiral Peter 20

Human Rights Watch 77

I

India 24, 94, 98

Indonesia 33

International Atomic Energy Agency (IAEA) 147, 155–6

International Court of Justice (ICJ) 112, 202

International Maritime Organization (IMO) 23

International Monetary Fund (IMF) 37, 186

INTERPOL 23

IOC (Indian Ocean Commission) 23

Iran and Iranian nuclear negotiations and deal x, xviii, xix, 8, 24, 33, 70, 149, 217

E3 plus 3 xviii, 148, 150–4, 155–76, 193, 214 (*see also under* China; France; Germany; Russia; United Kingdom; United States of America)

EU/ECOM coordination of negotiations 148–76, 193

Hassan Rouhani 149, 169

inspections 147, 155–6

Mohammad Zarif 152, 153–7, 158–9, 163, 164, 165–6, 167, 168, 169–71, 172–3, 174, 175, 176

Natanz and Arak nuclear facilities 147, 172, 173, 174

Non-Proliferation Treaty 147, 148–9, 154, 170

sanctions 147–8, 149, 159, 160, 161, 167, 168, 172, 176

Supreme National Security Council 148

uranium enrichment 147–8, 153–4, 155, 171

Iraq 93, 106

Ireland 12

Italy 6, 12, 42, 45, 92, 96, 200

J

Jahjaga, Atifete 126–7

Jalil, Mustafa Abdul 89, 99, 104

Jalili, Dr Saeed 148, 163

Japan 24, 92

EU/ECOM aid and support 33–4, 47, 49, 52–4

CA's visits 34, 48–53

earthquake and tsunami fatalities 47, 50–2

Fukushima nuclear plant 48, 217

prefab villages 52–3

Zuiganji Temple 49

Jibril, Mahmoud 89, 103–4

Jordan 56, 60, 96

K

Kandil, Hesham 61, 69, 76, 77

Kazakhstan 181, 208, 211, 212

Kenya 23, 24, 30
Kerry, John xviii, 23–4, 70–1, 85, 150, 153, 159–60, 162, 163, 164, 166–7, 168, 172, 173–4, 176, 177, 200–1, 203–6
Khrushchev, Nikita 195
Klement, Stephan 150, 170, 172, 175
Klitschko, Vitali 192, 196
Kosovo x, xvii, xix, 202, 217
  Albanian Kosovars 111
  Appeal Court in Mitrovica North 131, 136, 138, 142
  CA's visit 130
  customs revenue 125, 130
  EU/ECOM and negotiations with Serbia 112–13, 115–18, 119, 120–44
  EU civilian police team 113, 114
  Hashim Thaçi 113, 114, 115–18, 119, 120–6, 128–30, 131–44
  independence 111–12
  Integrated Border Management 120, 125, 130
  integrated justice/police system 123, 124, 129, 131, 136, 137–9, 142
  International Court of Justice 112, 113
  KFOR 113
  Liberation Army (KLA) 111, 113, 114
  north-Kosovo Serb population 113–14, 117, 121–2, 123, 124, 127–8, 129, 135, 136–9
  Serbian Orthodox monasteries and churches 112, 117, 122
  UN and NATO 111–12, 118, 122, 138
  US and negotiations with Serbia 118–20, 141, 143, 144
Kravchuk, Leonid 192
Kuchma, Leonid 192
Kurti, Albin 114
Kwaśniewski, Aleksander 183–4

L

Lagarde, Christine 186
L'Aquila earthquake (2009) 42, 45

Lavrov, Sergei 133, 154, 164, 165, 166, 167–8, 171–2, 173, 175, 176, 182, 189, 198–9, 201, 203, 204–5
Leakey, Lieutenant-General David 20
Lebanon 56, 94
León, Bernardino 60, 63, 64, 65–6, 67, 84
Leonid, Kuchma 192
Li Baodong 164, 165–6
Libya x, xix, xx, 55, 60, 87–8, 217
  Association of Election Observation 104
  Benghazi 87–8, 92, 100, 106
  Cairo Group 102
  CA's visits 87–8, 97–100, 104
  Colonel Gaddafi xix, 87, 88, 89, 91, 95, 102, 103, 106
  EU delegation 100–1, 103, 104, 105, 107
  EU/ECOM support following airstrikes 98–103, 105
  evacuation of EU nationals 90
  extraordinary EC meeting 90–2, 106
  G8 meeting 92–3
  jailing of Libyan nurses 89
  military airstrikes 97–8
  National Transitional Council (NTC) 89, 97, 98–100, 102, 103–4, 105
  NATO meeting 89–90
  'no-fly zone'/military action proposal 88, 90–7
  post-war continued unrest 104–7
  press, charities and human rights groups 100
  UN Security Council resolution 94
  Women's Rights Forum 104
Lisbon Treaty (2009) 4–5, 9, 10–11, 35
Lithuania 179, 184
Lucas, Han-Dieter 151, 156, 158, 162
Lukashenko, Alexander 208, 209–11, 212, 214–15
Lukin, Vladimir 194
Luxembourg 12

M

Ma Zhaoxu 151
Maidan protests (2013) 185–6, 187–93, 194–5, 197, 199
Malaysia Airlines flight MH17 207–8
Mandelson, Peter, Lord 1, 5, 15
Mansour, Adly 67, 68, 73–4, 75
Martin, Ian 105
Mauritius 23, 24
Médecins Sans Frontières 102
media/press see press/media
Medvedev, Dmitry 7, 94
Merkel, Angela 13, 15–16, 59, 91, 95, 185, 197, 200, 201, 202, 215–16
Michel, President 23
Middle East xx, 11, 57, 70, 88, 160
 see also Egypt; Libya
Miliband, David 14–15
Milošević, Slobodan 111, 118
Miozzo, Agostino 28, 100, 103
Mladić, Ratko 109
Mogadishu, Somalia 26, 28–9, 31
Mohamed, Mohamed Abdullahi 31
Mohamud, Hassan Sheikh 27, 29, 30–1
Moïse, President Jovenel 46
Moldova 179
Montenegro 111
Moran, Jim 60, 64, 65, 67, 68, 73, 85, 103, 105
Morocco 56, 96
Morrison, James 4, 8–9, 15, 16, 17, 18, 130, 150, 153, 154, 160–1, 162, 164, 169, 170, 174, 206
Morsi, Mohamed 58, 59–60, 61–6, 67, 68, 69, 70, 71, 72, 74, 76–84, 85, 86
Mothers (Bosnia-Herzegovina) 109–10
Moussa, Amr 59, 63, 64, 66, 92
Mozambique 23
Mubarak, Hosni 56–7, 59, 63, 67, 89
Mulet, Edmond 43
Munich Security Conference (2014) 113
Muslim Brotherhood 56–7, 59, 63, 65, 67–8, 69, 72, 73–4, 75–6

N

Nabiullina, Elvira 7
Natanz nuclear plant 147
National Salvation Front, Egyptian 63
National Transitional Council (NTC) 89, 97, 98–100, 102, 103–4, 105
natural disasters 33
 Haiti earthquake (2010) xx, 33–47
 Japan earthquake and tsunami (2011) 33–4, 47–54
 L'Aquila earthquake (2009) 42, 45
Nazarbayev, Nursultan 211, 212, 214
Nephew, Richard 160, 162, 175
Netherlands 12, 48, 208
New York Times 153
Nikolić, Tomislav 115, 119, 126–7, 130, 132, 133
Nobel Peace Prize nomination 144
Non-Proliferation Treaty 147, 148–9, 154, 170
North Atlantic Treaty Organization (NATO) xviii, xix, 13, 23, 24, 89–90, 97, 101, 111–12, 118, 136, 138, 143, 144, 182, 197, 213, 215
Norway 96
Nour Party, Egyptian 66
Nuland, Victoria xvii, 186, 192–3, 204

O

Obama, Barack xvii–xviii, 67, 157, 174, 206–7, 215–16
Operation Atlanta 20–1, 22–3
Operation Smile 45
Organisation of Islamic Cooperation (OIC) 102
Organization for Security and Co-operation in Europe (OSCE) 200, 205, 206, 207
Osman, Abdirahman 26

P

P5 plus 1 xviii, 148
Paet, Urmas 193

Party of the Regions, Ukrainian 181
Patterson, Anne 67
PES Party 12, 13–14, 15
Philippines 98
Ping, Jean 95
piracy xix–xx, 20, 21–6, 29, 30, 31
Poland 12, 193–4, 200
Political and Security Committee 25
Poroshenko, Petro 192, 196, 207, 209,
    211, 212–13, 214, 215, 216
Portugal 12
Potts, Rear-Admiral Duncan 25–6
press/media xiv, 18, 23, 39, 56, 91, 93,
    118, 123, 127, 133–4, 141, 144, 153,
    168, 175, 193, 206
Préval, Rene 41–2
Putin, Vladimir 7–8, 10, 95, 169, 182,
    189–90, 196, 197, 201–2, 209,
    210–15, 216

Q
Qatar 71, 96

R
Rasmussen, Anders Fogh 13
Ravanchi, Majid Takht 155, 169, 174
Red Crescent 102
Red Cross 52, 102
Reeker, Phil 119–20, 140, 142–3
Reinfeldt, Fredrik 16
Republika Srpska 124
Rice, Susan 157, 206
Romania 91
Rondos, Alex 27–8
Rouhani, Hassan 149, 169
Russia xviii, 6–8, 10, 92–3, 94–5, 106,
    111, 112, 133, 153, 214–15, 216,
    217
    Iran nuclear negotiations and deal
        148, 151–2, 158, 160, 161, 164–5,
        166, 167–8, 169, 171–2, 173, 193,
        214

    relations with Ukraine and post-2014
        annexation of Crimea 196–9,
        200–2, 203–6, 208, 210, 211–14,
        215, 216
    relations with Ukraine pre-2014
        annexation of Crimea 180–2,
        186–7, 189–90, 194, 195
Ryabkov, Sergei 16, 151–2, 161, 164, 169

S
Sabahi, Hamdeen 63, 64
Salafists 75
sanctions 147–8, 149, 159, 160, 161, 167,
    168, 172, 176, 189, 207
Sarkozy, Nicolas xix, 16, 87, 88, 89, 90,
    91, 93, 95, 96–7, 101
Saudi Arabia 71
Schmid, Helga 150, 153, 155, 156, 158,
    160–1, 162, 165, 167, 169, 170, 204,
    213
Schulz, Martin 12, 16
Second World War 111, 209
Serbia x, xvii, xix, 217
    Albanian Kosovars 111
    Appeal Court in Mitrovica North 131,
        136, 138, 142
    CA's visit 119
    customs revenue 125–6, 130
    EU/ECOM and negotiations with
        Kosovo 112–13, 115–18, 119,
        120–45
    Integrated Border Management 120,
        125, 130
    integrated justice/police system in
        Kosovo 123, 124, 129, 131, 136,
        137–8, 142
    International Court of Justice 112, 113
    Kosovan Serb refugees 113–14
    north-Kosovo Serb population
        113–14, 117, 121–2, 123, 124,
        127–9, 135, 136–9
    Orthodox Church 112, 117, 122
    the 'tank issue' 136, 138

Serbia (continued)
    UN and NATO 111–12, 118, 136, 138
    US and negotiations with Kosovo
        118–20, 144
Seychelles 23, 24, 30
Shafik, Ahmed 58, 59
Shala, Blerim 128
Sharaf, Essam 58
Sherman, Wendy 151, 153, 154, 156,
        157–8, 159, 160, 162, 163, 165, 167,
        169, 172, 206
Sikorski, Radek 193–4
Slovenia 111
Snow, Jon 144
Somalia xix–xx, 217
    CA's visit 26–9, 31
    civil war 19, 22, 28–9
    EU New Deal for Somalia 30
    fishing industry 19–20
    food and aid 19, 20, 22, 30
    government 19, 20, 26, 27, 28, 30–1
    land attack 25–6
    Mogadishu 26, 28–9, 31
    Operation Atlanta 20–1, 22–3
    piracy 20, 21–6, 29, 30, 31
    Seychelles conference 23, 24
    women of 31
Sorenson, Peter 110
South Africa 23, 28, 94
South Korea 6, 24
Soviet Union 180, 195
Spain 39, 42, 96
Srebrenica, Bosnia-Herzegovina 109–10
Stalin, Joseph 195
Steinmeier, Frank-Walter 193, 200
Strathclyde, Lord 'Tom' 1–2
Sullivan, Jake 157, 159, 163, 165, 171, 174
Sweden 16
Switzerland 200

T

Tadić, Boris 109, 112–13, 115
Tahiri, Edita 134

Tajani, Antonio 60, 61
Tanzania 24, 30
Tawadros II, Coptic Pope 66
terracotta army, China 218
Thaçi, Hashim 113, 114, 115–18, 119,
        120–6, 131–44
The Times 144
Timmermans, Frans 208
toxic waste 19
trade portfolio, EU 4, 5–6
Trump, Donald xviii, 3
Tunisia 55–6, 60, 89, 98, 104
Turkey 11, 33
Tusk, Donald 12
Tutankhamun tomb replica 61
Tymoshenko, Yulia 183, 184, 194, 195

U

Ukraine x, xvii, xviii, 8, 179, 216, 217
    Arseniy Yatsenyuk 187, 189, 196
    Association Agreement with the EU
        179, 180, 181, 184–5, 187, 189–90,
        207, 209, 211, 212–13, 215–16
    CA meets with opposition and
        activists 187, 191–2
    CA's visits 186–90, 191–2, 194–5,
        196–7
    election of new government (2014)
        207
    Eurasian Customs Union 181, 186,
        208–9, 211–15
    Maidan demonstrations 185–6,
        187–93, 194–5
    Malaysia Airlines flight MH17 207
    OSCE Special Monitoring Mission
        205, 206, 207
    Petro Poroshenko 192, 196, 207, 209,
        211, 212–13, 214, 215, 216
    Rada 184, 192, 195, 196, 201
    relations with Russia and post-2014
        annexation of Crimea 196–9,
        200–2, 203–6, 208, 210, 211–14,
        215, 216

relations with Russia pre-2014
  annexation of Crimea 180–2,
  186–7, 189–90, 194, 195
talks with EU/ECOM representatives
  186–7, 188–9, 191, 193–4, 201,
  203–5, 207, 208, 211–16
talks with Ukrainian crisis
  international contact group
  representatives 201, 203–5
and the US 192–3, 200–1, 203–4
Victor Yanukovych 179, 180–3, 184–5,
  186–7, 188–9, 191, 194, 212, 214
Vilnius Summit (2013) 179, 180,
  182–3, 184, 185
Yulia Tymoshenko 183, 184–5, 194,
  195
Ulyukaev, Alexei 211
UNICEF 27
United Arab Emirates (UAE) 71, 96
United Kingdom xviii, 4, 14, 33, 48, 90–1,
  92, 101, 106, 197, 200, 220
  Iran nuclear negotiations and deal
  148, 150–1, 156, 158, 160, 162, 173
United Nations (UN) 37–8
  Convention on the Law of the Sea 21
  Haiti 35, 38, 42–3
  Iran nuclear negotiations and deal 152
  Libya 88, 92, 94, 96, 102, 105, 106
  Resolution 1244 112, 113
  Security Council 88, 92, 94, 96, 106,
    112, 147, 148, 149, 155–6, 208, 217
  Serbia and Kosovo 111–12, 114
  Ukraine crisis contact group 200
United States of America (USA) xvii–xviii,
  xix, 6, 13, 14, 33, 57, 67, 89–90, 92,
  93, 94, 95, 118–20, 141, 143, 144,
  190, 192–3, 199
CA visits the White House 206
Iran nuclear negotiations and deal
  148, 149, 150, 151, 153, 154, 156,
  157–61, 162–7, 168, 169, 171, 172,
  173–5, 176, 193
Ukraine and Russian annexation of
  Crimea (2014) 192–3, 200–1, 203–6

V
Vale de Almeida, João 16
Van Rompuy, Herman 12, 16, 95, 185,
  201–2, 211
Vershbow, Sandy 136
Vilnius Summit (2013) 179–80, 182–3,
  184, 185
Vučić, Aleksandar 130, 131, 132–4,
  136–44

W
Westerwelle, Guido 160, 162, 163, 167,
  176
Wisner, Frank 57
Wood, Stewart 15
World Cup (2018), UEFA 215
World Food Programme 20, 22
World Trade Organization (WTO) xviii,
  7

X
Xi Jinping 169

Y
Yanukovych, Viktor 179, 180–3,
  184–5, 186–7, 188–9, 191, 194, 212,
  214
Yatsenyuk, Arseniy 187, 189, 196, 203
Yemen 56
Yousafzai, Malala 144
YouTube 193
Yugoslavia, collapse of 109, 110, 111

Z
Zapatero, José Luis 15, 60, 96
Zarif, Mohammad Javad 152,
  153–7, 158–9, 163, 164, 165–6,
  167, 168, 169–71, 172–3, 174,
  175–6
Zuiganji Temple, Japan 49